WRITING MARGINALITY IN MODERN FRENCH LITERATURE

Writing Marginality in Modern French Literature explores how cultural centres require the peripheral, the outlawed, and the deviant in order to define and bolster themselves. It analyses the hierarchies of cultural value which inform the work of six modern French writers: the exoticist Pierre Loti; Paul Gauguin, whose *Noa Noa* enacts European fantasies about Polynesia; Proust, who analyses such exemplary figures of exclusion and inclusion as the homosexual and the xenophobe; Montherlant, who claims to subvert colonialist values in *La Rose de sable*; Camus, who pleads an alienating detachment from the cultures of both metropolitan France and Algeria; and Jean Genet. Crucially Genet, typecast as France's moral pariah, charts Palestinian statelessness in his last work, *Un captif amoureux* (1986) and reflects ethically on the dispossession of the Other and the violence inherent in the West's marginalization of cultural difference.

EDWARD J. HUGHES is Reader in Modern French Literature at Royal Holloway at the University of London. He is the author of *Marcel Proust: a Study in the Quality of Awareness* (Cambridge, 1983) and *Albert Camus: 'Le Premier Homme' / 'La Peste'* (1995). His reviews appear regularly in *The Times Literary Supplement*.

CAMBRIDGE STUDIES IN FRENCH

Recent titles in the series include

WRITING MARGINALITY IN MODERN FRENCH LITERATURE

from Loti to Genet

EDWARD J. HUGHES

CAMBRIDGE
UNIVERSITY PRESS

PUBLISHED BY THE PRESS SYNDICATE OF THE UNIVERSITY OF CAMBRIDGE
The Pitt Building, Trumpington Street, Cambridge, United Kingdom

CAMBRIDGE UNIVERSITY PRESS
The Edinburgh Building, Cambridge CB2 2RU, UK
40 West 20th Street, New York, NY 10011-4211, USA
10 Stamford Road, Oakleigh, VIC 3166, Australia
Ruiz de Alarcón 13, 28014 Madrid, Spain
Dock House, The Waterfront, Cape Town 8001, South Africa

http://www.cambridge.org

First published 2001

Printed in the United Kingdom at the University Press, Cambridge

Typeset in Monotype Baskerville 11/12½ in QuarkXPress™ [SE]

A catalogue record for this book is available from the British Library

Library of Congress cataloguing in publication data

Hughes, Edward J. (Edward Joseph), 1953–
Writing marginality in modern French literature: from Loti to Genet / Edward J. Hughes.
p. cm. – (Cambridge studies in French)
Includes bibliographical references and index.
ISBN 0 521 64296 5
1. French literature – 19th century – History and criticism. 2. French literature – 20th
century – History and criticism. 3. Marginality, social, in literature. 4. Literature and
society – France – History – 19th century. 5. Literature and society – French – History – 20th
century. I. Title. II. Series.

PQ295.M37 H84 2001
840.9′355–dc21 00-063060

ISBN 0 521 64296 5 hardback

Contents

Acknowledgements

In writing this book, I have received generous help from many people. I am greatly indebted to my colleagues in the French Department, Royal Holloway, University of London for their support and encouragement, and to them and the College for allowing me generous research leave to work on this project; to the Arts and Humanities Research Board for funding additional leave to enable me to complete the book; and to the British Academy and the Central Research Fund of the University of London for funding a research visit to the Institut Mémoires de l'Edition Contemporaine (IMEC) and the Bibliothèque Nationale in Paris. I also thank the editors of *Paragraph: A Journal of Modern Critical Theory* and the *Journal of the Institute of Romance Studies* for permission to use material published in those journals and now absorbed into Chapter 1 (*Paragraph*, 18, 2 (July 1995); *JIRS*, 3 (1994–95)). Kind permission has also been received from the University of Glasgow to reproduce in Chapter 1 material from my article 'Cultural Stereotyping: Segalen against Loti', in Charles Forsdick and Susan Marson, eds., *Reading Diversity: Lectures du Divers* (University of Glasgow French and German Publications, 2000), pp. 25–38.

I am also grateful to Laura Marcus for her illuminating comments on an early draft of Chapter 2; to Patricia O'Flaherty for her painstaking reading of my chapter on Montherlant and her many excellent suggestions; and to members of the Aberdeen Critical Theory Seminar and the French Department of the University of Edinburgh for their engaging responses to a research paper on Genet that has been incorporated into Chapter 5. I thank warmly the many colleagues and friends who have encouraged me in my research, responded to individual queries, or been generous in exchanging ideas and making suggestions, especially Richard Bales, Malcolm Bowie, Celia Britton, Harry Cockerham, Antoine Compagnon, Abigail Descombes, Satanay Dorken, Peter Dunwoodie, Charles Forsdick, James Hiddleston, Annette Lavers,

Robert Lethbridge, Susan Marson, Cedric May, John O'Brien, John Renwick, Eric Robertson, Soizick Solman, Michael Syrotinski, Sonya Stephens, and Nicholas White. My thanks also go to Linda Bree and Rachel De Wachter for their unfailing help as editors, my copy-editor Ann Lewis for her great efficiency, the Cambridge University Press readers for their encouraging and highly cogent feedback and instructive suggestions, and to Michael Sheringham, who, since I first made tentative proposals for this study, has warmly encouraged me, offering invaluable advice about its content and overall direction. Finally, I thank Beatrice Lewis for her moral support over the years and friends and family, especially Kathleen, Roisha, and Eamonn, for their patience and help.

Abbreviations

I have used available translations of Proust, Camus, and Genet, making only very occasional modifications to these, and have supplied double page references. The translations of material from Loti, Gauguin, Montherlant, and Camus's early essays are my own.

AA	Paul Gauguin, *Avant et Après*, Paris: La Table Ronde, 1994.
Az	Pierre Loti, *Aziyadé*, Paris: GF-Flammarion, 1989.
CA	Jean Genet, *Un captif amoureux*, Paris: Gallimard (Folio), 1986.
Corr.	Marcel Proust, *Correspondance*, 21 vols., Philip Kolb (ed.), Paris: Plon, 1970–93.
CSB	Marcel Proust, *Contre Sainte-Beuve*, Paris: Bibliothèque de la Pléiade, 1971.
ED	Jean Genet, *L'Ennemi déclaré*, ed. Albert Dichy, Paris: Gallimard, 1991.
EK	Albert Camus, *Exile and the Kingdom*, trans. Justin O'Brien, Harmondsworth: Penguin, 1989.
Ess.	Albert Camus, *Essais*, Paris: Bibliothèque de la Pléiade, 1965.
FM	Albert Camus, *The First Man*, trans. David Hapgood, London: Hamish Hamilton, 1995.
JV	Jean Genet, *Journal du voleur*, Paris: Gallimard (Folio): 1949.
LRS	Pierre Loti, *Le Roman d'un spahi*, Paris: Omnibus, 1989.
MC	Pierre Loti, *Madame Chrysanthème*, Paris: GF-Flammarion, 1990.
ML	Pierre Loti, *Le Mariage de Loti*, Paris: GF-Flammarion, 1991.
NCE	Roland Barthes, *New Critical Essays*, trans. Richard Howard, New York: Hill and Wang, 1980.
NN	Paul Gauguin and Charles Morice, *Noa Noa*, Paris: La Plume, 1901.
OC	Victor Segalen, *Œuvres Complètes*, Paris: Laffont, 1995.
PH	Albert Camus, *Le Premier Homme*, Paris: Gallimard, 1994.

PL   Jean Genet, *Prisoner of Love*, trans. Barbara Bray, Wesleyan University Press, 1992.

RS   Henry de Montherlant, *La Rose de sable*, Paris: Gallimard (Folio), 1968.

RMP   Marcel Proust, *Remembrance of Things Past*, Harmondsworth: Penguin, 1989.

RTP   Marcel Proust, *À la recherche du temps perdu*, 4 vols., Paris: Bibliothèque de la Pléiade, 1987–89.

TF   Albert Camus, *The Fall*, trans. Justin O'Brien, Harmondsworth: Penguin, 1990.

TRN   Albert Camus, *Théâtre, Récits, Nouvelles*, Paris: Bibliothèque de la Pléiade, 1962.

Introduction

Writing in a state of shock following the killing of the US Black activist George Jackson in San Quentin prison in 1971, Jean Genet, who actively collaborated with the Black Panthers in the 1960s and early 70s, called on Western radicals to contest the mythologies on which White dominance was based. A colossal effort was needed, he insisted, to counter this hegemonic control: 'we must learn to betray the Whites that we are' ['il faut apprendre à trahir les blancs que nous sommes'].[1] Genet's outspokenness is unsurprising when we remember his well-established reputation as cultural dissident in France. The legacy of domination, he argues, disfigures those who perpetuate it. More noted for his use of the accusatory *vous* when addressing and castigating his Western bourgeois addressees, he employs the *nous* to underline and help shoulder, however momentarily, the burden of collective guilt surrounding racial injustice. This incitement to cultural self-betrayal regularly finds overdetermined expression in Genet, even if the extreme circumstances in which he is here writing help explain his forthrightness.

The call to collective self-scrutiny echoes a more general preoccupation with cultural self-image and value in modern French literature. The denigration of Europe by Camus's colonial-missionary protagonist in *Le Renégat* – 'down with Europe, reason, honour, and the cross' (*EK*, 44) ['À bas l'Europe, la raison et l'honneur et la croix'] (*TRN*, 1590) – anticipates Genet's promotion of self-betrayal and pinpoints the strains inherent in Western supremacism. Often the most virulent expressions of such Europhobia occur along ethnic interfaces, geographical margins, interstitial spaces in which cultural self-definition is simultaneously forged and contested. In the movement towards decolonization, a lexicon of insecurity marks the waning of influence. As Sartre writes in his preface to Fanon's indictment of colonization, *Les Damnés de la Terre*, the European, hitherto the imperious subject of history, is to become its object.[2]

In his preface to Fanon, Sartre eagerly trumpets the demise of the West, likening Europe to a vessel taking in water, or to a sick continent. But if his mocking invitation to cure Europe helps convey the atmosphere of cultural uncertainty in the post-war period, it may indirectly sanction a narcissistic return to beleaguered self-obsession. More generally, his exhortation, like Genet's call to self-betrayal, may be as much an invitation to European self-contemplation, however embedded in self-hatred, as to any consideration of otherness.

Sartre sponsored perceived marginal authors and causes of the period, often acting as cultural mediator between a metropolitan literary public and new radical voices. In a domestic context, his promotion of Genet, whom he assiduously touted as thief and social deviant in his *Saint-Genet: comédien et martyr*, is an example of the kudos that accrued to him through this exploitation of the celebrated social outcast. In fact, the work, seen by Sartre as 'the history of a liberation', was to have a paralysing effect on a resentful Genet.[3] *Saint-Genet* thus marks a potentially opportunistic espousal of *causes célèbres*, a scouring of shadowy fringes designed to secure for Sartre a vicarious *succès de scandale*.

Sartre also promoted a generation of emergent Francophone writers. He provided prefaces not just for *Les Damnés de la Terre*, but also for Memmi's *Portrait du colonisé*, précédé de *Portrait du colonisateur* and Senghor's *Anthologie de la Nouvelle Poésie nègre et malgache* of 1948. The Senghor preface takes the form of an essay, *Orphée Noir*, in which Sartre writes melodramatically of the new order that converts the European into the object of the African subject's gaze. We were used to seeing our greatness reflected, he insists, in the eyes of our African servants. But now, in a reversal of colonial paradigms, a would-be spectral black African imagination haunts a foregrounded colonial centre and France becomes exoticized and peripheral:

France is no more than a memory, a malaise, a white mist . . . a tormented hinterland. . . . Having drifted north, she is anchored near Kamtchatka. . . . Being is black. . . . We are mere accidents, remote and obliged to justify our customs and ways of doing things. . . . Under these tranquil and corrosive gazes, we are eaten through to the bone.[4]

The language of *Orphée Noir* suggests a form of cultural *Schadenfreude*, with Europe cast as a place of pathology and denied the cultural essentialism that historically it saw as its birthright. By the same token, the images of Africa that he proposes are wholly caricatural, as he flirts with racist stereotyping (dark eyes, dark skin, and a veiled cannibalism) and solar myth-making. Quoting from Césaire, 'Listen to the white world . . . Pity for our omniscient and naive conquerors', Sartre unsettles a philanthropic European complacency functioning in a colonial context.[5] Crucially, the ignorance that Césaire identifies at the heart of Western knowledge, while dismantling hegemonic cultural values, does not prevent Europe from being fascinated as much by its demise as by its former claims to glory.

A domestically generated Europhobia is central to the present study, which addresses contexts in which modern French writers, through contact with what a metropolitan consensus deems to be marginal, reflect on how cultural value and ethical authority are constructed, defended, and called into question. While Genet provides me with a chronological end-point, his energetic interrogation of the ways in which marginal cultures are perceived as deviant, foreign, dark, impenetrable, and Other implicitly sheds light on his predecessors. His campaigning embraced very openly issues of sexual politics, which he increasingly conjoins with the politics of race and social class. His last major work, *Un captif amoureux*, published in 1986, reflects on the West's policing of its borders. Having championed homosexuality and the victims of social marginalization in a national context in his earlier career, he now wrestles with the ethical dilemmas facing the sympathetic European eager to promote, but not expropriate, a cause and people (the Palestinians), whose dispossession is a direct consequence of Western *realpolitik*. *Un captif amoureux* is, then, a writing born out of recrimination, its author becoming Europe's apologist for what lies beyond its borders. In the words of Arnaud Malgorn, 'Genet the thief, the homosexual, the FLN militant, the West's witness at Sabra and Shatila, allows the Other to speak and his work . . . enables his reader to discover other legitimacies and so to discover himself as different'.[6]

Genet reflects keenly on his controversial engagement with not only the Palestinians but also the Black Panthers and the Baader Meinhof. He describes the Panthers as a dream-like presence adrift from the world of the dominant; they pursue a 'révolte poétique' (*CA*, 248) skirting round the edges of a hegemonic, stubbornly prosaic white culture. For Genet, seeing cultural dissidence as a poetry of unreality is not to hold it in check. Yet in the hands of his predecessors, the metaphors of dream and shadow regularly serve to contain and collapse radical difference. Chapter 1 explores Pierre Loti's exoticist evocation of the East. Significantly, the central protagonist in *Aziyadé*, to take just one of his novels, is the perplexed, wandering European, a British naval officer who literally polices Turkey at the time of the demise of the Ottoman Empire in 1878. Yet in donning the uniform of the Sultan's army and assuming the exotic identity of Arif-effendi, his intention is to relieve the sense of vacuity that mars his existence. Thus behind the Turkish dress lurks the desolate young boy back in rural England (*Az*, 89). The cure, then, for existential isolation is a phantasmagoric Istanbul.

The same compensatory logic is at work in Gauguin's autobiographical text *Noa Noa*, in which the painter-turned-writer offers a heady promotion of Oceania as a place that surpasses and reinvigorates a lethargic European *fin de siècle*. His enthusiasm for cultural exoticism is on the one hand a flagrant rebuttal of Parisian cultural norms; yet in another sense, with the commodification of his Polynesian work, a seemingly peripheral subject matter enjoys prestige in the late nineteenth-century Parisian art market. In this flirtation with other cultures, the evocation of a geographically remote otherness becomes imbricated with a promotion of Self and fluctuations in metropolitan taste.

In Proust's work, which I consider in Chapter 2, the debate on inside and outside, conformity and deviation, familiar and foreign, is highly developed. In his attempts to legitimize and make space for homosexuality, he reflects on what he sees as the constricting cultural geography of a heterosexual Europe. Getting beyond such orthodoxy entails the construction of an imaginary beyond the borders, claimed sexual deviance thus being accommodated symbolically in the colonial margins. The recourse to exoticism in the adjudication on sexual mores overlaps with Proust's analysis of the energies of xenophobia to form a psychosocial geometry, in which a hub of heterosexual conformity is set against a peripheral homosexuality.

Proust also insists provocatively on the analogous situation of Jew and homosexual, both figures being the butt of punitively normative cultures. He describes these inveterate marginals as 'shunning one another, seeking out those who are most directly their opposite, who do not want their company . . .; but also brought into the company of their own kind by the ostracism to which they are subjected, the opprobrium into which they have fallen' (*RMP*, II, 639) ['se fuyant les uns les autres, recherchant ceux qui sont le plus opposés, qui ne veulent pas d'eux . . .; mais aussi rassemblés à leurs pareils par l'ostracisme qui les frappe, l'opprobre où ils sont tombés'] (*RTP*, III, 18).[7] Proust thus describes the deep-seated ambivalence whereby the outcast shuttles between social acceptance and the accommodation afforded by exclusion and the flight from the centre.

In Chapter 3, I explore the exotic in Montherlant. In biographical terms, his travels to North Africa and sexual tastes recall those of Gide. But I include him not on account of his homosexuality or his revisitation of classical myth, but rather to analyse his reflections on colonization and cultural blindness. Issues of gender and sexuality are nevertheless inseparable from colonial discourse, as his novel of the early 1930s, *La Rose de sable*, demonstrates. Montherlant makes ambitious claims, describing his work as straddling anticolonialism and colonialist myth-making. He investigates, often melodramatically and with the mindset of his day, the French military legacy in colonial Morocco. With its conjunction of Arabophobic instincts and incipient xenophilia, *La Rose de sable* provides a reliable cultural barometer of the inter-war years. While often culturally authoritarian, the novel works to lay bare the violence underpinning such hierarchy. Brutalization impacts not only on the indigenous population but also on the novel's French-soldier hero. At its height, the drama precipitates a crisis in metropolitan values and destabilizes a hitherto sustaining discourse of patriotism.

The idea of the colonial fringes as the laboratory in which the colonizer's self-image is shaped finds an especially potent expression in the work of Camus. As a French Algerian, he occupied a peripheral position in relation to metropolitan tradition. Indeed, he protested his very particular kind of Europeanness, lived out on the limb that was French colonial culture in North Africa. When insurrection in Algeria forced France to reassess its position, Camus pleaded with characteristic stubbornness for the rights of the *petits colons*, the interstitial grouping to which he belonged. The strains between mother country and French Algerian border territory are central to Camus's work. In his analysis of the margins, tribal identity becomes fraught. Faced with French intolerance of the *petits colons*, who serve as an uncomfortable reminder of the colonial legacy, Camus appeals to history and confronts head-on the charge of abusive exploitation:

There must be . . . an end to this blanket condemnation of the French Algerians. Those in the metropolis who do not tire of hating them need to be reminded of the requirements of decency. When a French supporter of the FLN has the audacity to write that French Algerians have always seen France as a prostitute to be exploited, he needs to be aware that he is speaking irresponsibly about men whose grandparents, for example, opted for France in 1871 and left their native Alsace for Algeria, whose fathers died in large numbers in eastern France in 1914, and who themselves, twice mobilized in the last war, served on every front for this prostitute alongside hundreds of thousands of Muslims.

[Il faut cesser . . . de porter condamnation en bloc sur les Français d'Algérie. Une certaine opinion métropolitaine, qui ne se lasse pas de les haïr, doit être rappelée à la décence. Quand un partisan français du FLN ose écrire que les Français d'Algérie ont toujours considéré la France comme une prostituée à exploiter, il faut rappeler à cet irresponsable qu'il parle d'hommes dont les grands-parents, par exemple, ont opté pour la France en 1871 et quitté leur terre d'Alsace pour l'Algérie, dont les pères sont morts en masse dans l'Est de la France en 1914 et qui, eux-mêmes, deux fois mobilisés dans la dernière guerre, n'ont cessé, avec des centaines de milliers de musulmans, de se battre sur tous les fronts pour cette prostituée.][8]

In the embroiled debate about belonging and cultural affiliation, key elements in the power relation between centre and periphery emerge. Firstly, the essentially antagonistic nature of relations between French and French Algerians is revealed via a degraded sexuality, which captures the invective and anxiety that the North African fringes generate. Secondly, we have the feminizing of France, which sees itself as benign and munificent, Camus resenting the inference that the colonial margins act in an aggressively predatorial way. And thirdly, via the brothers-in-arms motif, the majority Muslim viewpoint is erased to the extent that it is conflated with that of the *petit colon*.

Camus's counter-discourse appeals to Frenchness and a legacy of heroic service to the nation. He rebuts the accusation of lurid exploitation, laying claim to a deeper, historically rooted Francophilia. Thus metropolitan disgust at the spectacle of *pied-noir* loyalism is the emotion generated by what, for the Parisian intelligentsia that Camus so chided, is the unwelcome reminder of a colonial past.

In attempting to define the margins, we are therefore necessarily involved in a simultaneous reflection on the status of the centre. Geoffrey Bennington reminds us how tempting it is to 'approach the question of nation directly by aiming for its centre or its origin'.[9] The satisfaction lies in identifying stories of national origins and founding mythologies, an example of which is Camus's tenacious will to position those on the edge at the centre of a national patrimony. But as Bennington adds, as soon as we look to the borders, the mythic origins are compromised because we are forced into an awareness of what lies beyond them. Thus the frontier 'closes the nation in on itself but also, immediately, opens it to an outside'. Bennington goes on to quote Edgar Morin:

All frontiers, including the membrane of living beings, including the frontier[s] of nations, are, at the same time as they are barriers, places of communication and exchange. *They are places of dissociation and association, of separation and articulation.*[10]

While Morin outlines the potential for communication along the border, the authors considered in the present study respond in different ways to the invitation to association posed by the Other. In each of the cases considered, definition of Self is provoked by the preoccupation with what is marginal and with the idea of the frontier. The polarities are typically North and South, the West and the rest, moribund and youthful, believer and infidel, health and pathology, the normal and the deviant, the familiar and the exotic. Such binarism itself fosters a politics of exclusion.

Genet headlines the violence spawned by borders and the insidious desire to recast relativities as imperious absolutes. Hence his insistence on a cultural geography that is always provisional:

Exoticism, the wonder you feel at what you see when at last you've crossed the ever-receding horizon. Beyond – but there's never any beyond except another changing horizon, necessarily a strange one, a foreign one. My long journeys became so familiar they concealed that crossing of the line, but in the end I thought that as I wrote this book I could make out, if only through a mist, not only France but also the West in general. . . . They had become utterly exotic to me, so that I went to France as a Frenchman might go to Burma. (*PL*, 338)

[exotisme, cet étonnement de voir enfin, quand on a franchi la ligne d'horizon qui sans cesse recule. Derrière elle, c'est qu'il n'y a jamais de derrière elle sauf la ligne d'horizon qui change et bien sûr c'est l'étranger. Ces longs voyages avec la familiarité entretenue justement là que me cachait cette ligne toujours franchie, c'est par l'effet d'une longue familiarité des voyages, presque d'une urgence, que, non la France seule mais l'Occident, je crus les distinguer en écrivant ce livre, mais les distinguer dans des brumes. Ils me parurent . . . l'exotisme suprême au point que j'allais en France comme un Français va en Birmanie.] (*CA*, 553)

While this decentring and the challenge to Western authority do not guarantee liberation from cultural hegemony, Genet delights in a distortion of the familiar and a conceptual relocation of France, thereby sealing his self-image as elusive migrant.

Readers may find my choice of authors eccentric. Unlike Proust, Camus, and Genet, Loti, Gauguin, and Montherlant are not canonical writers. Yet the works of each of these authors, major and minor alike, express a cultural malaise in which the insufficiency of Self regularly awakens a desire to explore as well as to police the exotic horizon. Were we to be guided solely by the canon, we might forget that Loti was a dominant figure in the *fin de siècle*, satisfying its appetite for the exotic, that Gauguin's fantastic paradise in *Noa Noa* connects with a tradition of exoticist curiosity in French literature, that Montherlant's Moroccan novel provides an exemplary depiction of the colonial mindset while trying to transcend it. The canon may exclude novels such as *Le Roman d'un spahi* and *La Rose de sable*, metaphorically removing from view reminders of the racist supremacism on which colonization was predicated. Yet if we readmit these texts and unpick sufficiently others such as *À la recherche du temps perdu*, we discover the common threads at the heart of Eurocentric fantasy. My chosen authors explore, anecdotally or theoretically, an often anxious exoticism, drawing out the social, ethical, and sexual tensions that this anxiety entails. Such tensions form provocative nexus-points, where the Western sexual dissident, to take just one recurring example, encounters the ethnic Other. These connections are in one sense wholly arbitrary. After all, why should the transsexual be likened to a Palestinian bomber, or the homosexual to a black African or a Jew? Why cast the North African Muslim or the Japanese bride as a child? Why see medieval France as pure, Algeria as having no history, or Polynesians as being androgynous. Yet we find these random projections, evaluations, and alliances in writers working ambiguously against and with a metropolitan bourgeoisie. Like Loti, Gauguin rails against a repressive West; like Camus's Cormery, the protagonist in Montherlant's *La Rose de sable* is obliquely positioned in relation to a cultural centre; like Genet, who attacks metropolitan values, Proust dismantles social consensus although in a radically different, much more veiled manner. But gesturing towards cultural difference in no way guarantees dialectical engagement with it. Indeed, it is often an ambivalent move, entailing the pursuit of private goals – sexual, political, aesthetic – and the collateral exclusion of the Other.

CHAPTER ONE

Without obligation: exotic appropriation in Loti and Gauguin

'We all call barbarous anything that is contrary to our own habits.'[1] Montaigne's celebrated call for cultural relativism provides us with an early example of a European, and more specifically French, tradition of questioning one's own cultural legacy through the invocation of difference. Occupying a central position in the French literary canon, 'Des cannibales' conflates a quasi-ethnographic self-scrutiny and the interrogation of other traditions. Thus behind Montaigne's defence of the non-European lies his denunciation of a barbarous European legacy, epitomized by the Wars of Religion in sixteenth-century France. This circuitousness, working back from the exotic to the domestic, forms a leitmotif in French literature. In Montesquieu's *Lettres persanes* (1721), for example, the Persians Usbek and Rica pen letters that convey a satirical view of France, as well as throwing light on the Orient. Interest in the exotic in nineteenth-century France was intense, with Ingres's erotic Oriental interiors and Delacroix's Morocco, the poetry of Hugo, Nerval, and Baudelaire, and the prose of Chateaubriand and Flaubert being among the most notable examples in a highly developed tradition. But again, the gesturing towards alterity implicit in such exoticism regularly involves Western projection and fantasy, and comes with a backhanded reference to domestic norms and values.

In the representation of a specifically Polynesian exotic, Bougainville's *Voyage autour du monde* of 1771 prompted Diderot's fictitious *Supplément au Voyage de Bougainville*, which highlights the deficiencies of European mores alongside their supposedly more primitive Polynesian equivalents.[2] Diderot makes ironically strong claims in respect of Tahitian culture in an oblique reflection on individual freedom in civilized society:

the savage life is so simple and our societies such complicated machines! The Tahitian is in contact with the origins of the world, the European with its old age. The distance between the Tahitian and us is greater than the distance

9

between a newborn child and a decrepit man. He understands nothing of our customs and laws, or he sees them as so many obstacles disguised in a hundred and one different ways; such obstacles can only awaken the indignation and disdain of someone for whom the instinct of freedom is the most deep-seated of all.[3]

If Diderot aims to jolt his reader out of cultural complacency, the attribution to the Polynesian of an infantilized simplicity and the insistence on tidy points of beginning and ending signal a clichéd binarism. While he stops short of any wholehearted endorsement of Tahitian ways, his flirtatious parable adumbrates a connection between Self and ethnic Other. Drawing on Freud, Julia Kristeva describes how the final and the original fascinate and trouble us.[4] In the debate about cultural value being constructed around a progressivist model of human development, an identitarian drama is thus externalized in the opposition between birth and death, liberty and restriction, Polynesian and European.

Diderot relates a fictitious dialogue between the Polynesian Orou and the Christian chaplain in which Orou signals the perversity of such traditions as celibacy in religious orders and monogamy.[5] Orou's concluding line ('you are more barbarous than we are'), a familiar retort in would-be sympathetic Western accounts of non-European cultures, reinforces the colonialist polarities of culture and nature, civilization and barbarism.[6] Diderot's highly schematic insistence on an emancipatory Polynesian simplicity anticipates aggressive claims about release from moral inhibition in the exoticist work of Loti and Gauguin. Here too, the risk is of commodifying the Other in order to guarantee a prestigious exotic.

Exploiting difference is not to be confused with disinterested access to the culture of the Other. As Kirk Varnedoe writes in his lucid discussion of Gauguin's legacy, each civilization invents the primitive that it needs, seeing in the Other, even of colonialist exploitation, a partial self-image, the preservation of an essential, original Self that pre-dates moral restriction and the burden of civilization.[7] Freud confirms the paradigm in *Civilization and its Discontents*, where he notes the West's idealization of primitive lifestyles as liberating, in contrast with the sacrifices the mature ego must endure in defence of civilization.[8]

Loti and Gauguin both exploit the otherness of Oceania. They had first-hand experience of Polynesia: Gauguin lived most of the last decade of his life in the Pacific Islands, first in Tahiti and then in the Marquesas Islands; and as Lieutenant Julien Viaud, Loti served in the French navy at a time of colonial expansion, travelling not just to

Polynesia but also to Africa, China, and Japan. Coincidentally, another uniformed officer, Victor Segalen, a naval doctor who charted the legacy of pathology and violence inflicted on Polynesian islanders by Western colonialists and adventurers, was to act as Gauguin's executor.[9] Arriving in Hiva Oa, Gauguin's final dwelling place, shortly after the painter's death in 1903, Segalen set about preserving not native culture but the primitivist legacy constructed by the self-proclaimed European savage.

Loti and Segalen have until recently been consigned to the literary margins, while Gauguin's celebrity as a primitivist painter has often obscured his work as a writer. Yet if late nineteenth-century bourgeois taste is anything to go by, Loti certainly was a dominant figure in the canon and his tales from Oceania formed part of the cultural lexicon of Parisian drawing rooms. His *Le Mariage de Loti* of 1880, which tells the story of an English naval officer's love for his young Tahitian bride Rarahu, enjoyed enormous popularity, running to a seventy-fifth edition by 1905. It served as required reading for soldiers, sailors, and administrators posted to Oceania, illustrating how today's often discarded text was the vade mecum for a whole generation embarking on colonial service.[10] The novel addresses, directly and in terms that often jar in a postcolonial age, questions of claimed moral authority and cultural value that shaped the history of French colonization. Indeed, if we are to believe one of France's most vigorous proponents of colonial expansion, Marshal Lyautey, Loti's first novel, *Aziyadé*, lamenting the demise of the Ottoman Empire, exerted more influence on public opinion in Europe in the years prior to the establishment of an independent Turkey than did Mustapha Kemal himself![11]

In a reinforcement of established cultural stereotypes, *fin-de-siècle* writers on France's colonial possessions restate the infantilism of the colonized and the empowering rejuvenation this offers. But they also protest that the civilization of 'these child-beings' has become moribund, in that these supposedly restorative spaces are now sites of disease and death caused by a pathogenic European presence.[12] In a letter to Jules de Gaultier, Segalen laments the 'painful civilizing experience undergone by these noble . . . countries'.[13] A decade earlier, Gauguin, writing about the death of the Polynesian King Pomaré in *Noa Noa*, announces the end of an era:

With him, Maori history came to a definitive end. . . . Alas, the civilization of the barrack-room, of trade and colonial administration won the day.
A profound sadness took hold of me.

[Avec lui se fermait l'histoire maorie. C'était bien fini. . . . La civilisation, hélas!
– soldatesque, négoce et fonctionnarisme – triomphait.
Une tristesse profonde s'empara de moi.] (*NN*, 40)[14]

Similar entropic accounts were already to be found in Loti's writing:
'Civilization has also been there too much, our stupid colonial civilization, all our conventions, customs, and vices, and the savage poetry disappears with the ways and traditions of the past' ['La civilisation y est
trop venue aussi, notre sotte civilisation coloniale, toutes nos conventions, toutes nos habitudes, tous nos vices, et la sauvage poésie s'en va,
avec les coutumes et les traditions du passé'] (*ML*, 52). But while Loti,
Gauguin, and Segalen all witness first hand the military might underpinning colonialism, they ambivalently dissociate themselves from the
same colonial rule that facilitates their exotic art.

In this picture of once vigorous cultures facing extinction in the wake
of colonization, a fundamental tension in European exoticism emerges.
Leconte de Lisle's 'The Last of the Maoris' ['Le Dernier des Maourys'],
published in 1889, encapsulates the ambiguity. The poem com-
memorates a Maori past, characterized by its traditions of freedom and
aggressive cannibalism, and the chief, the sole survivor of his race,
defiantly apportions blame for his tribe's demise to white settlers. The
tone of eulogy adopted in respect of the Maori by the author of the
Poèmes barbares is matched by a sense of violent disaffection from contemporary history and religion: 'it follows on from the natural repulsion that
we feel for that which kills us that I hate the times in which I live'.[15] Yet
Leconte de Lisle's revulsion for what is metaphorically lethal in French
society has a literal application in the colony, for the genocide hinted at
in the poet's choice of title is as much a consequence of European colonization as of inter-ethnic conflict in the Pacific. Thus the late nineteenth-century representation of the Polynesian is indissociable from the
rhetoric of morbid finality.

BETWEEN DISAFFECTION AND DENIGRATION: THE CASE OF PIERRE LOTI

Like Leconte de Lisle, Loti experienced disillusionment with contemporary France, his fiction promoting primitive ritual and archaism as anti-
dotes to republican contemporaneity. From the Istanbul of the decaying
Ottoman Empire in *Aziyadé* to the Tahiti of *Le Mariage de Loti* and
Nagasaki in *Madame Chrysanthème*, his naval-officer protagonist pursues a
series of liaisons with native women, while in *Le Roman d'un spahi*, the

marginalized soldier-hero, Peyral, serves in Senegal. Critics have rightly spelt out Loti's sexual opportunism and predatorial imagination, Lesley Blanch referring to the syndrome of 'living, loving, leaving'.[16] But his writing also has an important documentary function in that it charts the massive colonial expansion that facilitates his exoticism. At Mers el-Kébir in December 1869, the hunger and dispossession witnessed in Arab encampments cause him to lament 'the remains of a powerful nation that today succumbs, like the Natchez and so many others before it, to the merciless invasion of our civilization' ['ces débris d'une nation puissante qui succombe aujourd'hui, comme autrefois les Natchez et tant d'autres, sous la main de notre civilisation envahissante et impitoyable'].[17] In successive visits to Algeria, he reflects on the disfigurement of local culture, especially its architecture. And in *Le Figaro* in 1912, he roundly condemns the massacres that marked the early colonization of Algeria.[18]

But as Alain Quella-Villéger demonstrates, one episode in particular highlights Loti's engagement as a critical observer of colonial rule: the Tonkin expedition of 1883. Loti lambasts the government for sending to their deaths thousands of young French soldiers. In three articles, two of them unsigned, which appeared in *Le Figaro* in September and October 1883, he describes in lurid detail the massacre of Annamite civilians. His trenchant journalism fuelled intense criticism of the government of the day and hastened his recall, as Lieutenant Viaud, to France. The silencing of Loti (his accounts are nowhere to be found in the official *Histoire militaire de l'Indochine* of 1922) is an indirect tribute to his commitment to expose the scandal whereby, in Loti's formulation, Paris-based generals were sending young Breton sailors into a brutalizing campaign. Loti was later to censor his accounts of the Annam massacres in the *Revue de Paris* in 1897 and it is this expurgated version that Aimé Césaire condemns as sadistic and colonialist.[19]

The Annam scandal indicates that, far from cynically endorsing colonial policy, Loti was actively informing the public, through the pages of *Le Figaro*, of the realities of war in French Indo-China. His campaigning journalism does not excuse the racist stereotyping that peppers his fiction. But it illustrates how, within late nineteenth-century French culture, we have these eccentric, ambiguous voices, decrying colonial excesses while simultaneously articulating the crude prejudice of their day.

Denigration is certainly writ large in *Le Mariage de Loti*. How can we, the protagonist protests, born on the other side of the globe, begin to understand '*these incomplete beings*, who are so different from us, whose inner being remains mysterious and savage, and yet who demonstrate on certain occasions so much loving charm and exquisite sensitivity' ['*ces natures incomplètes*, si différentes des nôtres, chez qui le fond demeure mystérieux et sauvage, et où l'on trouve pourtant, à certaines heures, tant de charme d'amour, et d'exquise sensibilité'] (*ML*, 201; my italics). While the inferred plenitude of the civilized European is clear, incompleteness and lack also afflict the protagonist Loti, in that part of his mission in Polynesia is to establish contact with the family of his deceased older brother Georges, who had been married to a Tahitian. The quest for his nephew, seen as a young savage joined to Loti by a powerful blood-tie, introduces an intriguing hybridity spanning his native England and Polynesia (*ML*, 185–7).

Superficially, miscegenation suggests an interpenetration that gets beyond a casual exoticism. Yet Loti's projections involve an incorporation back into Westernness of the so-called savage. An ambiguous satisfaction marks the moment when the Tahitian wife of his brother recounts in her native tongue Loti's own childhood (*ML*, 185–7). In this narrating back of stories issuing from a cultural cradle in England, Loti's pleasure is to recognize himself in the speech and language of the Other. The exotic stands as a form of *déjà vu*, the Oceania that Loti now experiences becoming inseparable from the Pacific islands that he imagined earlier in Brightbury:

As a small boy living in the family home, my imagination would turn to Oceania; through the fantastic veil of the unknown, I had understood it and imagined it just as I find it today. – All these sites were DEJA VU, all these names known, all the characters are those who years ago haunted my boyhood dreams, so much so that at times I think it's today that I'm dreaming . . .

[Petit garçon, au foyer de famille, je songeais a l'Océanie; à travers le voile fantastique de l'inconnu, je l'avais comprise et devinée telle que je la trouve aujourd'hui. – Tous ces sites étaient DÉJÀ VUS, tous ces noms étaient connus, tous ces personnages sont bien ceux qui jadis hantaient mes rêves d'enfant, si bien que par instants c'est aujourd'hui que je crois rêver . . .'] (*ML*, 73; Loti's capitalization; ellipsis in the original)

The reversal of past and present confirms the view that the 'real' Tahiti can only ever be a shadow of the projected Tahiti of Loti's childhood. Thus, an oneiric Other is always already a product, a projection of the Self and, in this instance, literally recounts back to the European the story of his origins. Not only is exoticism then predicated on incomprehension and seduction, as Todorov observes, but it entails a tracking back from the periphery to within the Self.[20]

In Loti's first novel, *Aziyadé*, set in Salonika and Constantinople, cultural difference is depicted in similarly stereotypical ways. As with *Le Mariage de Loti* and *Madame Chrysanthème*, so long as the ship is in port, Lieutenant Loti can pursue his amorous adventures ashore. But once the order to set sail is issued, the liaison must end. Thus the ship crudely circumscribes interaction between European and Other, both chronologically and at a broader cultural level. Loti may protest his good faith, evidenced by his defection from Europe and his claimed validation of what the West discards, but the ring-fencing of contact remains an incontrovertible given.

'IL N'Y A D'URGENT QUE LE DÉCOR'[21]

The dramatization of contact with the Other dominates the opening pages of *Le Mariage de Loti*. In a ceremonial baptism conducted by three Tahitian noblewomen, the Polynesian names of Loti and Rémuna, both denoting flowers, are bestowed on the English officers Harry Grant and Plumket, both of whom cease to exist in Oceania, the text summarily announces (*ML*, 50). By a bizarre twist, the newly acquired Tahitian pseudonym Loti will become Viaud's *nom de plume.*[22]

In ideological terms, acquiring new identities is provocatively unproblematized, a change of name bringing effortless self-transformation. In *Aziyadé*, the same is true of a change of dress. Here, the restless protagonist, disguised as a Turk, heads off by night into Constantinople to meet up with his Circassian lover, Aziyadé. Slipping away from the naval vessel with his Macedonian manservant, Samuel, he assumes his new identity effortlessly: 'I remove the greatcoat covering my Turkish costume and *the transformation is complete*' ['j'enlève le manteau qui couvrait mon costume turc et *la transformation est faite*'] (*Az*, 60; my italics). The provocatively superficial change in no way diminishes the sureness of this Romantic conversion. In Loti's projection, Aziyadé too is all dress, so veiled that she becomes a formless white mass. Likewise, lavish furnishings fill the boat in which she travels as the clandestine lover, the stress on replenishment and supplementation underlining the incompletion and vacuity associated with the Other: 'One finds all the refinements of Oriental nonchalance, and it looks more like a floating bed than a boat' [On y trouve tous les raffinements de la nonchalance orientale, et il semblerait voir un lit qui flotte plutôt qu'une barque'] (*Az*, 60). The scene, which captures symptomatically the writer Loti's escape from his austere Huguenot background into Islamic decorativeness, underscores the place of dress, materials, and textures.[23] These are central to the exoticized description of the lovers and their temporary habitat, suggesting that this perilous union, formed 'so as to enjoy together the heady charms of the impossible' ['pour goûter ensemble les charmes enivrants de l'impossible'] (*Az*, 61), is consummated in the bringing together of exterior surfaces. Cultural transformation is thus to be realized unproblematically through accessories of dress rather than any deep conversion.

Barthes's elegant essay on *Aziyadé* has helped rescue the novel and its author from obscurity.[24] Identifying in the protagonist Loti a fanatical transvestism (*NCE*, 114), he catalogues the hero's tactical use of disguise – as Turk, sailor, Albanian, and dervish – to gain access to Aziyadé and infiltrate old Turkish culture. Analysing Loti's eventual decision to defend the ailing Ottoman Empire by donning the uniform of its army, Barthes highlights the ambiguity in Loti's desire to 'become a Turk in essence, i.e., in costume' (*NCE*, 115). As he wonders ominously whether or not he should enlist in the Sultan's army, Loti fantasizes about becoming the yuzbachi Arif, returning to Eyoub in uniform, and telling Aziyadé that he is not leaving after all (*Az*, 180). A cultural migration – *becoming* a Turkish officer and rescuing an impossible love – would thus be guaranteed ostensibly by pulling on ethnic dress.

The result of the protagonist Loti's successive reincarnations is that in willing this cultural migration, he studiously avoids the discourse of depth. He consciously refers to his *dream* of moving into Eyoub, the holy quarter of Istanbul, and assuming the name Arif. His Muslim neighbours treat the fiction with benign tolerance. They know he is a Western Christian, but no one takes umbrage at his Oriental fantasy, he reflects innocently, and they indulgently call him by his Turkish name (*Az*, 97). In a striking image of isolation, we see him alone in his apartment, 'all wrapped up in a fox-skin overcoat, and imagining that he is a dervish' ['bien enveloppé dans un manteau de peau de renard, et en train de se prendre pour un derviche'] (*Az*, 90). Loti's cultivation of superficiality is practised in a disarmingly self-aware manner. The injection of an intense theatricality and the aggressive promotion of surface textures suggest an effortless cultural appropriation. The transparency of the gestures is captured emblematically with his quickfire culture-switching in a café in the Galata region of Istanbul. For Loti: 'I went in through the main door dressed as a European, and left as a Turk [via the back door] onto the cul-de-sac' ['J'entrais en vêtements européens par la grande porte, et je sortais en Turc par l'impasse'] (*Az*, 134). The disarming trivialization of otherness is arresting. But these automatic gestures may attenuate the charge of an exploitative European imagination and suggest a self-deluding and, one is almost tempted to say (remembering the indulgence shown Arif/Loti by his Muslim neighbours), innocuous cultural migration.

Such a reading however ignores those instances where Loti shows an authoritarian indifference to the fate of the dying Aziyadé, who is the undoubted victim in this story of impossible love. Here, the otherwise naive promotion of fantasy becomes unquestionably wilful and predatorial. Nevertheless, Loti experiences self-delusion and not self-incrimination when, having crossed a frontier using his Ottoman passport, he reports that the authorities ignore his poor command of Turkish and allow themselves to be taken in by his beads and costume (*Az*, 175). The apparent complicity between an indulgent ethnic Other and Loti reinforces the mythopoeic order.

That dress should supersede ethical responsibility is precisely the aspect of *Aziyadé* that Barthes draws out when he comments on the protagonist Loti's insertion in the various tableaux of Turkish life: 'the goal of transvestism is finally (once the illusion of being is exhausted) to transform oneself into a describable object – and not into an introspectible subject' (*NCE*, 115). In subtracting introspection from the portrait of Lieutenant Loti, Barthes does not extract *Aziyadé* from the category of colonialist literature, in which the Other is regularly assigned to a negative vacuity. Rather, he exposes the European colonial imagination as a force that cavalierly dispenses with depth. Thus, the ready availability of local forms of dress parallels the accessibility of native spaces such as Loti's habitat in the holy quarter of Eyoub or the mosque (the empty mosque, as Barthes is quick to point out), which the Christian lieutenant transgressively enters.

Loti's compulsive transvestism finds its authoritarian correlative in a regressive politics, the imperious political fiat being as arbitrary as the automatism of dress switching. Likewise, in the novel's climactic finale, as the narrator decries the imminent demise of the Ottoman Empire, abandoned by the European powers in 1878, so Aziyadé's fate is sealed. Her death, like the imperial collapse, appears a necessary outcome, given the impossibility that marks the relationship with Loti. The graveyard where Aziyadé is buried – 'The cemetery did not convey the horror of our European cemeteries; its Oriental sadness was sweeter and also more imposing' ['Ce cimetière n'avait pas l'horreur de nos cimetières d'Europe; sa tristesse orientale était plus douce, et aussi plus grandiose']

(*Az*, 220) – is linked specifically with momentous political changes, 'when the destinies of men and empires reach decisive crisis points, when destinies are at an end' ['quand les destinées des hommes ou des empires touchent aux grandes crises décisives, quand les destinées s'achèvent'] (*Az*, 220–1). Similarly, the central protagonist, now far from his native Yorkshire and bearing arms for the Sultan, sees his transformation mirrored in a momentous contemporary history. In this way, Loti's private desire is realized within the very public domain of the dissolution of empire. Recording the sound of the Turks going to battle, the protagonist adopts a tone of elegiac grandeur: 'it was like the final hunting-down of Islam and the Orient, the swan-song of the great race of Genghis' ['on eût dit le suprême hallali de l'islamisme et de l'Orient, le chant de mort de la grande race de Tchengiz'] (*Az*, 221). As in *Le Mariage de Loti*, the exotic is here inseparable from an entropic order.

The conflation of surface and being in *Aziyadé* is picked up by Barthes, who enthuses: '*the person is nothing but this desired image which the garment permits us to believe in*' (*NCE*, 115; my italics). And the Turk of the old days that Loti longs to be is, in Barthes's words, 'a man of pure desire, cut loose from the Occident and from modernism, insofar as, in the eyes of a modern Occidental, one and the other are identified with the very responsibility of living' (*NCE*, 115).

The novel regularly denigrates contemporary Europe and republican democracy. The corollary is the idealization of scenes in the Turkish cafe, where pashas and ordinary folk mix: 'O Equality! unknown in our democratic nation, our Western republics!' ['Ô Egalité! inconnue à notre nation démocratique, à nos républiques occidentales!'] (*Az*, 135). In Loti's manipulative ethnography, Ottoman hierarchy becomes egalitarian. He commends the vigorous discussion of political developments in popular circles in Turkey, and contrasts this with the apathy obtaining in equivalent social groups back home. He longs for release from isolation, while railing against his own cultural legacy: 'I loathe all work that does not require physical, muscular effort, all science, all the conventional duties and social obligations of our Western countries' ['j'ai horreur de tout travail qui n'est pas du corps et des muscles; horreur de toute science; haine de tous les devoirs conventionnels, de toutes les obligations sociales de nos pays d'Occident'] (*Az*, 118). The cult of the vigorous body and the devaluing of the intellect are part of the regressive politics that remedy Loti's rootlessness. Imagining mundane pleasures, he dreams of finding acceptance in a socially obscure milieu: 'O to be a boatman in a gilt jacket, somewhere off Southern Turkey' ['Être batelier en veste dorée, quelque part au sud de la Turquie'] (*Az*, 118). Again, the sartorial detail encapsulates the dream of release from duty.

Tahiti and Istanbul emerge then as sites of irresponsibility, as Barthes infers. As we read in *Le Mariage de Loti*, Tahiti is another staging-post for Loti's fantasy: 'The whole country and my beloved girlfriend were going to disappear, like the decor for an act that has just ended . . .' ['Tout ce pays et ma petite amie bien-aimée allaient disparaître, comme s'é-vanouit le décor de l'acte qui vient de finir . . .'] (*ML*, 207; ellipsis in the original). Likewise, in the ball thrown by Queen Pomaré in honour of the departing naval officers, images of decadence predominate, the message being that European contact with the Tahitians is a party now over. Loti, Barthes's 'man of pure desire', leaves behind in Polynesia a culture described increasingly in moribund terms and summed up in the plight of Loti's wife, Rarahu, who expires 'in the abyss of eternal noth-ingness!' ['dans l'abîme de l'éternel néant!'] (*ML*, 227). Rarahu is, apply-ing Barthes's verdict on *Aziyadé*, 'the necessary name of the Forbidden, the pure form under which a thousand social transgressions can be accounted for' (*NCE*, 112). Thus taboo in the cultural fringes is explored without retribution or sanction.

A COMMODIFIED EXOTIC

The same unfettered licence marks *Madame Chrysanthème*. Here the cul-tural malcontent refers to his stop-over in Nagasaki as his little Japanese comedy (*MC*, 201). It is marked by surface appearances, costumes, and the heavily ritualized bodily expression of obsequiousness that the pro-tagonist Loti ridicules. Poses supplant psychological depth, so that the sleeping figure of Chrysanthème is welcomed for its decorativeness. The brevity of Loti's marriage to her is celebrated at the end of the novel in the nonchalant prayer to the Shinto god Ama-Terace-Omi-Kami: 'wash me clean and white from this little marriage in the waters of the river of Kamo . . .' ['lavez-moi bien blanchement de ce petit mariage, dans les eaux de la rivière de Kamo . . .'] (*MC*, 232). The disengagement is as painless as the initial search for a bride on arrival in Nagasaki is peremp-tory.

Acts of engagement are also associated with surfaces, literally so when, to mark his stay in Japan, Loti summons local tattoo artists, who inscribe on his chest the image of a chimera. The inscription is added to the collection of tattoos religiously accumulated in other exotic sites. Similarly, ritual closes this ambiguous encounter with the Other:

A farewell tea, for which we will use the greatest possible pomp. Besides, it's in keeping with my tradition of rounding off my exotic existences with a fete.

[Un thé d'adieu, alors, pour lequel nous déploierons le plus de pompe possible. Cela rentre dans ma manière, du reste, de clore mes existences exotiques par une fête.] (*MC*, 214)

These serial exotic existences tell us more about Loti than about the cultures visited. As he points out in his dedication of the novel to the Duchesse de Richelieu, the novel's three principal characters are himself, Japan, and the effect the country has on him. Like Rarahu and Aziyadé before her, Madame Chrysanthème catalyses the reactions of the colonial sailor.

In contrast with the Arabophilia found in *Aziyadé*, *Madame Chrysanthème* vilifies Japanese culture as ugly, grotesque, and miniature. While conceding that he overuses the adjective 'petit' (*MC*, 182), Loti proposes alternative pejoratives, likening Japanese women to dolls, puppets, and ornaments. They possess a 'childhood that persists to the end of their lives' ['enfance qui persiste jusqu'à la fin de la vie'] (*MC*, 81), Loti asserting that death matters less for 'this light, childlike people' ['ce peuple enfantin et léger'] (*MC*, 111).

The racism, often vicious and authoritarian, is stemmed in moments of cultural impenetrability: the erection of altars to the memory of deceased relatives, for example, arrests the denigration, as does the spectacle of two elaborately dressed, upper-class women, who exude superiority and thus an elusive difference: 'And as I stare at them, I muse: how different we are from the Japanese; how unlike them we are! . . .' ['Et je songe, en les dévisageant: comme nous sommes loin de ce peuple japonais, comme nous sommes de race dissemblable! . . .'] (*MC*, 186–7; ellipsis in the original). There is the occasional *mea culpa*, along with glimpses of sensitivity that are still couched in caricatural terms. Moments of epiphany such as an enormous red sunset reveal a hackneyed Romanticism and prompt Loti to feel almost at home. Cultural difference is crudely grasped, the singing of Madame Chrysanthème and her companion being likened to the thinking of a bird or the dreaming of a monkey. Notwithstanding this simian Other, Loti protests that he is shedding Western prejudices. Yet the claimed enlightenment cannot undo the trivialization of Japanese life, a point confirmed by Loti's self-image as a form of homunculus:

I am now getting accustomed to Japanese preciosity; I am becoming smaller and more mannered; I feel my thoughts narrowing . . .; I'm getting used to the ingenious pieces of small furniture, the doll-size writing-desks.

[Voici que je me fais très bien à ce Japon mignard maintenant; je me rapetisse et je me manière; je sens mes pensées se rétrécir . . .; je m'habitue aux petits meubles ingénieux, aux pupitres de poupée pour écrire.] (*MC*, 203).

The act of writing itself becomes diminutive, like the Japanese kitsch that it evokes.

Likewise, Loti's capacity for mimicry spells an always superficial engagement with cultural difference. In formal terms, the heavily fragmented nature of this short novel with its fifty-four chapters and regular use of ellipsis confirms the impression of non-engagement. The denigration is reinforced with the assertion that the encounter with Madame Chrysanthème does not belong to the tragic genre.

As in *Aziyadé* and *Le Mariage de Loti*, the European protagonist's quest for what he construes as genuine cultural difference draws him back to the archaic. He glimpses, among the thousands of newer dwellings in Nagasaki, older residences, 'probably the old, authentic Japanese Nagasaki that still survives . . .' ['probablement le vrai, le vieux Nagasaki japonais qui subsiste encore . . .'] (*MC*, 52; ellipsis in the original). While the disappearance of a mummified ancient Japan, inundated with Western artefacts and ways (*MC*, 228), causes him disappointment, the lament is self-interested in that he requires the difference that colonial service regularly provides. Hence the complaint: 'A time will come when the earth will be a boring place to inhabit, when it will be the same from one end to the other, and when you won't even be able to travel for a bit of amusement . . .' ['Il viendra un temps où la terre sera bien ennuyeuse à habiter, quand on l'aura rendue pareille d'un bout à l'autre, et qu'on ne pourra même plus essayer de voyager pour se distraire un peu . . .'] (*MC*, 50; ellipsis in the original).

But if this dislike of cultural homogenization betrays the exoticist's need for the palliative of a reified difference, there are moments when he finds life's *ennui* intolerable. Mortality haunts the protagonist Loti, who fears that he will never know the lands he dreamt of in his childhood. The death instinct is captured when, travelling ashore in Nagasaki in a tiny sampan, he refers to the vessel as a floating coffin and again as a small sarcophagus (*MC*, 55). The self-dramatization confirms the isolation of the exoticist and symbolically denies the cultural encounter.

The same conflation of mortality and the exotic occurs at a memorable moment late in *Aziyadé* when the European malcontent desires to extricate himself from a burdensome existential plight. Reflecting on the Islamic belief that Allah will carry his subjects into paradise by pulling on a lock of hair on their otherwise shaven heads, the young lieutenant asks who will carry him into paradise to escape a decrepit world: 'If only someone could give me the Muslim faith, how I would shed tears of joy embracing the green flag of the Prophet!' ['Si quelqu'un pouvait me donner seulement la foi musulmane, comme j'irais en pleurant de joie, embrasser le drapeau vert du prophète!'] (*Az*, 204–5).

We can connect Genet's injunction a century later to 'betray the Whites that we are' back to Loti's claimed apostasy.[25] At a biographical level, there is evidence of real Arabophilia in Julien Viaud's relationship with his Circassian mistress, Hatidjè Hanum. But the cultural reincarnation he dreams of remains mythopoeic.[26] Lieutenant Viaud's journal shows the novelist toying with the idea of becoming a Turk. He concludes whimsically that, as a French officer, he no longer has a role to play in Istanbul after the break-up of the Ottoman Empire ordered by the Treaty of Berlin in 1878.[27] At a fictional level, if the depiction of promised gratification in Japan and Oceania is regularly blighted by cultural intolerance, the denouement in *Aziyadé* offers an improbable resolution. For whereas in *Le Mariage de Loti* and *Madame Chrysanthème*, the ship setting sail spells narrative closure, *Aziyadé* ends with the realization of a desire for incorporation into ancient Ottoman culture, as Loti dies fighting in the service of the Sultan.

AN AMBIGUOUS AFROPHOBIA

In working from *Aziyadé* to *Le Roman d'un spahi*, we move from Arabophilia to Afrophobia.[28] Exotic dress, which so seduced the Turcophile hero in Istanbul, stands initially as a mark of radical alienation in *Le Roman d'un spahi*. Contemplating his brightly coloured spahi's uniform complete with fez, Loti's soldier-hero serving in Senegal, the Cevennol peasant Jean Peyral, asks accusingly why he has been turned into a half-African, a being apart. The loss of identity occasioned by the ambiguous colonial uniform confirms the dominant impression that Peyral is a figure of disaffection. Yet as Chris Bongie reminds us, the spahi comes to love his fez and sword and in the end chooses Africa over France.[29] While his five years of military service are a form of exile, during which the parental home is evoked with undiluted sentimentalism and narrow filial piety, Africa is also the stage for his initiation to sexual pleasure and for his death. As with Loti's other exotic locations, the spahi's life in colonial Senegal is represented stereotypically: black Africans are simian-like, and in the colonialist's projection, the continent exudes an immense solitude: 'O sadness of the land of Africa!' ['Ô tristesse de cette terre d'Afrique!'] (*LRS*, 258). In detail that anticipates the melodrama of Marlow's travels into the African interior in Conrad's *Heart of Darkness*, the river along which the spahis sail into battle is cast as 'the vestibule of great African solitudes' ['le vestibule des grandes solitudes africaines'] (*LRS*, 347). Not unexpectedly, the journey is the prelude to the spahi's death.

The equating of Africa with the primitive forces of sexuality and death is confirmed as the spahi anticipates his love encounter with the black girl Fatou, who is later to bear his child. For the spahi, the prearranged meeting with her under a baobab tree is a form of self-destruction. Hence the lurid contract – 'signing a sort of funereal pact with this black race' ['signer avec cette race noire une sorte de pacte funeste'] (*LRS*, 291) – becomes a self-fulfilling prophecy, since the spahi will die in battle. But unlike the fallen hero of *Aziyadé*, buried with full honours alongside 'fellow' defenders of Islam (*Az*, 222), the spahi's end is ambiguous in a different sense. Fatou honours the body where it lies on the battlefield before killing their child and taking her own life. The neat arrangement of these three unburied bodies, soon to be engulfed, the text insists, in the menacing night of the African interior, brings to a melodramatic finale the spahi's adventure.

If the intermarriage in *Le Mariage de Loti* intrigues the protagonist in search of his lost brother, the interbreeding in *Le Roman d'un spahi* leading to this macabre 'family' sacrifice on the battlefield releases vicious intolerance. Writing on the great taboo of miscegenation, Glissant protests that 'the damnation of that word' must be writ large.[30] But for contemporary colonial onlookers, Peyral's cohabitation with Fatou is scandalous and ensures that he is denied military promotion. His sadistic treatment of Fatou is mirrored in the perversions of racism affirmed by the child of their union: 'The child had not wanted its mother's blood' ['L'enfant n'avait pas voulu du sang de sa mère'] (*LRS*, 352); and, once born, it is endowed with a precocious bigotry, as it wonders how its Cevennol blood has been mixed with 'this impure negro race' ['cette impure race nègre'].

Despite the persistent racial blindness of the text, Peyral grows paradoxically closer to his African concubine. Reunited with her after a separation that he has unilaterally imposed, he now concedes, however grudgingly, that, unlike his young fiancée back in rural France, Fatou has been 'faithful in her own way' ['fidèle . . . à sa manière'] (*LRS*, 352). What unites them are 'these powerful bonds of great persistence that separation can scarcely destroy' ['ces liens puissants d'une grande persistance, que la séparation peut à peine détruire'] (*LRS*, 352). As the scene ends, the spahi, overwhelmed by his acute isolation, allows Fatou to slip an African amulet around his neck and share in his soldier's rations. However crudely sentimentalized the rapport, a curious, brief communion stands out against a backdrop of ethnic denigration and physical violence. The concluding triple death of spahi, concubine, and infant serves conflicting fantasies. At one level, the collective extinction of life symbolically reinforces a colonialist logic in which Africa and Africans no longer exist once the European ceases to behold them. But the choreography of the closing scene also gives expression to a reverie about cultural bonding across continents. Africa is indeed represented with stereotypical menace as the 'great mysterious continent inhabited by black men' ['grand continent mystérieux habité par les hommes noirs'] (*LRS*, 348), but in the spahi's experience, it offers, however contradictorily and parasitically, consolation for existential isolation. In its crudely stereotypical form, Africa thus provides what in a related context Marianna Torgovnick calls 'a heightened . . . primitive, . . . the screen on which we project our deepest fears and strongest desires'.[31] The locus of sadness and death (the lives of the soldiers in exile are described as being haunted by death (*LRS*, 321)), the continent is also a place of origins: 'At the geological beginnings of the earth, before the separation into day and night, the world must have had that calm sense of anticipation' ['Aux premiers âges géologiques, avant que *le jour fût séparé des ténèbres*, les choses devaient avoir de ces tranquillités d'attente'] (*LRS*, 323; Loti's italics).

Todorov reminds us that, a decade after the publication of *Le Roman d'un spahi*, Loti was elected to the Académie française in preference to Zola, the point being that the sadism and racist colonialism of the novel were no bar to its author's advancement.[32] The contradictions articulated in Loti provide access to the late nineteenth-century colonialist mind-set. The tradition makes uncomfortable reading for the liberal humanist and this may help explain the eclipse of his literary reputation for much of the twentieth century. Whether it be in his Arabophilia, his ingrained Afrophobia, or the fascination and denigration that mark his evocations of Tahitians and Japanese, we have essentialized portraits of the Other. Loti registers contradictory responses to alterity: the crude racist stereotyping; the sentimentalized laments for the *kasbah* in Algiers, old Nagasaki, and Ottoman feudalism, together with disaffection from the republican France of his day; the sense of outrage at the 1883 massacres in Annam; the inchoate awareness of cultural relativism. This patchwork of impressions reflects late nineteenth-century colonialist culture, coercive and yet also curious, obdurately supremacist and yet disturbed by the difference that the new colonial order makes available.

A EUROPEAN PALIMPSEST: MOERENHOUT'S MESSAGE

Differences in ways of seeing the world are the only source of scandal.

(Moerenhout).[33]

The quest for consolation beyond Europe that energizes Jean Peyral in *Le Roman d'un spahi* is also to be found in the writings of Paul Gauguin. While Polynesia, not colonial Africa, is Gauguin's place of primeval origination and closure, he too uses the language of compensatory other times and spaces in his *Ancien Culte Mahorie*, *Noa Noa*, and *Avant et Après*. Like Leconte de Lisle, he made extensive use of Jacques-Antoine Moerenhout's *Voyages aux Îles du Grand Océan* of 1837, a standard work of reference on Polynesia that he was reading soon after arriving in Tahiti in June 1891. Moerenhout, who had worked as American consul in the Pacific, focuses on the geography, ethnography, and history of the islands, and his *Voyages* represents authentic *in situ* observation.[34] This imbrication of ethnography and exoticism shows how Gauguin's account of the Pacific Other is derived from another European, creating the sense of a Western palimpsest of the primitive.[35]

Moerenhout plays up the idea of Polynesian brutality. Referring to the Aréoïs tribe, he invokes, like Cook before him, this society 'in which prostitution was a founding principle, and infanticide compulsory' (I, 495). Of the Tahitians, he writes stereotypically of their hedonism: 'Enjoyment was their sole aim' ['Jouir était leur seul objet'] (II, 171), a cliché echoed in the name Gauguin gives his final home in Hiva Oa, *La Maison du Jouir*. When not engaged in war, Polynesians are, in Moerenhout's account, carefree, unhindered by moral scruples, and firmly anchored in the present. They provide an antidote to the European *cogito* and the preoccupation with economic necessity, compensations that are duly endorsed by Gauguin in his eulogy of Polynesian ways.

Eschewing cultural hierarchy, Moerenhout promotes relativism as the only real vantage-point from which to represent anthropological diversity. Yet while he claims to be disinterested in his consideration of 'peoples we call savage' (I, 418), there are significant lapses into sensationalism. Evoking the appearance of certain tribal chiefs and distinguished warriors whose bodies are covered in tattoos, he protests: 'it is the inhuman savage in his most hideous appearance, the cannibal barbarian at his most disgusting; he is a tiger, a frightening monster who would drink human blood and devour quivering flesh' (II, 123). By equating Polynesian tradition with degradation, Moerenhout placates a Western need to see its own moral probity corroborated in this overdetermined spectacle of claimed perversity.

But if Moerenhout regularly invokes the distinction between the monstrous and the civilized, he infers at key moments that these categories are far from being mutually exclusive. Puzzling over what he assumes to be a socially sanctioned infanticide, he insists that a thin line separates violence and nurture:

but . . . if the child was not put to death immediately, if it was able to live for just half an hour, to be seen by or receive a caress from its mother, it was saved, and it was then taken care of in a way that contrasts inexplicably with the very practice of infanticide, as with so many other barbarian customs. (II, 189)

This life-and-death cradle drama stands as a paradigm for the precarious division between barbarism and civilization. In a disconcerting imbrication of claimed opposites, generous nurture and a murderous impulse overlap. For Moerenhout, these aberrant forms of behaviour are not exclusive to barbarism. Infanticide and euthanasia are, he surmises, historically conditioned practices, emerging from an earlier cataclysm that threatened the very survival of Polynesian culture. In a simulated reconstruction of that earlier civilization, he posits a system of religious beliefs as elaborate as that obtaining in nineteenth-century Europe (II, 214).[36] Adducing some form of seismic calamity, he postulates the submersion of a Polynesian continent, with vestiges of this once eminent civilization surviving on the islands that remained. The collective memory of behaviour induced by the cataclysm conditions the cultural eccentricities that the ethnographer now observes.[37] Thus infanticide recalls an earlier apocalyptic moment when such a practice ensured the preservation of civilized order. By thus retrieving the Polynesian from the category of the barbaric, Moerenhout's oxymoron conflates civilized and non-civilized, rendering morally explicable the spectacle of would-be bestiality.[38]

The pattern whereby vital necessity shapes cultural practice is confirmed when Moerenhout projects his conjecture about tribal catastrophe back on to Europe itself and fantasizes about a calamitous loss of high culture. With Europe submerged and only a few scattered islands remaining, he asks:

is it likely that . . . much would remain of the highly developed sciences, the fine arts that have reached a state of such perfection but which are concentrated in the plains where people tend to settle? Undoubtedly not. . . . [A]fter such a disaster, after the period of terror, consternation and disorder . . . is it at all surprising that the art of writing would be lost and that all that would remain of this edifying morality and . . . Christian dogma in the minds of the survivors would be a few vague notions. (II, 215–16)

Moerenhout's eccentric projection, linked to geophysical catastrophe, signals an intense form of European cultural self-doubt.[39] The anxiety that the centre might slide into barbarism haunts the civilized mind. Thus the ethnographic fantasy, while ostensibly focused on the Polynesian Other, readmits repressed European fears about the brittle foundations of its own civilization.

Gauguin, too, if we are to believe Segalen, was exercised by visions of apocalypse. Segalen depicts him as a Nietzschean hero restoring Polynesia to a vigorous hedonism.[40] In this mythical scenario, he imagines the painter, desperate to preserve a culture in ruins, dreaming about its petrification. The faces of this moribund people, convulsed, heroic, and beautiful, would be preserved in lava, Segalen fantasizes.[41] Nevertheless, the European desire to capture a claimed savage beauty entails, paradoxically and ambiguously, its reification. Native attributes are thus frozen in poses that placate the Western spectator who requires a commodified cultural difference.

We can end this brief digression on Gauguin's key source-text by considering two contrasting literary representations of the Polynesian's experience of Europe signalled by Moerenhout: the English poet William Cowper's reflections on Omaï, the Pacific companion whom Cook brought to England; and Jacques Delille's poem 'Des champs d'O-taïti, si chers à son enfance' ['From the fields of Tahiti, beloved of his childhood'], which dramatizes the exile of Potavéri, the young Tahitian who arrived in France with Bougainville.[42] In Cowper's reconstruction of the non-European mindset, the spectacle of English wealth, pomp, and manicured gardens will alienate Omaï from his native land:

> Thee, gentle savage! whom no love of thee
> Or thine, but curiosity, perhaps,
> Or else vain glory, prompted us to draw
> Forth from thy native bow'rs, to show thee here
> With what superior skill we can abuse

> The gifts of Providence and squander life.
> Thy dream is past; and thou hast found again
> Thy cocoas and bananas, palms and yams,
> And homestall thetch'd with leaves. But hast thou found
> Their former charms? . . . are thy simple friends,
> Thy simple fare, and all thy plain delights,
> As dear to thee as once?   (The Task)

Cowper sees the corruption of Omaï by the West as it pursues its voy-euristic and predatorial impulses. However, sensing more poetic beauty than truth in Cowper's assertion of a Western cultural victory, Moerenhout prefers Delille's perspective, in which Potavéri, pining for the flora of his native Pacific, finds it in the munificent gardens of Versailles:

> [A thousand things full of charm
> . . . He believes he can see again, and his tender soul,
> At least for an instant, rediscovers his homeland.]   (*Jardins*)

If, thanks to what is touted as the West's generous provision of exotic plants, the moment of epiphany restores the native to Oceania, it also seals the category of an unspoilt innocence. Thus, while Cowper and Delille propose superficially different conclusions (native taste is either corrupted or confirmed), both rely on a discourse of opposition in which the European presumes to know the innermost thoughts of the 'gentle savage'.

'. . . TERRIBLE DÉMANGEAISON D'INCONNU'[43]

Gauguin found inspiration not only in Moerenhout but also in the hugely successful *Exposition Universelle* of 1889. His work featured in an exhibition of the 'Groupe impressionniste et synthétiste' in a café situated within the precincts of the exhibition, and he was especially drawn to the human exhibits, the several hundred tribespeople from Dakar, New Caledonia, and Saigon whose habitats were reconstructed on the Champ-de-Mars.[44] The numbers flocking to see these emblems of difference confirm a metropolitan need for crude cultural simplification, while Gauguin's decision to go to Oceania can be seen as further indulging the curiosity aroused by the exhibition.[45]

In cavalier fashion, he claims direct access to the primitive, assuming the mantle of the *sauvage* and surrendering gloriously, as he fantasizes, to a higher, Maori authority: 'I held the paintbrush; the Maori gods directed my hand' ['je tenais le pinceau, les Dieux Maories dirigeaient ma main'] (*NN*, 26). This claimed passivity is not to be equated with Gauguin's cultural self-evacuation. Varnedoe makes the point that his primitivism was essentially a European construction, that his painting was more influenced by Degas and Cézanne than by the indigenous art of Oceania, and that his accounts of Polynesian life were often derivative (Moerenhout, as we have just seen, was a crucial source).[46] Varnedoe adds that if Gauguin is the father of primitivism in modern art, he is also the inheritor of a European tradition that gestures superficially to the pre-civilized. Pissarro, objecting that Gauguin was forever poaching, asserts in a letter to his son Lucien: 'today he is pillaging the savages of Oceania'.[47] Crucially, such plundering is not to be confused with an empathetic account of difference.

In an unapologetic usurpation of otherness, Gauguin exploits Polynesia to enhance his profile as primitive savage. His case is complicated by his contestation of colonialist culture. The autobiographical *Avant et Après*, a loosely structured narrative combining material on contemporary artists, bawdy anecdotes, and travel writing, also contains outspoken criticism of colonial authority. He cites the sexual predation of the civilizing bishop and the European judge while playing down his own.[48] He pours scorn on the 'infernal machine' ['machine infernale'] (*AA*, 168) of the Catholic Church for its commitment to temporal power, its denigration of Marquesan art, and its cynical exploitation of religious authority. He exposes the crude racism of Petit, the French governor of the Marquesas Islands who fantasizes about supplementing the dwindling native population by moving people from the over-crowded island of Martinique! He decries even more shocking commodification of the Other when colonialists, tired of shooting at game, target 'black flesh' ['la chair noire'] (*AA*, 213). Rejecting as rank hypocrisy the 'Liberté, Egalité, Fraternité' slogan, he condemns the practice of extortionate colonial taxation, where the colonized become merely a source of revenue and enjoy no inward investment.

Gauguin's indictment of colonial ways is not without contradiction. In a stinging letter to the authorities reproduced in full in *Avant et Après*, he berates a coarse and venal gendarmerie, as well as a French judge whose knee-jerk response to a tattooed face is to criminalize it. But he also asserts that prohibition of local alcohol drives the population from the towns and causes a labour shortage. The policy, he concludes pessimistically, will only drive the locals back to savagery (*AA*, 160). The contrast with statements made elsewhere about preserving savagery is clear. Likewise, while exposing the mindset of colonial functionaries, he shares many of the evolutionist assumptions that inform their administration. Reconstructing a dream of primordial chaos, he fantasizes about the origins of this now moribund race and appeals to 'the boldness of the unconscious' ['la hardiesse de l'inconscience'] (*AA*, 93). In an archaic landscape, he finds himself among strange, human-looking animals that are inferior to monkeys. The dream ends with Gauguin encountering an angel, who explains that these sub-simian figures are at a stage he once occupied, and that his own incompleteness will, in infinity, become full-ness in the hands of God. Gauguin thus shelters behind his 'bold unconscious' to relay the voice of nineteenth-century racism. The arbitrariness of colonial self-representation is further underlined by linking the colony to the Cythera of Greek antiquity, with its perpetual hedonism and perfect ignorance of the world of work (*AA*, 74).

PRIMITIVIST SELF-PROJECTION

As a self-publicist, Gauguin skilfully constructs his image as a primitive savage, asserting before leaving Paris in 1891:

I leave to find tranquillity, to be rid of the burden of civilization. . . . I need to immerse myself in virgin nature, see only savages, live as they do, with no other preoccupation than to render, as a child would, the conceptions of my brain with the sole aid of primitive means of art . . . which are the only true ones.

[Je pars pour être tranquille, pour être débarrassé de l'influence de la civilisa-tion. . . . j'ai besoin de me retremper dans la nature vierge, de ne voir que des sauvages, de vivre leur vie, sans autre préoccupation que de rendre, comme le ferait un enfant, les conceptions de mon cerveau avec l'aide seulement des moyens d'art primitifs . . . les seuls vrais.][49]

It is tempting to read these trenchant words of farewell as signalling a definitive break with his European roots. Yet reflecting on his departure from the cultural centre, first to Brittany in 1886, then to Martinique in 1887, and finally to Polynesia where he died in 1903, Gill Perry sees the flight to the perceived margins of civilization as a central element in late nineteenth-century avant-gardism and a preparation for the modern.[50] The cultural spin-offs of colonial conquest epitomize this realignment – the ethnographic museums, interest in the artefacts of colonized peoples, and the great vogue for Darwin-inspired theories of evolution.[51]

Gauguin assertively foregrounds an antithetical model of mutual exclusivity between civilized and savage. In a letter of 1890 to the artist Emile Bernard, he announces his withdrawal from the so-called civilized world and his planned visit to the Southern Hemisphere.[52] He writes in

1895 to the Swedish writer August Strindberg of 'the great clash between your civilization and my barbarism. The civilization from which you suffer. The barbarism that rejuvenates me' ['tout un choc entre votre civilisation et ma barbarie. Civilisation dont vous souffrez. Barbarie qui est pour moi un rajeunissement'].[53]

Before Tahiti, the prospect of securing a posting to Tonkin awakens dreams of an illustrious Oriental tradition. He insists that the West is rotten, and that 'Hercules can, like Antaeus, gain new strength on setting foot there' ['Hercule peut, comme Antée, prendre des forces nouvelles en touchant le sol de là-bas'].[54] The Greek legend of Antaeus acquiring chthonic energy provides a mythological gloss for the ingrained colonialist assumption that colonization would reinvigorate its agents. Similarly, the Hercules myth, with its celebrated twelve labours of conquest, including the slaying or taming of mythical animals, the killing of enemies, and the conquest of the Amazons, suggests subliminally the policing and physical domination in what colonization euphemistically called *la pacification*.

Gauguin's nostalgia contrasts with the earlier, highly influential progressivist histories of the Enlightenment that saw ever more rational cultures replacing barbarianism.[55] While his argument is predicated on the same teleological principle of human evolution, his regressivist instinct delivers an overstated Europhobia. Following his first trip to Tahiti between 1891 and 1893, he concludes triumphantly in *Noa Noa* (the title of which signifies 'very fragrant' in Tahitian): 'I leave two years older and feeling twenty years younger, more *savage* than at the outset and much more *knowledgeable*. Yes, the savages . . . have taught me to know myself better, they have taught me my own truth' ['Je pars, vieilli de deux ans, rajeuni de vingt ans, plus *barbare* qu'à l'arrivée et bien plus *instruit*. Oui, les sauvages . . . m'ont fait me mieux connaître moi-même, ils m'ont dit ma propre vérité'] (*NN*, 237; Gauguin's emphasis). In Gauguin's aggressive reversal, Oceania civilizes and restores the weary, ignorant European.

The long correspondence with his painter friend and agent Georges-Daniel de Monfreid highlights their shared attempts to valorize what urban bourgeois culture discards. Writing from a retreat in the mountains, Monfreid refers to the therapeutic benefits of fleeing the centre. Savage life, he insists, is more rational than its civilized counterpart and the animality within us must be rediscovered and a harmonious balance established between body and mind.[56] Metropolitan bourgeois living, by contrast, breeds disease and disequilibrium.[57]

Gauguin's disaffection assumes various guises: Orientalism, primitivism, and the wholesale rejection of bourgeois family morality, progress,
and the cult of the machine; it does not amount to cultural empathy.[58]
His arguments are often reliant on a sclerotic binarism:

Savages! That word inevitably came to my lips when I looked at these black
people with their cannibal teeth. However, I could already glimpse their real,
strange grace. . . . I was a savage to each one of them just as they were to me.
And were they wrong or was I?

['Sauvages!' Ce mot me venait inévitablement aux lèvres, quand je considérais
ces êtres noirs, aux dents de cannibales. Déjà, pourtant, j'entrevoyais leur grâce
réelle, étrange. . . . Comme chacun d'eux pour moi, j'étais pour chacun d'eux
un sauvage.
   Et, d'eux et de moi, qui avait tort?] (*NN*, 49)

The conundrum superficially suggests an incipient cultural relativism, as
Gauguin converts himself tokenistically into the object of the Other's
gaze. His more normal vantage point, however, is that of the always-
waiting-to-be-seduced European spectator, as this gloss on indolence
confirms:

Is it a case of insouciance, frivolity, capriciousness? Could it be – who knows! –
the deepest form of philosophy. Beware of luxury! Avoid developing the need
and the taste for it . . .

[Est-ce là de l'insouciance, de la légèreté, de la versatilité? Serait-ce – qui sait!
– de la plus profonde philosophie? – Prends garde au luxe! Prends garde d'en
contracter le goût et le besoin . . .] (*NN*, 82; ellipsis in the original)

By elevating inaction to the level of a superior form of knowledge,
Gauguin condemns two key elements in European capitalism, the work
ethic and wealth accumulation. The recurring indolent pose is axiomatic
in the Tahitian paintings, with works such as *Femmes de Tahiti, Cavaliers sur
la plage*, and *Ils ne travailleront pas aujourd'hui* all depicting deliverance from
humdrum, alienating labour.

   A scene in *Noa Noa* where Gauguin voices his anxiety as an artist draws
its potency precisely from the backdrop of utilitarianism. His Polynesian
male companion, Jotéfa, with whom he has been felling trees for use in
sculpture, congratulates the artist on his social usefulness: 'I'm sure
Jotéfa is the first person in the world to have spoken to me in such terms,
in the language of the savage or the child, for you have to be one or the
other . . . to imagine that an artist is *someone useful*' ['Je crois bien que
Jotéfa est le premier homme au monde qui m'ait tenu ce langage, – ce
langage de sauvage ou d'enfant, car il faut être l'un des deux . . . pour

s'imaginer qu'un artiste soit – un *homme utile*'] (*NN*, 84; Gauguin's emphasis). What Europe castigates as Gauguin's moral irresponsibility thus converts into Tahitian recognition of his social service, the painter becoming a semi-divine maker of men (*NN*, 124). A claimed new order, based on an infantilized, savage Other, gives the artist a prestige that 'adult', 'civilized' Europe withholds.

The cameo confirms Gauguin's taste for fantastic self-projections. Similarly, his descriptions of Maori women are occasions for licentiousness and unqualified sadism. His vicious assertion that 'they all harbour a latent desire to be raped' ['Toutes ont le désir latent du viol'] (*NN*, 52–3), is symptomatic of the fantasies harboured by a predatorial European male imagination. As Peter Brooks reminds us, the West's fascination with the bodies of other cultures finds an acute expression in Gauguin's painting and writing, where the exotic is inextricably bound up with erotic aggression.[59]

ANDROGYNY AND DISSIDENCE

If misogyny confirms a male-centred hierarchy of cultural value, Gauguin's fascination with androgyny unsettles it.[60] This emerges with particular force in the description of Jotéfa, with whom Gauguin, cast as first-person narrator, enters the forest. Primitive nature, then, is the stage for the encounter with radical difference:

And in that forest, that solitude, that silence, there were just two of us, – he a very young man, and I, almost an old man, with my soul stripped of so many illusions, my body weary from so much effort and that long and fatal legacy of vices from a society that was morally and physically sick!

He walked in front of me with the animal suppleness of his graceful androgynous form. . . .

Was it a man walking there . . .?

[Et dans cette forêt, dans cette solitude, dans ce silence, nous étions deux, – lui, un tout jeune homme, et moi, presque un vieillard, l'âme défleurie de tant d'illusions, le corps lassé de tant d'efforts, et cette longue, et cette fatale hérédité des vices d'une société moralement et physiquement malade!

Il marchait devant moi, dans la souplesse animale de ses formes gracieuses d'androgyne. . . .

Était-ce un homme qui marchait là . . .?] (*NN*, 85–6)

A decrepit Europe is thus incarnate in the ageing body of Gauguin, who craves release from a civilization that perverts and debilitates. Europhobia finds a variety of expressions here. Unlike the earlier references to male heterosexual predation, vigour and suppleness are now ascribed to the androgyne. And while the erotic impulse is partly displaced on to nature, the fixation with Jotéfa, the animalized, androgynous Other, remains.

At the heart of Gauguin's fantasy is the drama of undecidability. The potential misidentification detaches the Polynesian from traditional gender categories. In constructing this site where a male/female binarism falters, Gauguin speculates that sexual difference, so celebrated and fetichized in the West, is less prevalent in Polynesia:

With these naked tribes, as with animals, sexual difference is much less accentuated than in our own climate. Thanks to the artifices of belts and corsets, we have managed to convert woman into an artificial being, an anomaly . . . that we carefully maintain in a state of nervous weakness and muscular inferiority, by sparing her tiring work, that is to say opportunities for physical development. Thus . . . our womenfolk no longer have anything in common with us, a state of affairs that may have grave moral and social consequences.

[Chez ces peuplades nues, comme chez les animaux, la différence entre les sexes est bien moins accentuée que dans nos climats. Grâce à nos artifices de ceintures et de corsets, nous avons réussi à faire de la femme un être factice, une anomalie . . . que nous maintenons avec soin dans un état de faiblesse nerveuse et d'infériorité musculaire, en lui épargnant les fatigues, c'est à dire les occasions de développement. Ainsi . . . nos femmes n'ont plus rien de commun avec nous, ce qui ne va peut-être pas sans de graves inconvénients moraux et sociaux.] (*NN*, 86)[61]

In this pseudo-ethnography, Gauguin alleges the alienating power of societally imposed norms governing the Western female body, while self-indulgently delighting in the spectacle of muscular Tahitian women. Working within a predictably tidy dualism, he claims that the women have something virile about them, the men something feminine (*NN*, 86). By generating these mobile sexual identities, the self-styled *vieux civilisé* allows himself to be puzzled by scenes of sexual indifferentiation of his own creation. He feigns shock and outrage too. Struck by the androgynous appearance of the young man in the forest, he claims to sense relief when he eventually sees the man's chest: 'the androgyne had disappeared. . . . Once again, I was at peace' ['l'androgyne avait disparu. . . . La paix rentra aussitôt en moi'] (*NN*, 87). The impression of disturbance and arousal projected by sexual ambiguity is thus apparently stemmed with the fixing of gender identity. But, as with the radical discarding of utilitarianism and monogamy, the blurring of gender undoes another category of late nineteenth-century cultural conformity: heterosexual difference.[62]

The veiled homosexual nature of the scene is reinforced as Gauguin describes how, with his hands bleeding, he joyously hacks away at the rosewood tree, all the while mindful that his aggressive instinct aims to appease some unidentified 'divine brutality':

It wasn't the tree I was striking. . . . And yet I would have gladly heard the joyous sound of my axe hitting other trunks once I had felled this one.

[Ce n'est pas sur l'arbre que je frappais. . . . Et pourtant j'aurais volontiers écouté chanter ma hache sur d'autres troncs encore quand celui-ci fut à terre.] (*NN*, 89)

The crescendo of physical effort, purportedly to deliver the raw material for sculpture, heralds transparently a quasi-sexual climax and a personal epiphany, the metaphorical cutting down of the old Gauguin. The moment, commemorated in verse, assumes the weight of an important rite of passage, a hymn of farewell, we are encouraged to believe, to European narcissism: 'Destroy in you the love of Yourself!' ['Détruis en toi l'amour de Toi-même!'] (*NN*, 89). While the taking of fruit from the tree in Genesis triggers Adam's fall and enslavement to toil and hardship, the momentous tree-felling in *Noa Noa* has wholly felicitous consequences. Gauguin sees it as signalling an end to European self-absorption and trumpets this vigorous reincarnation unproblematically as the supreme victory over a nefarious civilization.

The assertion of purity suggests a knowing simplification, the act of revenge of civilization's victim. Paradoxically, Gauguin's ostensibly Europhobic dissidence reconstructs many of the continent's prejudices: the infantilization of the Other, the narcissistic hedonism, and the identification of Tahiti as a site of unbridled sexuality. In Gauguin's exotic *ailleurs*, axiomatic European values are purportedly contested and yet circuitously reinstated.

In his iconoclastic fantasies, Gauguin anticipates arguments that feature in *Civilization and its Discontents*. Freud's thesis is well known, namely that innate human aggression acts potentially as a giant obstacle to culture and that the same aggression, channelled through the super ego, can be directed punitively against the ego: 'Civilization, therefore, obtains mastery over the individual's dangerous desire for aggression by weakening and disarming it and by setting up an agency within him to keep watch over it, like a garrison in a conquered city.'[63] In contrast, Gauguin proposes a tropical idyll in which libidinal drives are freely explored.

Freud contests the assertion that the primitive mind-set is culturally uninhibited and thus superior, dismissing as exoticist fallacy the assumption that the colonized lead more fulfilled and simple lives away from the claimed complications of civilization. Rejecting this primitivist euphoria, he speculates:

As regards the primitive peoples who exist today, careful researches have shown that their instinctual life is by no means to be envied for its freedom. It is subject to restrictions of a different kind but perhaps of greater severity than those attaching to modern civilized man.[64]

Freud's censorious riposte to the discontents dismisses the idea of a compensatory primitive freedom. Insisting that the mature ego must repudiate the oceanic, that is the feeling of limitlessness in which separation between the ego and the world is blurred, he further likens the ego to Rome, the Eternal City establishing its boundaries and hierarchy.[65]

Gauguin is unequivocal about his incorporation into Polynesian culture. *Noa Noa* provides him, he argues, with the opportunity to orchestrate this meeting of primitive and European styles. In addition to doing the illustrations, he will author the 'native' tranches of the text, while the poet Charles Morice will compose its 'civilized' pages. Writing to Monfreid in 1902, a year after publication, he wonders if, as a newcomer to writing, his naive style might be superior to that of the 'rotten' *civilisé*, Morice. The composite nature of *Noa Noa* becomes quickly transparent, Morice's florid contributions, often in verse, contrasting with the painter's less affected evocations of Polynesian life. Yet even allowing for Gauguin's boast about his half-Peruvian origins or his status as naive writer, we are left with the provocative assertion that he can convincingly re-create the perspective of the so-called barbarian.[66]

In assuming the voice of the *sauvage*, Gauguin practises a form of cultural ventriloquy. As he evokes life with his young bride Téhura, the constructed polarities of European perversion and Polynesian transparency are deliberately reversed. He depicts himself not as imperious male subject but as anxious lover, alongside his Protean spouse:

[Téhura] was sometimes very sensible and loving, sometimes very wild and frivolous. Two contradictory beings in one – to say nothing of the many others . . . – who contradicted one another . . . she was double, triple, multiple; the *child* of an *ancient* race.

[[Téhura] était tantôt très sage et très aimante, tantôt très folle et très frivole. Deux êtres contraires – sans compter beaucoup d'autres . . . – en un, qui se démentaient mutuellement . . . elle était double, et triple, et multiple: l'*enfant* d'une race *vieille*.] (*NN*, 135; Gauguin's emphasis)

While still locked within a colonialist binarism, Gauguin recasts himself improbably as passive recipient of an unpredictable, threatening alterity. Highlighting the infantile and the ancient, he reaffirms the preoccupation with origins and finality central to nineteenth-century French evocations of Polynesian culture.

A FALTERING MIGRATION

As Nicholas Wadley reminds us, the intended audience for *Noa Noa* was Parisian, Gauguin dramatizing his role as inhibited European, in love with a young Polynesian bride.[67] The centrality of artifice confirms the contradictions in his claimed cultural migration.[68] Indeed the self-proclaimed enemy of culture is incapable of abandoning the value systems that feed his malaise.

The same impossibility of migration dominates Gauguin's painting, where *civilisé* and *sauvage* regularly stand juxtaposed. Wadley makes the point that the figures depicted seldom touch, still less embrace each other.[69] Alignment and contiguity, replicating a pattern of separateness between European and Polynesian, are the dominant modes of configuration. The *dramatis personae* in *D'où venons-nous? Que sommes-nous? Où allons-nous?* ['Where do we come from? What are we? Where are we going?'], which was to have been Gauguin's swansong before his failed suicide in 1897, includes two shadowy figures, who '[record] near the tree of science their note of anguish caused by this science itself, in comparison with the simple beings in a virgin nature, which might be the human idea of paradise . . .'[70] In Gauguin's gloss, crippling European self-consciousness and Polynesian ease again stand in tidy opposition.

A similar interface structures *Contes Barbares* ['Savage Tales'] of 1902, in which the painter Meyer de Haan looms with animal menace to the left of a scene of idyllic harmony, dominated by the refined figure of the young Polynesian woman Tohataua. De Haan's enlarged eyes and clawed feet give him a pronounced diabolic quality, which is enhanced by the uncompromising segregation in the painting. Moreover, as Malingue points out, it is the presence of De Haan which enables Gauguin to entitle the painting *Contes Barbares*.[71] With its internal partitioning, the canvas works through gradations of European animality and Polynesian refinement, reconfirming the inversion of primitive and civilized on which Gauguin insists in *Noa Noa*. Crucially, it is as if the quest for difference and the exotic reaches its goal not in the figures of Oceania but rather in the European himself. The inversion confirms

Kristeva's point in *Étrangers à nous-mêmes* that the Self in reality encompasses what it conventionally projects on to the Other. Europe finds its own barbarism in the animalized figure of De Haan, just as it finds a constructed primitivism in the Gauguin who co-authors *Noa Noa*.

The limits of Gauguin's exoticism are evident in Segalen's story, apocryphal or otherwise, about the painter taking a small colony of Maoris with him to Hiva Oa to escape the stranglehold of the French colonial system. In keeping with Maori ritual, Tioka and Gauguin drink each other's blood in a deeply fraternal form of communion. But when Gauguin is enjoined by his new brother to swap names, he insists on the sovereignty of the individual. In Segalen's account, 'The Master violently refused, and with a look of rage that Tioka had never suspected . . ., he said in a low voice: "Paul Gauguin! Never! Paul Gauguin does not surrender his identity . . ."' Segalen glosses the outburst, reflecting on the clash of cultures and 'the revolt of a proud *individualism* . . . in which the *Self* is unique, untouchable, entirely self-contained, and of supreme value. – This contrasts with the impersonal instincts of the Inoa tribe' (Segalen's italics).[72] While alert to the cultural collision, Segalen exonerates Gauguin and endorses the myth of sexual hedonism.

The image of the painter fending off an invasive communitarian *sauvagerie* gives the lie to any easy absorption into Polynesian culture. As Monfreid explains to Gauguin, however, the latter's reputation in Europe rests precisely on the belief that he has indeed secured some form of mythical, seamless insertion into the culture of Oceania. Writing in November 1902, he reminds Gauguin of the need to safeguard his status as the cultural dissident gone native in Oceania. Indeed talk from Gauguin about returning to Europe (and there was much of it) unsettles his correspondent, for whom the artist's self-imposed absence is intimately linked with his success. Thus a powerful logic linking remoteness and prestige operates within the field of European high culture. Monfreid counsels:

It is to be feared that your coming back would disturb the work of incubation taking place in public opinion with regard to you: you are currently the legendary, unheard of artist who dispatches his disconcerting, inimitable works from farthest Oceania, the definitive works of a great man who has disappeared, as it were, from the world. . . . In short, you enjoy the immunity of the glorious deceased, you have passed into the history of art. – And in the meantime, the public is learning to appreciate your work.[73]

Reflecting on the commercialization of art, Monfreid's letter explores image-making and reputation. Exile from Europe is variously described as a form of glorious death, immunity from the everyday, and a guarantee of status. Hence the commercially central place of the exoticized margins. Paris, the cultural capital of the nineteenth-century world, educates the appetite for what is deemed peripheral: 'Let this work reach its completion. It is only beginning', Monfreid cautions, aware of the link between legend and its commodification.[74]

The same myth-making colours Morice's melodramatic notice in the French press announcing Gauguin's second departure for Tahiti in 1895:

Tomorrow, leaving Paris, France, Europe – with no hope of return – is a great artist, positively disgusted with the atmosphere of hydrogenous gas . . . that we inhale in the West. . . . Yes, Gauguin is right to leave, and you have to envy him for having a free homeland [in the South Pacific] that can alleviate the pain of the land he is leaving.[75]

By deliberately playing up the poisonous atmosphere of Europe and the remoteness of Polynesia, Morice forges his collaborator's reputation for risk-taking and inaccessibility. At the same time, the juxtaposition of a polluted Paris and an idealized Tahiti suggests a *fin-de-siècle* culture that is wholly familiar with these congealed images of Self and rejuvenating Other.

*

As self-styled adventurers, Loti and Gauguin parade their rebellion against the restrictive moral, religious, sexual, and economic codes of Europe. Yet the aggression in the claimed migration captures symptomatically an inability to engage dialectically with the otherness made visible by colonization. The challenge posed by difference exercises not just opponents of colonial officialdom such as Gauguin but also officers in uniform like Loti, whose professional position made exotic cultures geographically close if still conceptually opaque.

Segalen, another serving officer who post-dates both authors, proposes contrasting evaluations of their achievements. The author of an 'Hommage à Gauguin', he hails his predecessor as the European who dreams of restoring to Polynesia the hedonistic lifestyle that colonization has destroyed.[76] The desire to emulate the master influences his *Les Immémoriaux*, an attempted reconstruction of a Tahitian Golden Age that laments the decline in that civilization already signalled in Moerenhout, Loti, and Gauguin. In a letter to Monfreid of April 1906, Segalen writes of wanting to reproduce in words the style of Gauguin's painting and praises 'the illumination of a whole race that permeates his Tahitian work'.[77]

Yet he shows no such indulgence towards Loti, branding him a vulgar exoticist. In his *Essai sur l'exotisme*, he insists with aloofness that incomprehensibility and impenetrability are the hallmarks of the exotic, accusing Loti of penetrating difference, of being 'in a state of mystic intoxication and unaware of the [exotic] object . . . and . . . hopelessly mixed up with it' (*OC*, I, 758). Yet while Segalen asserts his ability to preserve difference, his claims remain fundamentally ambiguous: 'Let us not flatter ourselves that we can assimilate customs, races, nations, others; on the contrary, let us rejoice in the fact that we can never do so, thereby reserving for ourselves the enduring pleasure of feeling difference' (*OC*, I, 751). He thus appears to be energized not by a sense of ethical obligation but rather by the urge to guarantee a rarefied exotic pleasure, in other words to contemplate a still commodified otherness. James Clifford makes the point that by the end of Segalen's career, the Self and not the Other has become exotic and that 'it is the opening of a fissure in the subject' that constitutes what Segalen labels 'the Diverse' ['le Divers'].[78]

With hindsight, the promotion of Gauguin and dismissal of Loti appears arbitrary. While there is admittedly nothing comparable to Segalen's theorization of otherness in Loti and Gauguin, we nevertheless find familiar shared perspectives in the works of all three: the infantilization of the Polynesian Other, the lament for a moribund culture, the denunciation of Western pathology, the strident defection from France. Taken together, they demonstrate how the *fin-de-siècle* European exoticist, when confronted with difference, responds with a contradictory mixture of curiosity, awe, ignorance, and derision. Segalen protests that otherness needs to be impenetrable. Yet both Loti's apparently effortless cultural transvestism and Gauguin's self-proclaimed savagery reject such irreducibility. Their blinkered, authoritarian domestication of a silenced alterity exemplifies the response to cultural difference in the age of high colonialism.

CHAPTER TWO

Exemplary inclusions, indecent exclusions in Proust's
Recherche

MIRAGES OF DESIRE

If the conspicuous exotic in the works of Loti, Gauguin, and Segalen contrasts markedly with the Francocentric world of *À la recherche du temps perdu*, obsession with the Other is no less real in the novel. While Segalen delights in the preservation of a resistant difference, such irreducible alterity frequently awakens an aggressive frustration for Proust's Narrator. Yet desire in the *Recherche* also spawns its own exotic, as Proust recycles the hackneyed motifs that Loti and his generation handed down to him. Hence the Africanist nostalgia when he writes:

Like those mirages that encourage the traveller to continue walking in the desert, in the desert of life . . . a pair of blue-grey eyes, above a white bodice, gives us the mirage of an assuagement that renews our desire to press on.

[Comme ces mirages qui donnent au voyageur la force de marcher dans le désert, dans le désert de la vie . . . des yeux bleu gris, au-dessus d'un corsage blanc, nous donne le mirage d'un assouvissement qui nous redonne le goût de marcher.][1]

Given the ironic fluctuations in literary fashion, it is easy to overlook just how much Proust's generation was influenced by Loti. While his slide into obscurity for much of the twentieth century is not in question, David Sweetman rightly insists on Loti's 'commanding influence' in the closing years of the nineteenth century.[2] Proust's work, by contrast, encountered initial resistance and incomprehension before occupying a central place in the literary canon. Around the age of twenty, he cites Loti and Anatole France as his favourite authors.[3] The endorsement is confirmed in his correspondence, where we find that, like his mother, he was an avid reader of Loti.[4] At a dinner at the Grand Hotel in Cabourg in 1908, mention of Constantinople prompts Proust to quote by heart a page from *Aziyadé* on the exotic city.[5] And as late as 1920, he writes to thank Fernand Vandérem for an article

41

praising the representation of childhood in *Combray*, Tolstoy's *Memoirs*, and Loti's *Le Roman d'un enfant*.[6]

In a manner that parallels Proust's own early enthusiasm for *Le Mariage de Loti*, Marcel's adolescent experiences of sexual desire in the *Recherche* are intricately connected to the exotic. He trains his sights on the band of young girls whom he first sees coming ashore, as he fantasizes, on the beach at the Norman seaside town of Balbec. Noted for their separateness and difference, the *jeunes filles en fleurs* comprise an 'inhuman world' ['ce monde inhumain'] (*RMP*, I, 851; *RTP*, II, 151), a tribe apart governed by a bird's logic that the bourgeois holiday-makers find impenetrable. As 'the zoophytic band of girls' (*RMP*, I, 914) ['la bande zoophytique des jeunes filles'] (*RTP*, II, 210), they are Proust's recondite equivalent of the animalized figures that people the exotic landscapes of Loti and Gauguin. The girls are central to what the Narrator labels an encounter between civilized and barbarian, and exude physical vigour, sadistic pleasure, and unintellectuality (*RMP*, I, 888; *RTP*, II, 186). The motifs of rejuvenation and irresponsibility echo the discourse of 'exotic nonchalance' (*ML*, 71) that we find in *Le Mariage de Loti* and *Noa Noa*. The girls are demonized, playing Mephistopheles to Marcel's Faust (*RMP*, I, 914; *RTP*, II, 210). Desire itself is conceived of as a quest for an opposite that is unavailable and exists outside the Self. The Other *is* desire: 'like a *simple objectification, unreal and diabolical,* of the temperament diametrically opposed to my own, *of the semi-barbarous and cruel vitality* of which I, in my weakness, my excess of tortured sensibility and intellectuality, was so destitute' (*RMP*, I, 914) ['comme une *simple objectivation irréelle et diabolique* du tempérament opposé au mien, *de la vitalité quasi barbare et cruelle* dont était si dépourvue ma faiblesse, mon excès de sensibilité douloureuse et d'intellectualité'] (*RTP*, II, 210; my italics). In this adaptation of the *fin-de-siècle* motif of a tired European intellectualism, the primitive and diabolical are synonymous with the Other, possession of whom will invigorate an emasculated Self.

Assimilation of the stranger exercises the Narrator to the point where Marcel's pursuit of the *jeunes filles* becomes a form of cannibalism. He crudely compares the woman desired to the fish that eludes the fisherman day after day, before ending up on his plate (*RMP*, I, 854; *RTP*, II, 154). The same urge, while camouflaged, persists in a more theorized reflection on the destruction of difference:

we know no rest until we have converted these aliens into something that is compatible with ourselves, the mind being in this respect endowed with the same kind of reaction and activity as our physical organism, which cannot abide the infusion of any foreign body into its veins without at once striving to digest and assimilate it. (*RMP*, 1, 859)

[nous n'avons de repos que nous n'ayons converti ces étrangères en quelque chose qui soit pareil à nous, notre âme étant à cet égard douée du même genre de réaction et d'activité que notre organisme physique, lequel ne peut tolérer l'immixtion dans son sein d'un corps étranger sans qu'il s'exerce aussitôt à digérer et assimiler l'intrus.] (*RTP*, II, 159)

Whereas in Marcel's adolescent melodrama, savagery is attributed tendentiously to the Other, the mature Narrator's biological digression inverts the paradigm to show a cannibalizing, predatorial Self. Moreover, while Proust's *Recherche* explores a domestic, national context, the language of primitive desire on the beach at Balbec echoes the intolerant assimilation of difference to be found in the exotic writing of Loti and Gauguin.

THE MAPPING OF HOMOSEXUALITY

Proust's audacious promotion of homosexuality entails even greater reliance on the exoticist tradition and involves a simultaneous inscription in his novel of important broader social tensions. In his attempts to defend and promote what he apocalyptically calls the accursed race of sexual marginals, important socio-historical elements force themselves into prominence. In particular, questions of ethnic and national identity, already in sharp focus in the age of high colonialism, colour the depiction of sexuality. Thus the Narrator's anagnorisis in the area of homosexuality triggers a broader political and cultural recognition, the ramifications of which reach well beyond mundane social scandal.

The section of the novel in which this awakening to the world of homosexuality is celebrated is *Sodome et Gomorrhe*. It opens with what is, to adopt the Narrator's categorization, an *exposé* on the workings of homosexual attraction. This is an inaugural text, partitioned off materially from the rest of the novel as the self-contained Part I of the volume. In addition to the appeal to biblical archaism in the *Sodome et Gomorrhe* title, we have an epigraph from Vigny, the tonality of which is no less redolent of apocalypse: 'Woman will have Gomorrah and man will have Sodom' ['La femme aura Gomorrhe et l'homme aura Sodome']. If the apocalypse associated with primitive desire in Loti and Gauguin is associated with a distant ethnic Other, the calamity occasioned by desire in Proust summons up a remote, biblical past.

While Vigny's alexandrine prescribes a strict, binary opposition, modelled on the Genesis story, Proust's text radically unwrites the tidiness of the gender division, offering in place of a cæsura along gender lines, a set of complex and mobile sexual identities, variously mediated through a number of textual antecedents – not just the Bible, but also an extensive botanical treatise that borrows extensively from Maeterlinck's *L'Intelligence des fleurs*, and contemporary press coverage of a European colonial war.[7] Alongside Proust's botany and entomology, then, we have the curious conjunction of a contemporary colonial politics and a scene of archaic calamity. The attempt is to vindicate homosexuality by grounding it in a seemingly timeless nature and simultaneously appealing to the pressing claims of contemporary history. Proust thus indirectly proposes a mapping of homosexuality, to the extent that his text brings into play a symbolic cartography in which sexual mores are located often in spaces beyond Europe.

In getting homosexuality on to the map, Proust exploits both anecdote and theoretical speculation. The treatise, with its allure of discursive authority, is the mode of writing adopted in the incipit of *Sodome et Gomorrhe*, where the Narrator offers a thirty-page excursus on the nature and claimed origins of homosexuality. It is an exposition prompted, ostensibly, by that important moment in the diegesis when Marcel happens to catch sight of Charlus and Jupien in the courtyard of the Guermantes residence in Paris. Significantly, the sexual intrigue triggers abundant hypothesizing and calls up a subversive political agenda.

The reflections on the social organization of sexual desire – and especially outlawed forms of desire – reveal intellectual seriousness and fantasy in equal measure, a point made by Malcolm Bowie in his comparative study of Freud and Proust.[8] Bowie stresses how both writers 'conferred unusual epistemic privileges upon "aberrant" configurations of desire; both were impassioned relativists in their surveys of sexual behaviour yet had recourse to the strong-minded categories of their age in their moments of moral or intellectual exhaustion'.[9] In Proust's case, the epistemology in play is coloured by contemporary European imperialism. Marcel lies hidden just off the Guermantes courtyard, but his attempts to change position to hear what Jupien and Charlus (now inside Jupien's shop) are saying are transformed into an act of improbable military adventure. As Marcel skirts recklessly round the open courtyard, the Narrator advances three reasons for his bravado: first, impatience; secondly, an obscure memory of his boyhood voyeurism at Montjouvain, when he had seen Mlle Vinteuil and her lesbian lover; and finally, a reason unfolded with initial reluctance, but identified as being crucial:

I hardly dare confess to the third and final reason, so childish does it seem, but I suspect that it was unconsciously decisive. Ever since, in order to follow – and see controverted – the military principles enunciated by Saint-Loup, I had been following in close detail the course of the Boer War, I had been led on from that to reread old accounts of travel and exploration. These narratives had thrilled me, and I applied them to the events of my daily life to give myself courage. When attacks of illness had compelled me to remain for several days and nights on end not only without sleep but without lying down, without tasting food or drink . . ., I would think of some traveller cast up on a shore, poisoned by noxious herbs, shivering with fever in clothes drenched by the salt water, who nevertheless in a day or two felt stronger, rose and went blindly on his way, in search of possible inhabitants who might turn out to be cannibals. (*RMP*, ii, 630)

[Enfin j'ose à peine, à cause de son caractère d'enfantillage, avouer la troisième raison, qui fut, je crois bien, inconsciemment déterminante. Depuis que pour suivre – et voir se démentir – les principes militaires de Saint-Loup, j'avais suivi avec grand détail la guerre des Boers, j'avais été conduit à relire d'anciens récits d'explorations, de voyages. Ces récits m'avaient passionné et j'en faisais l'application dans la vie courante pour me donner plus de courage. Quand des crises m'avaient forcé à rester plusieurs jours et plusieurs nuits de suite non seulement sans dormir, mais sans m'étendre, sans boire et sans manger . . ., alors je pensais à tel voyageur jeté sur la grève, empoisonné par des herbes malsaines, grelottant de fièvre dans ses vêtements trempés par l'eau de la mer, et qui pourtant se sentait mieux au bout de deux jours, reprenait au hasard sa route, à la recherche d'habitants quelconques qui seraient peut-être des anthropophages.] (*RTP*, iii, 10)

To which the Narrator adds that, if the Boers heroically expose themselves in open country to British attack, then Marcel can surely handle the reduced theatre of operations that is the Guermantes courtyard! I have quoted extensively here to convey the sensationalized representation of imperial warfare, of explorers shipwrecked and likely to face death at any moment. Talk of travellers coming ashore in Africa and facing cannibalization has a Conradian ring to it.[10] It could also be a page straight out of Loti's *Le Roman d'un spahi*, where Peyral pursues what France sees as a scandalous sexual relationship before dying in battle. This is the terrain that Proust instinctively works back to in order to situate another form of sexual taboo, not Peyral's cohabitation with the black African girl but Charlus's homosexual liaison with Jupien. An exoticized, would-be barbarous Africa thus becomes home to an unspeakable sexual perversion. And as with Loti, pathology and mortality are suggestively triggered in Proust's reflection on primitive sexual desire.

The overall effect is to seal a curious conjunction of spaces: private and public, sexual and military, erotic and heroic, home and colonial, and, more anecdotally, a Parisian courtyard and the South African veldt. The sickly Marcel, seemingly ensconced in a dehistoricized introspection, now enjoys heroization on a turbulent European colonial stage. At Balbec, Marcel's quest for the would-be savage *jeunes filles* was also subject to fantastic overestimation. Desire brings other radical transformations, the bird-like girls at Balbec anticipating the man-insect and the man-bird that Charlus and Jupien become in their courting ritual (*RMP*, II, 628; *RTP*, III, 8). While relocating the desiring subject in nature is an entirely conventional topos, Proust works more provocatively through a range of analogies, from a populist fear of being cannibalized to erudite but no less intense reflection on the assimilation of the Other.

Charlus too engages in exotic self-promotion. Reflecting on his sexual interest in a tram-driver, he comments grandly: "'For it happens to me at times, like the Caliph who used to roam the streets of Baghdad in the guise of a common merchant, to condescend to follow some curious little person whose profile may have taken my fancy'" (*RMP*, II, 632) ["'Il m'arrive en effet, comme le calife qui parcourait Bagdad pris pour un simple marchand, de condescendre à suivre quelque curieuse petite personne dont la silhouette m'aura amusé'"] (*RTP*, III, 12). As in *Aziyadé*, the Oriental city stands stereotypically as a site of illicit desire. Likewise, punishment for transgression is exoticized in both novels, the spectre of divine retribution signalled in the words taken from Daniel: V, 25, 'Mané, Thécel, Pharès', appearing both in *Sodome et Gomorrhe* (*RMP*, II, 636; *RTP*, III, 16) and as the title for Section IV of *Aziyadé*.[11] Primitive desire thus has its own erudite archaism.

The sexual encounter between Charlus and Jupien that energizes Marcel's imaginatively charged surveillance triggers a series of bizarre reincarnations. Marcel may apologize for introducing the historical realities that are adumbrated, seeing them as mere footnotes to the psychosexual drama unfolding in the Guermantes courtyard. But in reality, the impulse to explore the sexual margins occupied by Jupien and Charlus calls up, as though logically, the equally neglected practices of the colonial arena.

Fredric Jameson's essay, *Modernism and Imperialism*, examines the relationship the modernist text sustains with the European imperialist ambiance in which it is produced. He characterizes modernism as being apolitical, as turning away from the social world associated with realism, and valorizing increased subjectivism, introspection and the supremacy of art.[12] These categories are confirmed by the many aestheticized readings of *À la recherche* that are available. For Jameson, the dilemma facing modernism involves what he terms the 'meaning-loss' that is the product of colonialism. At its crudest, most material level, colonialism, he argues, entails part of the economic system being located beyond the metropolis:

> Such spatial disjunction has as its immediate consequence the inability to grasp the way the system functions as a whole. Unlike the classical stage of national or market capitalism, then, pieces of the puzzle are missing; it can never be fully reconstructed; no enlargement of personal experience (in the knowledge of other social classes, for example), no intensity of self-examination . . ., no scientific deductions on the basis of the internal evidence of First-World data, can ever be enough to include this radical otherness of colonial life, colonial suffering and exploitation, let alone the structural connections between that and this, between absent space and daily life in the metropolis.[13]

We can use Jameson's trenchant politicized reading of modernism as a bridge to an historicized reading of the opening pages of *Sodome et Gomorrhe*. In Marcel's discoveries about the world of homosexuality, fragments of a colonial reality, however trivialized, force their way into prominence. In his attempts to establish meaning for what he sees in the Guermantes courtyard (which represents emblematically, given its social prestige in the novel, one of Jameson's 'metropolitan centres' par excellence), Marcel looks to the fringe areas of Africa and Arabia. A marginalized sexual orientation, hitherto excluded and unseen, comes to be instated via another incorporation, this time of absent, non-Western spaces. In their exoticized forms, they help resolve the Narrator's representational difficulties by being coextensive with what is, for the unlikely colonial foot-soldier-cum-voyeur Marcel, the radical alterity of homosexuality.

It is no coincidence that the Narrator's very first step, in *Sodome et Gomorrhe*, is to address the question of space, in the form of the textual space necessary for the revelations about Charlus's sexuality. The text begins:

> The reader will remember that . . . I . . . had made a discovery which concerned M. de Charlus in particular but was in itself so important that I have until now, until the moment when I could give it the prominence and treat it with the fullness that it demanded, postponed giving an account of it. (*RMP*, II, 623)

> [On sait que . . . j'avais . . . fait . . . une découverte, concernant particulièrement M. de Charlus, mais si importante en elle-même que j'ai jusqu'ici, jusqu'au moment de pouvoir lui donner la place et l'étendue voulues, différé de la rapporter.] (*RTP*, III, 3)

With the *exposé* on homosexuality inaugurating the volume, the marginal thus becomes, in structural terms, central. Moreover, the boundaries of the excursus on homosexuality are co-terminous with Part I of

Sodome et Gomorrhe. This conscious allocation of textual space mirrors Vigny's formulation quoted earlier: 'La femme aura Gomorrhe et l'homme aura Sodome'. Thus a heavily exoticized homosexuality is accommodated.

Marcel freely indulges in what he terms the contemplation of the botanist, pondering specifically the question of the fecundation of plants by bees. His daring *rapprochement* of human sexuality and botany is well known.[14] But this is no lapse into a dehistoricized science. For what exercises Marcel's mind is political diplomacy when, in his silent surveillance of the plants, he wonders if the insect will miraculously arrive from afar: 'the arrival, almost beyond the possibility of hope (across so many obstacles of distance, of adverse risks, of dangers), of the insect sent from so far away as ambassador to the virgin who had been waiting for so long' (*RMP*, II, 624) ['[cette] arrivée presque impossible à espérer (à travers tant d'obstacles, de distance, de risques contraires, de dangers) de l'insecte envoyé de si loin en ambassadeur à la vierge qui depuis longtemps prolongeait son attente'] (*RTP*, III, 4). The Narrator's dramatic reconstruction derives its power from its anthropocentric insistence on a world of envoys, diplomatic missions, and high-risk conquest. The male insect-ambassador undertakes a lengthy, heroic voyage, culminating in union with the female virgin-flower. While the risks and spaces evoked are not narrowly colonial, the heroic exertion overseas of political influence and power actively informs Proust's presentation of homosexuality. In that sense, via the literally promiscuous circuit of envoy/insect/homosexual, the pursuit of perverse sexual pleasure and the exemplary performance of patriotic duty coalesce, sexual deviance thus occupying the centre ground of bourgeois nationalist consensus.

Proust chooses a provocative metaphor from domestic politics when he likens the social organization of homosexuality to

a freemasonry far more extensive, more effective and less suspected than that of the Lodges, for it rests upon an identity of tastes, needs, habits, dangers, apprenticeship, knowledge, traffic, vocabulary, and one in which even members who do not wish to know one another recognize one another immediately by natural or conventional, involuntary or deliberate signs which indicate one of his kind to the beggar in the person of the nobleman whose carriage door he is shutting, to the father in the person of his daughter's suitor, to the man who has sought healing, absolution or legal defence in the doctor, the priest or the barrister to whom he has had recourse; all of them obliged to protect their own secret but sharing with the others a secret which the rest of humanity does not suspect and which means that to them the most wildly improbable tales of adventure seem true, for in this life of anachronistic fiction the ambassador is a bosom friend of the felon, the prince, with a certain insolent aplomb born of his aristocratic breeding which the timorous bourgeois lacks, on leaving the duchess's party goes off to confer in private with the ruffian. (*RMP*, II, 639–40)

[une franc-maçonnerie bien plus étendue, plus efficace et moins soupçonnée que celle des loges, car elle repose sur une identité de goûts, de besoins, d'habitudes, de dangers, d'apprentissage, de savoir, de trafic, de glossaire, et dans laquelle les membres mêmes qui souhaitent de ne pas se connaître, aussitôt se reconnaissent à des signes naturels ou de convention, involontaires ou voulus, qui signalent un de ses semblables au mendiant dans le grand seigneur à qui il ferme la portière de sa voiture, au père dans le fiancé de sa fille, à celui qui avait voulu se guérir, se confesser, qui avait à se défendre, dans le médecin, dans le prêtre, dans l'avocat qu'il est allé trouver; tous obligés à protéger leur secret, mais ayant leur part d'un secret des autres que le reste de l'humanité ne soupçonne pas et qui fait qu'à eux les romans d'aventure les plus invraisemblables semblent vrais; car dans cette vie romanesque, anachronique, l'ambassadeur est ami du forçat; le prince, avec une certaine liberté d'allures que donne l'éducation aristocratique et qu'un petit bourgeois tremblant n'aurait pas, en sortant de chez la duchesse s'en va conférer avec l'apache.] (*RTP*, III, 18–19)[15]

Proust's giant fresco suggests a teeming world of secret, homosexual connections which itself constitutes a thriving form of social inclusiveness. The forces regulating this fraternity, which brings together envoy and criminal, beggar and aristocrat, range from liberal egalitarianism to a virulent social elitism. Thus an all-pervasive homosexuality, grounded in dislocation and anachronism, generates an exotic sociology, in which improbable alliances are forged across the social strata. A dense matrix of common traits – gestural, linguistic, psychological – force even the most secretive of homosexuals into some form of reluctant self-disclosure. The confidence with which the homosexual fraternity extends its network is captured stylistically in the lexical density and resourcefulness of the description. The gravitational forces at work in the area of sexual preference are similarly reflected at the level of syntax: thus, in the arrangement of syntagms, each subject – confessor, patient, defendant – after a period of deferral and textual separation, eventually and inexorably finds its desired object. Through the logic of these very carefully imbricated syntactical connections, a new homosexual grammar or law is being written.

Charlus himself, in declaring his sexuality, occupies a strikingly marginal position. Abandoning all affectation, the aristocrat in him assumes his medieval incarnation. Given the cult of medievalism in Proust's novel, the connection will appear familiar. Yet this confident appeal to anachronism forms another element in the Narrator's fantasticated account of homosexual desire: 'Pale as a marble statue, his fine features with the prominent nose no longer received from an expression deliberately assumed a different meaning which altered the beauty of their contours; no more now than a Guermantes, he seemed already carved in stone, he, Palamède xv, in the chapel at Combray' (*RMP*, ii, 625) ['Pâle comme un marbre, il avait le nez fort, ses traits fins ne recevaient plus d'un regard volontaire une signification différente qui altérât la beauté de leur modelé; plus rien qu'un Guermantes, il semblait déjà sculpté, lui Palamède xv, dans la chapelle de Combray'] (*RTP*, iii, 5). Exoticized in a temporal sense, a statuesque Charlus, his sexual desire now uncovered, stands squarely for a medieval, aristocratic lineage. 'Desire always proceeds towards an extreme archaism', Barthes observes, interpreting the feudal nature of the protagonist Loti's desire captured in the cultivation of old Ottoman order in *Aziyadé*.[16] In Charlus's case, the anachronism is compounded in the description of him already carved, as the moment of his desire announces a future petrification in the medieval statuary of the Combray church. Significantly, the moment of homosexual truth restores a seemingly cohesive Golden Age, in which arrogance and violence give way to harmony. The paradigms of alterity within which Charlus's sexuality is inscribed are thus provided by a remote medieval past, colonial actuality, and dislocations in the class system. Moreover, the appeal to the natural implies a desire to convert this marginality into the social normality to which the deviant aspires.

The Narrator vigorously pursues other potential antecedents and models for the socially marginalized homosexual lover:

Perhaps, to form a picture of these, we ought to think, if not of the wild animals that never become domesticated, of the lion-cubs, allegedly tamed, which are still lions at heart, then at least of the negroes whom the comfortable existence of the white man renders desperately unhappy and who prefer the risks of life in the wild and its incomprehensible joys. (*RMP*, ii, 647)

[Peut-être, pour les peindre, faut-il penser sinon aux animaux qui ne se domestiquent pas, aux lionceaux prétendus apprivoisés mais restés lions, du moins aux noirs, que l'existence confortable des blancs désespère et qui préfèrent les risques de la vie sauvage et ses incompréhensibles joies.] (*RTP*, iii, 26)

The Narrator's reckless use of anthropocentric and more specifically Eurocentric stereotypes situates him squarely within the colonialist tradition. He floats a crude animal analogy before scuppering it, replacing it with a no less dubious comparison involving blacks. At a time when the European colonization of Africa and beyond was at its height, Proust chooses the colony in which to simulate the conditions of extreme danger facing the homosexual, now cast as the colonized contending with invasion. In the Narrator's fantastic sexual geography, which is inflected by the racism of his day, Africa becomes an idealized space, in which heroic blacks, repelled by images of white comfort, are the risk-takers. Homosexuals are similarly outraged by heterosexual ease. The opposition, while flawed with the essentialization fundamental to racism, becomes heavily moralized, with its insistence on the imaginative and ethical superiority of black (and homosexual) asceticism. Like the Polynesia of *Noa Noa* or the Africa of *Le Roman d'un spahi*, Proust's 'dark continent' appears fleetingly as the escape route from moral restriction. As with Gauguin and Loti, his association of the Other with sexual desire is random and predatorial. No less arbitrary is his animalization of the homosexual. Yet in looking beyond Europe to articulate social taboo, Proust reinforces the tradition whereby the forbidden is regularly accommodated beyond the West. The combination of suppression and revolt recalls Freud's seductive argument that 'civilization behaves towards sexuality as a people or a stratum of its population does which has subjected another one to its exploitation'.[17]

If, for Jameson, the reality of empire is occluded in modernism, writing homosexuality in *À la recherche du temps perdu* means reinstating a hitherto shelved colonial history. In both cases, alterity, be it that of the colonized or the would-be sexual deviant, acquires a moral superiority. But the ability to see it, the Narrator argues, requires a sixth, almost divine, sense:

Each man's vice (we use the term for the sake of linguistic convenience) accompanies him through life after the manner of the familiar genius who was invisible to men so long as they were unaware of his presence. . . . Ulysses himself did not recognize Athena at first. But the gods are immediately perceptible to one another, like as quickly to like, and so too had M. de Charlus been to Jupien. Until that moment, in the presence of M. de Charlus I had been in the position of an unobservant man who, standing before a pregnant woman whose distended outline he has failed to remark, persists, while she smilingly reiterates 'Yes, I'm a little tired just now', in asking her tactlessly: 'Why, what's the matter with you?' But let someone say to him: 'She is expecting a child', and suddenly he catches sight of her stomach and ceases to see anything else. It is the explanation that opens our eyes; the dispelling of an error gives us an additional sense. (*RMP*, ii, 635–6)

[Le vice (on parle ainsi pour la commodité du langage), le vice de chacun l'accompagne à la façon de ce génie qui était invisible pour les hommes tant qu'ils ignoraient sa présence. . . . Ulysse lui-même ne reconnaissait pas d'abord Athéné. Mais les dieux sont immédiatement perceptibles aux dieux, le semblable aussi vite au semblable, ainsi encore l'avait été M. de Charlus à Jupien. Jusqu'ici je m'étais trouvé en face de M. de Charlus de la même façon qu'un homme distrait, lequel, devant une femme enceinte dont il n'a pas remarqué la taille alourdie, s'obstine, tandis qu'elle lui répète en souriant: 'Oui, je suis un peu fatiguée en ce moment', à lui demander indiscrètement: 'Qu'avez-vous donc?' Mais que quelqu'un lui dise: 'Elle est grosse', soudain il aperçoit le ventre et ne verra plus que lui. C'est la raison qui ouvre les yeux; une erreur dissipée nous donne un sens de plus.] (*RTP*, III, 15)

The Narrator's impatient reference to linguistic convenience signals indirectly the need for a radically new discourse, a need that triggers hasty reconfigurations, including not only the animalization and Africanization of the homosexual but now also his divinization. Moreover, pregnancy, itself offering a literal trace of heterosexual activity, paradoxically corroborates a homosexual reality and eclipses the division between the normative and the aberrant. Would-be perversity thus collapses semantic categories and spawns enigma in pursuit of social realignment.

WHERE VICE MEETS VIRTUE: JUPIEN'S BROTHEL

The exoticization of war-time Paris, described in *Le Temps retrouvé* as a place of sexual promiscuity, is centred around the evocation of Jupien's male brothel. As Marcel and Charlus walk along the street, the city is described in stereotypically Orientalist terms. The Seine is likened to the Bosphorus, while a crescent moon reinforces the sense of eastern exoticism:

And – a symbol perhaps of the invasion foretold by the defeatism of M. de Charlus, or else of the cooperation of our Muslim brothers with the armies of France – the moon, narrow and curved like a sequin, seemed to have placed the sky of Paris beneath the oriental sign of the crescent. (*RMP*, III, 836)

[Et, symbole soit de cette invasion que prédisait le défaitisme de M. de Charlus, soit de la coopération de nos frères musulmans avec les armées de la France, la lune étroite et recourbée comme un sequin semblait mettre le ciel parisien sous le signe oriental du croissant.] (*RTP*, IV, 387–8)

The Narrator's hesitant evaluation of the scene is inseparable from collective cultural memory. Certainly, the claimed fraternal presence of Muslim armies (drawn from what was euphemistically called *la plus grande France*), shows Proust using uncritically the clichéd language of a would-be benign colonialist order. No less predictable is the crescent moon, announcing fear of incursion from the East, while subliminally triggering archaic memories of Christian conquest of the infidel. The inference is that in this Constantinople of the West, homosexuality awakens both curiosity and a desire on the part of a heterosexual consensus to repress it. Charlus confirms the impression of a palimpsestic representation of the East when he boasts: '"Don't you see all the Orient of Decamps and Fromentin and Ingres and Delacroix in this scene?"' (*RMP*, III, 837) ['"Est-ce que tout l'Orient de Decamps, de Fromentin, d'Ingres, de Delacroix n'est pas là-dedans?"'] (*RTP*, IV, 388). The list is proof that the Western phenomenon of Orientalism regularly functions in a self-sustaining, citational way.[18] In an early manuscript draft, Proust goes further, likening the scene in wartime Paris to the sensuous Istanbul of *Aziyadé* before adding in a burst of racial sensationalism that the sky-blue uniforms of the international troops take us beyond the 'colonial Orient' of Loti and into the country of 'the "manhunt"' ['la "chasse à l'homme"'].[19] Thus Proust's gradations of difference replicate the lurid stereotyping of high colonialism.

If Charlus calls up modern pictorial sources to find the East, the Narrator invokes an older, and for him favourite, intertext, the *Thousand and One Nights* (*RMP*, III, 837; *RTP*, IV, 388). Recalling how, on first entering the male brothel, he had thought he was going to the rescue of someone being beaten, he asserts that it was a re-enactment of another story in the *Thousand and One Nights*, in which a woman, transformed into a dog, is beaten voluntarily, so as to be restored to her former human self (*RMP*, III, 862; *RTP*, IV, 411).[20] Not only does the reference orientalize Charlus's flagellation but it ties an exoticized violence and defeat to homosexuality. Moreover, reference to the *Thousand and One Nights* textualizes and exoticizes this desire.

In Charlus's Oriental cameo, we have a further twist in the sexual comedy the Narrator constructs around him. As his eye catches a passing Senegalese soldier who fails to stop, Charlus comments regretfully: '"But how unfortunate that to complete the picture one of us two is not an odalisque!"' (*RMP*, III, 837) ['"Mais quel malheur, pour compléter le tableau, que l'un de nos deux ne soit pas une odalisque!"'] (*RTP*, IV, 388). He thus rounds off his fantasia by positing his reincarnation as one of Ingres's concubines in a sultan's seraglio. The echo of Ingres's crowded Eastern interiors is especially suggestive at this juncture in *Le Temps retrouvé*, as it anticipates the busy crowd scene in Jupien's brothel. But in another stage in Marcel's deferred recognition of sexual activity, he fails initially to recognize the brothel for what it is. In fact, he naively wonders if, in reaching the hotel, he has stumbled upon a nest of spies, and all this before hearing a sound of chains that convinces him he is about to witness a great crime. Hence the mock heroic image of Marcel: 'so that it was at once with the pride of an emissary of justice and the rapture of a poet that I at length, my mind made up, entered the hotel' (*RMP*, III, 840) ['et c'est à la fois avec une fierté de justicier et une volupté de poète que j'entrai délibérément dans l'hôtel'] (*RTP*, IV, 391). The double image of the protagonist, grandly cast as protector of the law and as voluptuary, anticipates the combination of outrage and fascination that Marcel registers once he realizes he is not in a nest of spies but in a male brothel. The discovery, announcing a shift from espionage to homosexuality, leaves Marcel as the ingenuous upholder of a heterosexual law.

The insistent play within the brothel scene between legality and criminality, chastity and promiscuity, is epitomized in Jupien's story of the man who, on being approached by Charlus, suspects him of being a spy. Jupien reports matter-of-factly: "'And he was greatly relieved when he realized that he was being asked to sell not his country but his body, which is possibly not a more moral thing to do, but less dangerous and in any case easier'" (*RMP*, III, 860) ["'Et il s'est senti bien à l'aise quand il a vu qu'on ne lui demandait pas de livrer sa patrie, mais son corps, ce qui n'est peut-être pas plus moral, mais ce qui est moins dangereux et surtout plus facile'"] (*RTP*, IV, 409–10). In Jupien's words, stripped of all sentimentalism, we find an intriguing convergence of political and sexual morality. In the alternatives enumerated – selling one's country or one's body – Proust feigns to underpin and in reality undermines the politics of bourgeois heterosexual nationalism. He appeals mock heroically to an ethics of national loyalty, while unsettling the very bases on which such loyalty rests. Here again, the accommodation of homosexuality generates a politics which, in its corrosive irony and playfulness, strains to the limit the status quo.

Homosexual desire weakens another central plank in the bourgeois order, the hierarchy of social class. Thus Charlus's long-standing aristocratic disdain for the middle classes has become, in old age, his exclusion of all but the lowest classes. In this cultivation of social inferiors, he is following, we are told, in the footsteps of predecessors such as the Duc de La Rochefoucauld who, according to Saint-Simon, lived out their last years in the company of their domestics (*RMP*, III, 860; *RTP*, IV, 409). As an emblem of anarchy, homosexual desire thus randomly disturbs the categories of class and race alike.

The testing of consensus continues when Jupien, apologizing for his role in running the brothel, explains to Marcel that, were he to cater solely for *bona fide* residents in his hotel, he would never make ends meet. His impish conclusion, "'Here, contrary to the doctrine of the Carmelites, it is thanks to vice that virtue is able to live'" (*RMP*, III, 859) ["'Ici c'est le contraire des carmels, c'est grâce au vice que vit la vertu'"] (*RTP*, IV, 409), inverts the religious notion of expiation for the sins of many as practised by a few. In Jupien's dialectical model, vice and inversion become providential and even sacrificial in their shoring up of virtue.

*

The depiction of homosexuality poses representational challenges in *À la recherche*, and releases intense speculative energy and inventiveness, as well as crude exaggeration and prejudice. In mapping this transgressive sexual zone, the Narrator develops analogies and connections that are heavy with socio-cultural connotations. We have seen figures of the homosexual as explorer, black African, caliph of Baghdad, figure from the Orient, as bee, as flower, as pregnant woman, as inhabitant of Sodom and Gomorrah, as the vice that guarantees virtue, as Athena, as inverted snob shunning the bourgeoisie and collapsing the social order, and, by inference, as cannibal. No less exotic are the reincarnations of the spectator Marcel as heroic European abroad, Ulysses, Boer guerrilla, botanist, and entomologist.

The range of risky analogies deployed shows Proust at full stretch imaginatively in his attempt to represent and rehabilitate an outlawed sexuality. In doing so, he works in the exotic geographical and cultural margins that European colonialism makes available. In the case of Jupien's brothel, he subversively queries the bases of cultural orthodoxy by conflating the exigencies of patriotism and sexual pleasure. Proust is indiscriminate and unpredictable in his depiction of homosexuality. The comfortable parochialism whereby the accursed race is made up of very much home-grown freemasons illustrates a desire to see homosexuality legitimized, to have outside become inside, to cloak would-be vice in respectability. Yet the effect of these myriad analogies is to make the *apologia* strongly promiscuous in its representational variety.

Proust's accounts both subvert and underpin the political order that shapes them. Colonialism provided opportunities for extravagant myth-making, not just for Proust but also for less celebrated predecessors such as Loti and Gauguin. Many of the *exotica* in *Sodome et Gomorrhe* are by-products of the colonial imagination. But in addition to Proust's parasitical speculation, there is the inference that, in homosexuality as with the ethnic Other, there exists a force capable of resisting the desire for a hegemony that is both Western and heterosexual. Genet draws together the forces of ethnicity and sexuality in a powerful statement of dissidence in *Un captif amoureux*, as we shall be seeing later. In a style that could only have pleased Genet, Jupien flirtatiously rewrites the Carmelite code of vice and virtue, as the novel pursues its subversive appropriation of established Christian morality.

The Narrator of *À la recherche* thus explores the radical otherness of desire, both heterosexual and homosexual. In a style reminiscent of the Surrealist map of the world in which non-European sites are magnified and a self-styled rationalist Europe is made minuscule, Proust charts a *mappa mundi* of alterity, guided by popular prejudice and fantasy as well as often erudite speculation.[21] The excess that this represents signals the paradoxes and strains inherent in European cultural self-definition more generally. The meaning-loss in colonialism identified by Jameson is converted into a tentative, if still hackneyed, meaning-gain in *À la recherche*, as homosexuality acquires signification in new spaces beyond Europe. Putting it more polemically, if the colony regularly provides a safety valve for metropolitan order (the shipping to Algeria of Parisian revolutionaries of 1848 and displaced Alsatians in 1871 signalled in Camus's *Le Premier Homme* provides a good example), so the *Recherche* plays with relocating overseas the sexual dissidents of its day.[22]

THE PLACE OF XENOPHOBIA

> The stakes . . . where we burn our enemies, or those designated as such, give off a good heat to the collective soul. The very effort . . . helps purify us.
>
> (Memmi)[23]

Proust's exploration of perceived sexual orthodoxy and deviance also triggers virulent expressions of political and national conservatism. Perversely, it is the most prominent homosexual of all, Charlus, who plays the old card of fierce national pride and uncompromising moral orthodoxy, in an attempt to conceal, and yet also obliquely to express, his sexual preferences.

The parameters of a narrow Christian nationalism govern the comedy that unfolds as Charlus meets Marcel's Jewish friend, Bloch. While Bloch immediately arouses Charlus's sexual interest, the latter responds initially by concealing that interest:

I told [M. de Charlus] that it had been very kind of him to say that he hoped to see Bloch again. The Baron gave not the slightest sign of having heard my remark, and as I repeated it four times without eliciting a reply, I began to wonder whether I had been the victim of an acoustic mirage when I thought I heard M. de Charlus utter those words. 'He lives at Balbec?', crooned the Baron in a tone so far from interrogatory that it is regrettable that the written language does not possess a sign other than the question mark to end such apparently unquestioning remarks. (*RMP*, II, 1141)

[Je dis à M. de Charlus qu'il avait été bien aimable de lui dire qu'il espérait le revoir. Pas un mouvement ne révéla chez le baron qu'il eût entendu ma phrase, et comme je la répétai quatre fois sans avoir de réponse, je finis par douter si je n'avais pas été le jouet d'un mirage acoustique quand j'avais cru entendre ce que M. de Charlus avait dit. 'Il habite Balbec?' chantonna le baron, d'un air si peu questionneur qu'il est fâcheux que la langue française ne possède pas un signe autre que le point d'interrogation pour terminer ces phrases apparemment si peu interrogatives.] (*RTP*, III, 489–90)

The comic persistence of Marcel's interventions finally provokes the most glancing of enquiries from Charlus, the melodic nature of which belies a latent but insistent desire. So oblique is the query that the Narrator reflects, with a combination of irony and regret, on the absence in the French language of some diacritic form of question mark that might capture Charlus's pianissimo enquiry. Finding a language for homosexuality is thus as urgent as finding a space for it. Prompted by the punctual manifestation of desire in Charlus's operatic 'Il habite Balbec?', the Narrator's metalinguistic speculation demonstrates how Charlus's homosexual play generates offcentredness, taking place at the limit points of language, just as elsewhere sexual deviance leads us to the West's distant colonial fringes.

The sequel to this particular episode has its own complications. Learning that Bloch's family are staying at a local residence known as 'La Commanderie', Charlus explains that properties thus named had historical links with the Order of Malta, of which he, Charlus, is a member. Not satisfied with his exhibition of Christian erudition, he launches into an hysterical anti-semitic tirade, castigating Bloch and other Jews for acquiring properties with names such as Priory, Abbey, Minster, Chantry:

'So your friend lives at the Commanderie, the wretch! What sadism! You must show me the way to it', he added, resuming his air of indifference, 'so that I may go there one day and see how our former domains endure such a profanation.' (*RMP*, II, 1142)

['Votre ami habite La Commanderie, le malheureux! Quel sadisme! Vous m'indiquerez le chemin, ajouta-t-il en reprenant l'air d'indifférence, pour que j'aille un jour voir comment nos antiques domaines supportent une pareille profanation.'] (*RTP*, III, 490)

In unveiling the libidinal energies at work in Charlus's diatribe, the Narrator constructs a comedy that is simultaneously political and sexual. He glosses the political element, commenting on '[t]his speech, anti-Jewish or pro-Hebrew – according to whether one pays attention to the overt meaning of its sentences or the intentions that they concealed' (*RMP*, II, 1144) ['[c]e discours antijuif ou prohébreu – selon qu'on s'attachera à l'extérieur des phrases ou aux intentions qu'elles recelaient'] (*RTP*, III, 492). Significantly, the desire of the body, mediated through language, is further articulated in Charlus's parade of anti-Jewish invective. The two poles of surface anti-semitism and deep pro-Jewishness, resting on an apparently secure language/pre-language divide, suggest the conflict attendant on the expression of libidinal desire. Moreover, satisfying that desire exacts a political and ethical price. Asked what Bloch's Paris address is, Marcel can only say that his father's offices are in the Rue des Blancs-Manteaux. Charlus's predictably shrill reply further strains the Narrator's diagnosis of latent pro-Jewishness:

'Oh, isn't that the last word in perversity!' exclaimed M. de Charlus, *appearing to find a profound satisfaction in his own cry of ironical indignation.* 'Rue des Blancs-Manteaux!' he repeated, dwelling with emphasis upon each syllable and laughing as he spoke. 'What sacrilege! To think that these White Mantles polluted by M. Bloch were those of the mendicant friars, styled Serfs of the Blessed Virgin, whom Saint Louis established there.' (*RMP*, II, 1142–3)

['Oh! quel comble de perversité, s'écria M. de Charlus, *en paraissant trouver, dans son propre cri d'ironique indignation, une satisfaction profonde.* Rue des Blancs-Manteaux, répéta-t-il en pressurant chaque syllabe et en riant. Quel sacrilège! Pensez que ces Blancs-Manteaux pollués par M. Bloch étaient ceux des frères mendiants, dits serfs de la Sainte-Vierge, que saint Louis établit là.'] (*RTP*, III, 491; my emphasis)

Charlus's potted local history and its celebration of an immaculate, Christian past reinforces rather than dispels enigma. To dismiss it as mere pretext, as a front for underlying homosexual desire, would be to subtract the central element of linguistic parade that is integral to Charlus's pleasure. The Narrator himself concedes the point when he identifies the possibility that on the ironic surface of his tirade, the Baron appears to experience a deep satisfaction.

The cultivation of surface in the depiction of homosexuality is not exclusive to the *Recherche*. Robert Fraser links Proust and Wilde, documenting Wilde's rejection of the rhetoric of depth and authenticity and his aggressive promotion of surface.[24] Likewise, Jonathan Dollimore sees Genet subverting the opposition between surface and depth and using the links between paradox and perversity against punitive heterosexual regimes: 'Genet . . . like Wilde, produces both anarchic pleasure and subversive knowledge inseparably.'[25]

For Proust, language becomes the site of Charlus's subversive pleasure. In fact his deliberate and sensuous recital of the street name, with its connotations of monastic asceticism, is evidence that his virulent outburst, far from announcing a future pleasure beyond language, becomes the only sensual gratification available.[26] The prospect of love and desire existing within language alone strains the Narrator's categories of philo- and anti-semitism. For in this perspective, Charlus's outburst ceases to be pretext and becomes the only text available. Paradox is thus a central weapon in Proust's representation of perversity.

The linguistic surface of Charlus's diatribe forcefully demonstrates a striking convergence of anti-semitic and sexual energies. In the light of Freud, we can see in Charlus's abuse a case of desire placated at a social, ethical cost.[27] For the Narrator of the *Recherche*, the hysterical denigration of Jews ostensibly acquires little prestige. Indeed he dismisses it as a charade, albeit a fairly spectacular one. He uncovers the migration of desire, which in this instance finds its way into a heavily ironic expression of anti-Jewishness. The excess permitted by caricature is symptomatic of the displaced gratification that Charlus finds in the mediated form of verbal invective. But desire again requires the Other to be made exotic in an essentialized way, a point clearly signalled in Charlus's distasteful approval for the ghetto: '"But after all a ghetto is all the finer the more homogeneous and complete it is."' (*RMP*, II, 1143) ['"Mais enfin un ghetto est d'autant plus beau qu'il est plus homogène et plus complet"'] (*RTP*, III, 492). The ring-fencing of difference that Segalen sees as a requirement of the exotic becomes, in Charlus's hands, a bigoted endorsement of punitive segregation.

Before leaving the episode, we need to consider a final detail in Charlus's diatribe. He settles on an incident that occurred in medieval times in the Rue des Blancs-Manteaux area: '"a strange Jew . . . boiled the Host, after which I think they boiled him, which is stranger still since it seems to suggest that the body of a Jew can be equivalent to the Body of Our Lord"' (*RMP*, II, 1143) ['"un étrange juif . . . avait fait bouillir des hosties, après quoi je pense qu'on le fit bouillir lui-même, ce qui est plus étrange encore puisque cela a l'air de signifier que le corps d'un juif peut valoir autant que le corps du bon Dieu"'] (*RTP*, III, 492).[28] Charlus's

ostentatious display of Christian deference in no way conceals his face-
tious sophistry. He is clearly pursuing a series of oppositions that the doctrine of transubstantiation makes available – the visible host and the
notion of Christ's real presence, the appearance of bread and the divine
reality. It is precisely the terms of this opposition that he exploits for perverse effect, when he argues that the execution of the Jew on grounds of
sacrilege is itself an insult to God and thereby sacrilegious.

This relates to the question of desire and language. In the absence of
Bloch, Charlus settles for the vitriolic language of his feigned anti-semitism; and it is in this porous language, however imperfectly it holds his
desire, that the only presence of Bloch is possible. Elsewhere in Proust's
novel, the terms of the eucharistic transformation are recalled with
familiarity, for example when the boy Marcel sees his mother's bedtime
kiss as 'a host for an act of peace-giving communion in which my lips
might imbibe her *real presence*' (*RMP*, I, 14) ['une hostie pour une communion de paix où mes lèvres puiseraient sa *présence réelle*'] (*RTP*, I, 13;
my emphasis); and again when the adult Marcel finds in Albertine's
tongue an almost sacred nourishment (*RMP*, III, 2; *RTP*, III, 520).
Subliminally, the ingestion of the loved one adumbrated in eucharistic
communion provides an echo of the cannibalizing urge of the desiring
subject discussed earlier. But the fleeting moments of satisfaction in corporeal adhesion contrast with the more usual absent body, of the mother
who must socialize, of Albertine out and about in Paris; or, in Charlus's
case, of the absent Bloch.

In evoking the medieval Jew, Charlus toys with a complex set of connotations: real presence and absence, profane irony and sacred literal-
mindedness, Christian triumphalism and Jewish defeat, reverence and
sacrilege, Self and Other. Desire triggers both a busy search in the
present for Bloch's addresses in Balbec and Paris, and the medieval persecution of the Jew. The remote chronology provides access to the figure
whom Dollimore identifies as embodying pre-sexological perversion,
namely the religious heretic.[29] Resurrecting one of what Dollimore labels
the 'lost histories of perversion', Proust's deviant invokes an old Christian
hegemony, defined topographically in the form of an intolerant, medieval Paris. By occupying this ideologically central ground, Charlus
significantly transfers what are his *ex-centric* sexual preferences, couching
them in a discourse marked by narrow conformity and an intolerance of
deviation. His erotic tastes, which elsewhere in *À la recherche du temps perdu*
come close to incriminating him, here make him paradoxically a stout
and yet ironic defender of a closed Christian world order.

Proust's fictional model corroborates Foucault's observations on the nineteenth-century discourse of sexual perversity. What Foucault calls '"reverse" discourse' entails 'homosexuality [. . . speaking] in its own behalf, to demand that its legitimacy or "naturality" be acknowledged, often in the same vocabulary, using the same categories by which it was medically disqualified'.[30] In the case of Charlus, sexual deviance is cloaked in a legitimizing Christian hegemony and in the sectarian nationalism that assumes a heterosexual consensus.

The view that social and political cultures are often written and defined along their margins finds corroboration, then, in Charlus's diatribe. But while we perceive an active process of relegation from a perceived centre to the periphery, there is a sense in which the centre requires such peripheral deviance, in other words that Christian orthodoxy thrives on provocative non-Christian sacrilege, just as heterosexual 'virtue' needs homosexual 'vice'. In his *Langage Tangage ou Ce que les mots me disent*, Michel Leiris reflects playfully on the connotations of marginality: 'marginal – allergic to the pond in which the majority swim' ['marginal – allergique à la mare où l'on nage en majorité'].[31] Leiris's Surrealist punning pairs marginality and allergy, so that what stands outside consensus is pathological. Difference spells ailment and handicap. More accurately, the response of difference to the spectacle of the same is one of acute reaction to a disease-inducing majority.[32] Leiris's scrutiny of the cognate term, xenophobia, is equally incisive: 'xenophobia – a harmful fit of bile or madness affecting what is beautiful and fixed?' ['xénophobie – accès nocif de bile ou folie au beau fixe?'].[33] Leiris's question mark alerts us to the multiple semantic possibilities adumbrated in his witty gloss. At the level of internal rhyme, 'beau' calls up the 'pho-' in 'phobie' but also 'xéno-', the Greek *xenon*, meaning strange or foreign thing. So where is the beauty? While the suggestiveness of the rhyme makes difference as beautiful as the phobia it induces, the pairing 'beau fixe' connotes a sense of pleasure in cultural homogeneity. The pleasure is doubled in the semantic uncertainty (which element is nominal and which adjectival in 'beau fixe'?), leaving us with an identity that is beautiful by virtue of its fixity, and fixed by virtue of its beauty. Prompted by the encounter with the Other, forms of illness, both physical and mental, thus invade the collective native body and consciousness.

Xenophobia is explored with similar relish in Proust's novel. His appetite for paradoxical reconfigurations of the foreign and the familiar is evidenced by the Narrator's scrutiny of some very different residents of the Grand Hotel at Balbec. The Jewish homosexual Nissim Bernard (a modern-day sexological counterpart of Charlus's medieval religious pervert) pursues his fantasies, which the Narrator describes with Orientalist extravagance:[34]

[Nissim Bernard] loved moreover all the labyrinth of corridors, private offices, reception-rooms, cloakrooms, larders, galleries which composed the hotel at Balbec. With a strain of oriental atavism he loved a seraglio, and when he went out at night might be seen furtively exploring its purlieus. (*RMP*, II, 874)

[[Nissim Bernard] aimait d'ailleurs tout le labyrinthe de couloirs, de cabinets secrets, de salons, de vestiaires, de garde-manger, de galeries qu'était l'hôtel de Balbec. Par atavisme d'Oriental il aimait les sérails et quand il sortait le soir, on le voyait en explorer furtivement les détours.] (*RTP*, III, 239)

Promiscuity is thus located in the labyrinth, traditionally associated with the idea of a savage city, where wild fantasies are freely indulged.[35] In a carefully engineered contrast, the hotel also houses two travelling domestics whom Marcel befriends, Marie Gineste and Céleste Albaret. Crucially, the Narrator builds the contrast between the outsider Nissim Bernard and the servants around a division of space within the Grand Hotel, which functions as a theatre under Aimé's directorship. An ostensibly moral upstairs contrasts with a depraved downstairs:

While, venturing down to the basement and endeavouring at the same time to escape notice and to avoid a scandal, M. Nissim Bernard, in his quest of the young Levites, put one in mind of those lines in *La Juive*:

> O God of our Fathers, come down to us again,
> Our mysteries veil from the eyes of wicked men!

I on the contrary would go up to the room of two sisters who had come to Balbec with an old foreign lady as her maids. They were what the language of hotels called two *courrières*. . . . Born at the foot of the high mountains in the centre of France, on the banks of rivulets and torrents (the water flowed actually under the family home . . .), *they seemed to embody the spirit of those waters*. (*RMP*, II, 874–5)

[Tandis que se risquant jusqu'aux sous-sols et cherchant malgré tout à ne pas être vu et à éviter le scandale, M. Nissim Bernard, dans sa recherche des jeunes lévites, faisait penser à ces vers de *La Juive*:

> Ô Dieu de nos pères,
> Parmi nous descends,
> Cache nos mystères
> À l'œil des méchants!

je montais au contraire dans la chambre de deux soeurs qui avaient accompagné à Balbec, comme femmes de chambre, une vieille dame étrangère. C'était ce que le langage des hôtels appelait deux courrières. . . . Nées au pied des hautes montagnes du centre de la France, au bord de ruisseaux et de torrents (l'eau passait même sous leur maison de famille . . .), *elles semblaient en avoir gardé la nature.*] (*RTP*, III, 239–40; my emphasis)

In an exaggerated opposition, Nissim Bernard explores the basement in search of low homosexual pleasure, while Marcel ascends to visit the seemingly immaculate sisters. In this burlesque casting, virtue operates in a narrowly national setting, while vice pursues its labyrinthine course in an underworld ruled by mock-Judaic religious practices. The incorporation of Fromental Halévy's nineteenth-century opera *La Juive* extends the opposition, Jewish textuality and citation contrasting with the illiteracy of the servants. A manuscript variant reinforces the preoccupation with spatial arrangements, attributing stereotypically to Nissim Bernard an Oriental taste for the intrigue and complication of the night (*RTP*, III, 1475). With the hotel itself a body housing perceived high and low instincts, his enjoyment of its multiple entrances subliminally suggests promiscuous forms of sexual pleasure.

The fantasies about sexual licence and Judaic otherness are thrown into relief by the domestics, who are unrepentantly xenophobic: 'without knowing anything of history or geography, they heartily detested the English, the Germans, the Russians, the Italians, all foreign "vermin", and cared, with certain exceptions, for French people alone' (*RMP*, II, 878) ['sans savoir l'histoire ni la géographie, elles détestaient de confiance les Anglais, les Allemands, les Russes, les Italiens, la "vermine" des étrangers et n'aimaient, avec des exceptions, que les Français'] (*RTP*, III, 243).[36] Proust's Narrator is thus exploring a concordance of ethnic stereotypes, in which complication is seen as Oriental, while an aggressive simplicity originates in a central French location. The latter topos is as constructed and overdetermined as its Eastern correlative, the text moving deftly between these equally exotic constructions of rabid nationalism and lurid Orientalism. Yet the divide between foreign and national that is meant to underwrite the dichotomy between homosexual and heterosexual is compromised when we remember the Narrator's ironic detachment from the polarities he is describing, an irony that facilitates the sliding scale of vices and virtues in the *Recherche*. In geographical terms, Marcel's intermediate position is underlined by his being literally on the coast, adrift both from the sisters' would-be utopian birthplace in the heart of France (the seat, quintessentially, of Leiris's *beau fixe*) and Nissim Bernard's Orient.

Underpinning the xenophobe's position is the stubborn, self-congratulatory belief in the nation as the locus of the unchangeable and the beautiful, what Francis Mulhern in a parallel context calls 'the guarantee of integrity'.[37] But if the travelling domestics of the Balbec hotel appear to embody notions of home and centre, their xenophobia reveals unexpected sexual tensions. On one level, the pristine beauty of the sisters promises a desexualized pleasure for Marcel, at a time when he worries about Albertine's alleged lesbianism – as though xenophobia might quell an alarming alterity. But their conversation, rather like that of Charlus, is suffused with libidinal energy. In the verbal banter of Céleste, the more forward of the two domestics, we find the xenophobe manipulating an elaborate maternal language:

They often came in the morning to see me when I was still in bed. . . . Céleste would say to me. 'Oh! little black devil with raven hair, oh deep-dyed mischief! I don't know what your mother was thinking of when she made you, you're just like a bird. Look, Marie, wouldn't you say he was preening his feathers, and the supple way he turns his head right round, he looks so light, you'd think he was just learning to fly. Ah! it's lucky for you that you were born into the ranks of the rich. . . . There he goes, now, look, he's spilling his milk. Wait till I tie a napkin round you, because you'll never do it for yourself, I've never seen anyone so helpless and clumsy as you.' (*RMP*, ii, 875–6)

[Elles venaient souvent le matin me voir quand j'étais encore couché. . . . Céleste me disait: 'Oh! petit diable noir aux cheveux de geai, ô profonde malice! je ne sais pas à quoi pensait votre mère quand elle vous a fait, car vous avez tout d'un oiseau. Regarde, Marie, est-ce qu'on ne dirait pas qu'il se lisse ses plumes, et tourne son cou avec une souplesse? il a l'air tout léger, on dirait qu'il est en train d'apprendre à voler. Ah! vous avez de la chance que ceux qui vous ont créé vous aient fait naître dans le rang des riches. . . . Voilà qu'il . . . répand son lait, attendez que je vous mette une serviette car vous ne sauriez pas vous y prendre, je n'ai jamais vu quelqu'un de si bête et de si maladroit que vous.'] (*RTP*, iii, 240–1)

In describing a process of general infantilization, Céleste stubbornly returns to Marcel's conception, birth, and infancy. In this xenophobic space, the young adult Marcel is depotentiated, returning to a state of helpless dependence on the forceful mother Céleste. It is a regression that Marcel resists in part and his struggle to prevent Céleste from putting a napkin on him prompts her to exclaim: 'Marie, look at him, bang, he's shot straight up on end like a snake' (*RMP*, ii, 876) ['Marie, regarde-le, bing! voilà qu'il s'est dressé tout droit comme un serpent. Un vrai serpent, je te dis'] (*RTP*, iii, 241). The implicitly phallic image of a serpent-like Marcel heightens the veiled sexual comedy that is conducted and amplified through language itself – as, for example, when Céleste again draws attention to the idea of erection in a manner sufficiently displaced to preserve a semblance of playful innocence:

'Look, his hair's standing on end, puffing out with rage like a bird's feathers. Poor *ploumissou*!' Here it was not only Marie who protested, but myself, for I did not feel in the least like a grand gentleman. But Céleste would never believe in the sincerity of my modesty and would cut me short: 'Oh, what a bag of tricks! Oh, the soft talk, the deceitfulness! Ah, the cunning rogue! Ah, Molière!' (This was the only writer's name that she knew . . .) (*RMP*, II, 876)

['Regarde, ses cheveux se hérissent, ils se boursouflent par la colère comme les plumes des oiseaux. Pauvre *ploumissou*!' Ici ce n'était pas seulement Marie qui protestait, mais moi, car je ne me sentais pas seigneur du tout. Mais Céleste ne croyait jamais à la sincérité de ma modestie et, me coupant la parole: 'Ah! sac à ficelles, ah! douceur, ah! perfidie! rusé entre les rusés, rosse des rosses! Ah! Molière!' (C'était le seul nom d'écrivain qu'elle connût . . .)] (*RTP*, III, 241; Proust's emphasis)

Céleste's verbal ingenuity, her playing sensually with alliteration – recalling, incidentally, Charlus's sensuous anti-semitic tirade – is a form of seduction through language. The absence of any overt sexual contact between Marcel and Céleste enables the sexual drama-in-language to proceed, and Céleste's possession-taking climaxes in the suggestive string of vocatives, with the final mention of Molière haphazardly inferring a sealed national patrimony.

The text also enables us to identify a punitive, castrating Céleste. Her 'cutting [him] off' acquires a threatening if buried meaning on the stage of verbal seduction, where pleasure is taken in language; or again, when she captures Marcel as '"Oh, perfect miniature, finer than the most precious you could see in a glass case"' (*RMP*, II, 877–8) ['"Ô miniature parfaite, plus belle que la plus précieuse qu'on verrait sous une vitrine"'] (*RTP*, III, 242–3). The image of a reified Marcel, a curio in the possession of Céleste, dramatically confirms both the control she wields and Marcel's open flirtation with her crude ethnic and moral certainties. Indeed her xenophobia and rejection of difference demonstrate an aggressive insistence on sameness.[38]

Far from being a haven of idyllic, desexualized pleasures, the domestics' living-quarters thus represent a cultural pressure chamber in which xenophobic and sexual energies merge. Moreover, the appeal to ostentatious religiosity belies a subtext of barely repressed desire as Céleste exhorts her sister: '"There, Marie, look at him sipping his milk with a reverence that makes me want to say my prayers. What a serious air! . . . He's just like a child"' (*RMP*, II, 877) ['"Tiens, Marie, regarde-le boire son lait avec un recueillement qui me donne envie de faire ma prière. Quel air sérieux! . . . Il a tout des enfants"'] (*RTP*, III, 242).

Conniving in the outpouring of prejudice and stereotype, Marcel introduces two outside figures into the conversation: the wayward Nissim Bernard and Marcel's exhausted father, burdened with professional responsibility. On cue, Marie delivers on the vice and the virtue that they respectively represent: of Marcel's father, she says that his life is one of perpetual sacrifice, whereas in commenting on Nissim Bernard's behaviour, she indulges her sense of moral outrage: "'Ah! Monsieur, there are things I wouldn't have believed could exist until I came here'" (*RMP*, II, 877) ["'Ah! Monsieur, c'est des choses que je n'aurais pas pu croire que ça existait; il a fallu venir ici'"] (*RTP*, III, 242). Nissim Bernard thus joins Freud's category of 'people left over to receive the manifestations of [communal] aggressiveness'.[39] The return of the repressed in the spaces of the hotel enables us to contrast its basement, housing the desire for homosexual gratification and for an ethnic Other, and the attics, where a narcissistic refusal of difference accompanies a heterosexist and xenophobic maternalism.

Yet the brutalizing clarity of the polarization is repeatedly undone by the Narrator. Reflecting on the sisters' language, he is forced to conclude that their primitive enthusiasm borders paradoxically on affectation:

I have never known people so deliberately ignorant, who had learnt absolutely nothing at school, and yet whose language was somehow so literary that, but for the almost wild naturalness of their tone, one would have thought their speech affected. (*RMP*, II, 875)

[Je n'ai jamais connu de personnes aussi volontairement ignorantes, qui n'avaient absolument rien appris à l'école, et dont le langage eût pourtant quelque chose de si littéraire que sans le naturel presque sauvage de leur ton, on aurait cru leurs paroles affectées.] (*RTP*, III, 240)

Proust comes close to deconstructing the would-be primitive discourse of the sisters. By robbing their speech of its claim to naturalness, he exposes their seemingly artless xenophobia as a historically grounded, social identity. The point is confirmed in one of Marie's final flourishes in praise of Marcel: "'He can do the most insignificant things, and you'd think that the whole nobility of France, from here to the Pyrenees, was stirring in each of his movements'" (*RMP*, II, 877) ["'il peut faire les choses les plus insignifiantes, on dirait que toute la noblesse de France, jusqu'aux Pyrénées, se déplace dans chacun de ses mouvements'"] (*RTP*, III, 242). The slapstick grandeur of a mythical, eternal France in which meaning and value are coterminous with its frontiers is sufficiently transparent to unsettle the 'cultural liminality' of the nation.[40]

Céleste and her sister embody the racist bigotry of their day. At the slightest mention of a foreign guest at the hotel, they perform an elaborate mime, their mouths and hands becoming the mouths and hands of the outsiders. Wistfully the Narrator wants to preserve 'these admirable comic masks' (*RMP*, II, 878) ['ces admirables masques de théâtre'] (*RTP*, III, 243), marvelling at the grotesque, automatic impersonations of cultural difference. For the domestics, Marcel's otherness is at the level of social class (Céleste insists that he would never have survived outside the ranks of the rich). But crucially, the stereotypes that mark xenophobic denigration also shape her judgements of Marcel, who remains an exotic plaything in her hands. Compressed into the few pages of text that evoke the domestics, we have a compendium of the clichéd responses to alterity already seen in *fin-de-siècle* exotic writing: the reification and miniaturization of Marcel, recalling, for example, the depiction of the doll-like Japanese in *Madame Chrysanthème*; his animalization (he is a bird, a moth, a serpent, a squirrel; or again his nails are claw-like, like some of the animalized subjects of Gauguin's painting); his infantilization (Céleste boasts that he will never grow old); his demonization (he is a little black devil); his essentialization (he is malice and deceitfulness incarnate, or again he *is* his dress, like Aziyadé – '"he is all furs and lace"' (*RMP*, II, 876) ['"il n'est que fourrures et dentelles"'] (*RTP*, III, 241), quips Céleste on seeing a photograph of him as a child).

Pampered by the two domestics, Marcel delights in their company. He is enthralled by their racist language and cultural intolerance. Ironically, they are barely tolerated in the hotel because of their social class, although Marcel dismisses as hilarious the suggestion from the hotel manager that he should see less of them. For Marcel, they are better company than anyone else at the hotel, which leaves us to reflect on his fascination with prejudice. These victims of class exclusion are also the active agents of the chauvinism of their day. Inferior in a hierarchy of social class, they vaunt their sense of superiority in a hierarchy of race.

COUNTER-SITES

Central to social spaces such as the Grand Hotel at Balbec are what Foucault sees as the practice of social relations and the spatial distributions accorded to them.[41] Foucault identifies in particular the heterotopia: 'a kind of effectively enacted utopia in which the . . . other real sites that can be found within the culture are simultaneously represented, contested, and inverted'.[42] The category includes 'crisis heterotopias' (especially common, he observes, in so-called primitive societies), to be read as privileged or sacred or forbidden places reserved for groups in a state of perceived crisis in relation to the rest of society – adolescents, women menstruating, pregnant women, the elderly, and so on. There are also heterotopias of deviation, inhabited by those whose behaviour deviates from the norm: the prison, the rest-home, the psychiatric hospital.

Counter-sites are central to social relations in *À la recherche*. Jupien's male brothel in *Le Temps retrouvé* may be read as a space of compensation. Other sealed spaces in the novel include: the upstairs toilet in the Combray house (*RMP*, I, 172; *RTP*, I, 156) from which the young Marcel surveys the surrounding countryside while masturbating; the tight circle of the Verdurin salon, with its elaborate system of social inclusions and exclusions; the claustrophobic Paris apartment occupied jointly by Marcel and Albertine in *La Prisonnière*. These locations enable their occupants to survey and often to contest an external reality. They reflect the importance of the closet, the lobby, the bedroom, and the garret, as well as the tight-knit salon, in that these venues stand as epistemologically charged locations impacting on more public spaces and broader forms of social organization.[43]

The sites focused on in this chapter – the colony, the medieval time capsule, the monastic locations in an imagined Christian city, and the spatial configuration offered by the hotel at Balbec – act as counter-sites, from which cultural norms are read, defined, and subverted. In Charlus's case, his oblique expression of sexual preferences finds its heterotopia in a reconstructed, fiercely anti-semitic Christendom. In Kristeva's compact formulation, 'Seduced by Bloch, Charlus suppresses such feelings with perfect bad taste'.[44] In adopting an archaic model, the Baron is identifying not only a spatial disjunction but also other times, or what Foucault terms heterochronies.[45] Charlus's goal, then, is to shape a space and a time of compensation, in which his lunatic anti-semitic diatribe provides him with a surrogate sexual pleasure.

The Grand Hotel in Balbec is an epistemologically favoured venue in Proust's novel, providing a view of the world in microcosm not only through the living quarters of its bourgeois residents but also in two key sites: Nissim Bernard's stereotypically immoral basement and the domestics' superficially idyllic attic rooms. Access to these sites is difficult, anticipating Foucault's observation that the heterotopic site is not like a public place. While Proust's Narrator insists on their separateness, these locations are nevertheless inextricably connected, in that the pleasures of moral self-justification indulged in by Marie and Céleste require the co-presence of an Other, vilifiable on the grounds of sexual or ethnic difference. The domestic derives its virtue precisely from its ability to disparage the unfamiliar.

In these exclusive, protected spaces, the mythopoeic and perverted language of racial purity and origins is aggressively invoked. Kristeva alerts us to the syndrome of purity and perversity in *À la recherche* when she writes about Marcel's infatuation with the Duchesse de Guermantes. Like the domestics, the aristocrat embodies an old French tradition, in which Marcel finds, as Kristeva incisively observes, 'the purest and therefore the most perverse courtly tradition'.[46] Seen in this light, any appeal to a mythical French centre or to a founding moment of monastic greatness remains as perverse a construct as xenophobia.

A final borrowing from Leiris reconnects with Proust's psychology of chauvinism: 'xenophobia: cross-eyed idea of the mob at the cenotaph and in the whorehouse' ['xénophobie: idée bigle de la faune des cénotaphes et des boxons'].[47] What to the mind of civic probity are the discrete categories of the sacred (the seat of national memory in all its heroic status) and the profane are thus promiscuously conflated in the energies of xenophobia. Proust was wholly alert to the workings of desire in the formation of an ideological consensus. *À la recherche du temps perdu* shares the subversion in Leiris's definition, signalling, through xenophobia, the confluence of hackneyed nationalist emotion and raw heterosexual desire.

*

Reflecting on racial intolerance and cultural straitjacketing, Proust's Narrator recalls Charlus's divided loyalties at the time of the First World War. The Germanophilia that he recklessly parades in war-time Paris (*RMP*, III, 797–815; *RTP*, IV, 352–68) prompts Kristeva to see him as a misfit within a nationalist consensus, as an hermaphrodite not just in sexual terms: 'Unable to belong to a single sex, he is unable to belong to a single nation . . . he is a part both of the "body France" and of the "body Germany"'.[48] That Proust should take pleasure in disturbing both national and sexual identities is reinforced when his Narrator hypothesizes that the quarrels of nations replicate the struggles of individuals. As Marcel reflects on those who, driven on by hope and blind desire, are individual cells in 'the body France' (*RMP*, III, 798) ['[le] corps-France'] (*RTP*, IV, 353), Charlus is presented as a prescient figure, adrift from the constricting nation. His interstitial position, straddling boundaries, is commended by Marcel for its insight and detachment: 'he was very

intelligent and in every country fools form the bulk of the population'
(*RMP*, III, 799) ['Il était très fin, les sots sont en tout pays les plus nombreux'] (*RTP*, IV, 354).

Suspicious of collective opinion, Proust underscores the opposition
between the distorting passion that inflects militant nationalism and
disaffection. The miracle of patriotism, the Narrator suggests, lies in its
capacity to generate social cohesion, to the extent that one sides as seam-
lessly with the nation as one does with oneself in a lovers' quarrel (*RMP*,
III, 800; *RTP*, IV, 354–5). Proust thus homes in on the libidinal charge in
xenophobia, an energy that we can now explore further in
Montherlant's portrait of colonial culture in *La Rose de sable*, where
private and public obsessions again coalesce.

CHAPTER THREE

Claiming cultural dissidence: the case of Montherlant's La Rose de sable

The colonies are made to be lost. They are born with the cross of death on their forehead.

['Les colonies sont faites pour être perdues. Elles naissent avec la croix de mort au front . . .']¹

POLITICAL LOYALISM AND THE 'MISSION CIVILISATRICE'

Montherlant wrote *La Rose de sable* while living in Algiers between September 1930 and February 1932. He saw the work, which he classified as being anticolonialist, as a conscious reaction against the centenary celebrations of the French arrival in Algeria and *L'Exposition coloniale* of 1931. With hindsight, he defines his project as 'writing a novel in which one of the characters would embody the struggle between the most traditional colonialism and anticolonialism' ['écrire un roman dont un des personnages incarnerait la lutte entre le colonialisme le plus traditionnel et l'anticolonialisme'].² Montherlant was exercised at this period by what he termed the moral and social question of the European's dealings with the African.³ He nevertheless refused to publish his novel then, claiming that, for reasons of patriotism, it was inappropriate to release a work openly critical of the French presence in Morocco at a time when other European powers, especially Italy, harboured colonial ambitions in respect of North Africa. Not until 1968 did the novel appear in its entirety.⁴ Montherlant recalls that France was regularly denigrated in the pre-war years by Nazi Germany and Fascist Italy and that he was anxious not to provide them with a propaganda coup. The result of the delayed publication, he argues in the 1967 *Avant-propos* to the novel, is that his work may be read thirty-five years on as a historical document. If he stresses political and patriotic necessity, Montherlant makes no reference to his active homosexuality in North Africa which provided powerful private reasons for keeping under wraps what has been read as a novel of veiled homosexual transgression.⁵

Notable contemporaries of Montherlant did voice their disapproval of a so-called civilizing mission that was delivering a legacy of barbarism. In 1928, the campaigning journalist Albert Londres reported in *Le Petit Parisien* on the conditions in which the Brazzaville-Océan railway in the Congo was built, the two hundred kilometres of track being laid at a cost of 17,000 black African lives. The scandal of slave labour, summed up in Londres's catchphrase 'one negro per sleeper', was also reported on by Gide in his *Voyage au Congo*, where he condemned the project as 'a frightening consumer of human lives'.[6]

Given the outspokenness of these colonial testimonies, we may justifiably wonder how anticolonial *La Rose de sable* actually is. The central figure in the novel, a young French officer serving in the desert of southern Morocco, is what elsewhere Proust calls an exemplary 'cell of the body-France' (*RMP*, III, 798) ['une . . . cellule du corps-France'] (*RTP*, IV, 352). From being a naive, reactionary enthusiast of the colonial mission of *la France protectrice*, buoyed up by what he takes to be his innate ethnic superiority, Lieutenant Auligny undergoes a crisis of cultural values, as the case for anticolonialism slowly dawns on him. Central to this conversion is his emotional attachment to a young Bedouin girl Rahma, whom he treats paternalistically but who unsettles his blinkered colonialist mindset. The result is his disabling depression, and he asks to be transferred from the frontline to avoid fighting against the indigenous population. But in the ironic denouement to this 'predicament of colonial culture', to adapt Clifford's terminology, this would-be pacifist, who has withdrawn to Fez, meets his death at the hands of Muslim insurrectionaries, thereby becoming a martyr to the cause of an ostensibly enlightened French presence in North Africa.[7]

If Montherlant claims to be exercised by patriotic caution in relation to hostile European neighbours, we may well ask if these instincts ever abandon him. *La Rose de sable* bears many of the crude hallmarks of European denigration, Montherlant himself conceding that he speaks of North Africans in ways that are potentially shocking (*RS*, 13). Nevertheless, his novel, he claims, goes against the colonial grain and begins a process of re-evaluation in respect of assumed values, a fact acknowledged by critics in 1968 soon after the work appeared. Pierre Kyria, writing in *Combat*, comments that the novel would have had greatest impact in the period following the Second World War when decolonization was becoming imaginable.[8] Although potentially radical in its impact, Montherlant's portrayal replicates the cultural myopia of its day, while admittedly exposing many negative images of French colonial arrogance. Auligny's associate, Guiscart, for example, who has dropped out of conventional bourgeois life, observes sarcastically that the first two gifts made by the French to the Muslims of Africa are hedonism and tuberculosis (*RS*, 263). Colonization thus brings, as we have already seen with Loti and Gauguin, its own pathology as well as sexual predation, of which Guiscart is a cynical beneficiary (*RS*, 456). Likewise, Auligny occasionally abandons dogmatic patriotism and sees culture as something situated and constructed. Thus he queries the use of the term 'brigandage' to describe the Moroccan resistance to colonial rule, when, half a century earlier, the French sniper who is also resisting foreign invasion destroys a Prussian convoy and is hailed a national hero. While these misgivings are symptomatic of an emerging debate about colonization that helps shape the novel, such movement does not grant Montherlant immunity from cross-examination by the postcolonial reader.

'LYAUTEY L'AFRICAIN' AND THE LEGACY OF MILITARISM

Militarism is central to Montherlant's project. The novel's peritexts, particularly its epigraphs and the 'Note' that serves as a postface, are largely drawn from military sources. The work comes in two parts: a love story, the title of which, 'Les Cueilleuses de branches' [The Wood Gatherers] refers to the young Bedouin women of the Moroccan desert (one of whom becomes Auligny's 'rose de sable' or desert rose); and a second section, seen by Montherlant as the political half of the text, entitled 'Mission providentielle'. Leaving aside the seemingly unproblematic separation of love in the colonies and politics, talk of a providential mission is undoubtedly contentious, for it sees the French colonial presence as a civilizing force, the work of destiny. As the epigraph to Part II plainly shows, the immediate source for the title is the writing of Louis-Hubert-Gonzalve Lyautey, one of the foremost figures in French colonial history who was to rise to the rank of Marshal of France:

... The races whom we have the providential mission of introducing to the ways of industry, agriculture and economics, and also, it has to be said, to a higher moral plain, a fuller life.

[... Les races que nous avons la mission providentielle d'ouvrir à la voie industrielle, agricole, économique, et aussi, oui, il faut le dire, à une plus haute vie morale, à une vie plus complète. (ellipsis in the original)][9]

In 'Lyautey l'Africain', as he came to be known, we find the colonial discourse of Montherlant's day in its most seductive military formulation.[10]

He remained Resident-General of Morocco from the foundation of the French protectorate there in 1912 until 1925, having served in Indo-China and Madagascar in the 1890s and then in Algeria. One historian sums up his Moroccan legacy as delivering 'a benevolent autocracy and conscientious feudalism', and indeed at a diegetic level in *La Rose de sable*, Auligny demonstrates a similar style of manipulation in his affair with Rahma.[11]

Montherlant's source text is the article, 'On the Colonial Role of the Army', in which Lyautey attempts to give theoretical respectability to the role of the military overseas. The work reached a wide audience in the *Revue des Deux Mondes* in January 1900. It argued that military order and control were to precede economic exploitation, these twin objectives securing the grander aims of the *mission civilisatrice*. Against Lyautey's moral typecasting, predicated on the superiority of the colonizer, we can set Barthes's observation that the aim of official colonial discourse is to disguise a cynical reality as noble morality.[12] And indeed Celestino's verdict in Montherlant's *Le Chaos de la Nuit* is that Lyautey was fundamentally dishonest, inventing accounts of Moroccan insurrection to justify colonialist military aggression.[13]

Montherlant tempers Lyautey's high moral tone with a second epigraph, taken from Lieutenant Charles Lagarde's *Une promenade dans le Sahara*: 'People had spoken to me about the Arabs' hatred for the French. The only thing that strikes me is French hatred for the Arab' ['On m'avait parlé de la haine des Arabes pour les Français. Je ne suis frappé que par la haine du Français pour l'Arabe] (*RS*, 325). These twin epigraphs show Montherlant balancing contrasting military testimonies, the one corroborating European technical and moral superiority, the other decrying xenophobic intolerance. Superficially they suggest conflicting perspectives. Lyautey himself paints a picture of colonial life marked by its calculating ambivalence. Speaking at the 'Congrès des Hautes Études Marocaines' at Rabat in May 1921, he reminds his French academic audience that they are in the land of Ibn Khaldoum and Averroes and cites 'the elegant formulation of Colonel Berriau, "this race is not inferior, it is different"'. Yet he promotes military force at a ceremony in Casablanca in July of the same year, insisting that the only army is that constituted by the entire nation.[14] This osmosis of people and military to form a colonialist consensus finds expression in *La Rose de sable* where Auligny's obsessive mother is deeply wedded to militarism and harbours delusions of national grandeur in respect of her son.

Lyautey's contribution to the legitimization of French colonial rule was colossal. Long before becoming a member of the Académie Française in 1912, he gained celebrity for wielding the pen as a young officer, not unlike his fellow academician Loti as we saw in Chapter 1. In an article in the *Revue des Deux Mondes* of 15 March 1891, entitled 'Le Rôle social de l'officier dans le service universel' ['On the Social Role of the Officer in Universal Military Service'], he promulgates his paternalistic views.[15] The officer's responsibility, he argues, is to act as educator to the nation's youth and to 'enkindle in his men the *spirit* of his mission' (p. 11; Lyautey's italics). He is to 'build up the morale of the worker and conqu[er] his heart' (p. 27). In short, his duty is to accomplish the *mission morale* of educating his inferiors and winning their loyalty. In this form of visionary, aristocratic politics, Lyautey concedes that the social role he envisages for the officer might be a 'generous utopia, a seductive illusion' (p. 22). Winning the hearts of the proletariat and the colonized is Lyautey's twofold aim, the logic of educating the entire nation being to 'raise' the colony in turn to the civilized levels of the French metropolitan centre.

THE COLONIAL EXHIBITION OF 1931

Lyautey's paternalism finds exemplary expression in his plans for the *Exposition coloniale*, a commemoration that he masterminded in 1931. In his grandiose vision, a working-class Paris would turn its back on Communism once it had sampled the images of colonialism on view at the exhibition. Indeed his decision to plant what he calls 'our colonial shoots in [the] popular world' of Vincennes in south-eastern Paris is central to his grand social design.[16] The exhibition promised to take its visitors on a 'Tour of the world in a day' and its success (it drew half a million visitors on its last day alone, 15 November 1931) demonstrates how Lyautey was tapping into a deep vein of popular approval. The exhibition confirms two key features of metropolitan France's response to the colonial periphery in the inter-war years, namely the widespread acceptance of colonization and a deep-seated indifference to the conditions obtaining in *la plus grande France*.[17]

A Communist contemporary of Lyautey, Henri Cartier, whose *Comment la France 'civilise' ses colonies* was published in the wake of the exhibition, also envisaged a twinning of the proletariat and the colonized, but not for the paternalistic ends envisaged by the Marshal. The Tonkinese coolie in revolt against French torture is, he urges, the greatest ally of the Parisian worker. But Cartier's voice is very much a minority one in the inter-war years. He quotes disapprovingly from *La Vie socialiste* of 13

November 1928 lines that exemplify what Barthes calls 'the moralization of language': 'Colonization is a duty, a necessity, a right, colonization is a factor in human progress' and castigates socialists, or 'social-imperialists' as he prefers to call them.[18] One of Cartier's targets, Albert Sarraut, a former Governor General of French Indo-China and one-time Minister for the Colonies, declares that equity and solidarity are the guiding principles in France's treatment of the colonized, who are seen as the younger, less developed brothers of the colonizer (p. 75). The lofty discourse of generous protection captures the mindset of the day and, more particularly, the value-system of Auligny in *La Rose de sable*.

The consensus on colonial legitimacy was not absolute. The socialist Léon Blum, vilified by Cartier, was in fact lukewarm about the 1931 exhibition, calling, in the socialist newspaper *Le Populaire* of 7 May 1931, for 'fewer celebrations and speeches and more human intelligence and justice'.[19] This hesitation becomes unbridled militancy in the Surrealist pamphlet, 'Ne visitez pas l'Exposition coloniale' ['Do not visit the Colonial Exhibition'], signed by Breton, Éluard, Aragon, Char, and others in the same year.[20] The manifesto, which called for the immediate evacuation of the colonies, protested against the distorting power of white influence, referring to the colonized as 'men whom one can legitimately see as less perverted than ourselves'. At a counter-exhibition, 'La Vérité sur les Colonies' ['The Truth about the Colonies'], inaugurated in October 1931, the Surrealists exhibited indigenous art, Soviet achievements were vaunted, and damning photographic evidence of colonial rule was put on display. These dissenting voices, together with the populist curiosity for Lyautey's Vincennes extravaganza, complete with exotic aquarium, provide a spectrum of opinions and attitudes within which to read Montherlant's novel of anticolonialist awakening.[21]

Given the problematic addressed in *La Rose de sable*, Lyautey's observations on the twin weapons of moral improvement and physical coercion are especially resonant. Montherlant begins his novel with Lyautey warning against the likely political and military impact of French condescension in respect of the colonized:

In our overseas possessions, we face a moral crisis, a political malaise, especially in Indo-China. The explanation lies in our tendency to consider as inferior those races placed under our authority. It is unjust to treat Berbers, Annamites, Arabs, and Malagasies with a disdain and a condescension that incite hatred and store up future revolts.

[La France extérieure est en proie à une crise morale, à un malaise politique, surtout en Indochine, qui a son origine dans la tendance que nous avons à considérer comme inférieures les races placées sous notre autorité. Il n'est pas juste de traiter les Berbères, Annamites, Arabes, Malgaches avec une condescendance dédaigneuse qui fait naître la haine et prépare les révoltes de demain. (Lyautey)] (*RS*, 17)

While Breton and the Surrealists speak of the perverting course of colonial history, Lyautey's condemnation of French superiority is self-serving: respect will safeguard against future disorder, while the veiled fist of militarism and an intentionally cosmetic discourse of moral protection will, in combination, deliver political and commercial development.

Montherlant's key source text, Lyautey's *Lettres du Tonkin et de Madagascar*, was itself dedicated to General Gallieni, whose instructions to the colonial soldier Lyautey wholeheartedly endorses in his 'On the Colonial Role of the Army'. In pursuit of the euphemistically named 'pacification' of the colony (as Barthes notes, mystification in bourgeois language turns war into peace), Gallieni counsels the use of military might and political acumen.[22] And it is politics, Gallieni suggests, that will render the colony susceptible to European commercial exploitation.[23] Cartier, by contrast, reproduces a photograph depicting summary colonial justice – three severed, 'pacified' Indo-Chinese heads – alongside a studio portrait of Governor General Pasquier and the caption 'The Executioner of Indo-China'.

If Gallieni plays down punitive militarism, his sanitized version of control is a restatement of the civilizing mission. It parallels the pious evocation of exemplary service in *La Rose de sable*, where sentimentalism emerges as a central arm of colonial propaganda. Lyautey too paints idealized pictures of the small groups of colonial soldiers diligently managing newly acquired territory as they would small holdings back home. In the localized world of *la petite colonisation*, settlement means the reproduction of sameness rather than any engagement with otherness. In his propagandistic loyalism, he extols his men's 'qualities of order, foresight, ingenuity, and also of endurance, cordiality, and good humour!'[24] The fetishistic insistence on the small-scale shifts attention away from any moral questioning of greater colonial aims, just as in *La Rose de sable*, Lieutenant Auligny will keep a diary 'for the day-to-day history of the penetration' ['pour la petite histoire de la pénétration'] (*RS*, 370).

Lyautey was calculating in his prescriptions for the management of the colonial fringes. Writing from Marrakesh in the early days of the French protectorate, he appeals to rationalism to secure social order:

[Morocco] must not be ruled by force. The rational method . . . for which I have been sent here and no one else . . . is the continual interplay of politics and military force.[25]

But however much he prides himself on reason, the irrational lies at the heart of Lyautey's cultural authoritarianism. His authority assumes a significantly erotic twist when, reflecting on his early, unofficial incursions from Algeria into Morocco long before the establishment of a protectorate, he writes revealingly: 'This *pénétration discrète* of Morocco which I began clandestinely and which has scarcely begun, is so passionate a feeling that to leave would truly be a cruel disappointment for me.'[26] A feminized Morocco acts like an aphrodisiac on its future protector.

Montherlant's own, less elegant military theorizer, Lieutenant Auligny, lives out the contradictions inherent in the mismatch of a theory of civilizing mission and the practice of military coercion. By framing the young lieutenant's dilemma with the lapidary pronouncements of Lyautey and other military figures, Montherlant paves the way for a combined exploration of the discourse of colonial legitimization and the first faint pulses of anticolonialism.[27] These elements fuel Auligny's identity crisis, triggering an ideological debate about supremacist nationalism and the denial of autonomy to the colonized.

ULTERIOR MOTIVES: COLONIALISM'S 'ARRIÈRE-PENSÉES'

In the opening chapter of *La Rose de sable*, stereotypes of national self-congratulation abound. The protagonist's xenophobic dismissal of Jews, Moroccans, Spanish, and English (*RS*, 21–2) paints a picture of complacency that Montherlant deliberately overplays, as a prelude to Auligny's later, faltering conversion to ethnic tolerance. Whereas Spanish sounds disagreeably like the crackle of machine-gun fire, hearing French warms him like a ray of sun (*RS*, 25). The nation as sun and centre is no random metaphor. Auligny, hearing the sound of religious song coming from the mosque, not only likens it, viciously and ignorantly, to two dogs picking up each other's barking, but also returns to the heliocentric metaphor: 'Not surprising that the sun sets when it hears that. It's disgusted' ['Pas étonnant que le soleil se couche quand il entend ça: il est écœuré'] (*RS*, 40).

Guiscart, the disaffected European voluptuary, takes Auligny to task, systematically rebutting caricatural images of the North African as thief, fanatic, fatalist, and abuser of animals (*RS*, 34). By debunking each of these myths, Guiscart robs the xenophobe of the pleasure afforded by effortless negative stereotyping. He also advances an alternative explanation for racist bigotry:

The colonizers have another reason for particularly slandering the colonized. They feel they have acted wrongly towards them. It's an old law and doubtless one of the vilest in human nature.

[Les colonisateurs ont une autre raison de calomnier particulièrement les colonisés: ils se sentent dans leur tort à l'égard d'eux. C'est là une vieille loi, et sans doute une des plus viles, de la nature humaine.] (*RS*, 35)

Guiscart thus pinpoints a cycle of ill-treatment and denigration, reference to the French failure to honour promises made to the Dey reinforcing the point. The correctives provide an early sign that *La Rose de sable* unsettles the norms of self-congratulatory colonialist fiction.

Exploitation is rife in the novel: at an academic level, the French Orientalist, Combet-David, plagiarizes the work of his Tunisian collaborator, Yahia, without whom his reputation would be non-existent (*RS*, 112) and his translations from the Arabic destined for European consumption crudely distort the local culture and idiom; militarily, punitive action is systematically directed against insurrectionaries; and in sexual terms, Guiscart, despite his pointedly anti-colonial jibes, operates parasitically. In Auligny's case, the exploitative instinct is regularly checked by the fear that the French presence might in reality be more repressive than civilizing. But the five related forms of possession in the *mission civilisatrice* identified by Seán Hand (the spatial and the temporal, the verbal, the visual, the sexual, and the economic) are all in play in Auligny's treatment of the adolescent Bedouin girl, whom he pays in return for sexual favours.[28] One of his first acts is to rename her. The narrator rationalizes Auligny's dislike of the name Rahma, which conjures up belly-dancing and Lyautey's Colonial Exhibition. But by choosing to call her Ram (*RS*, 132) Auligny renders her essentially androgynous, since Ram is an Arab surname, the male and female first-name equivalents of which are Rahim and Rahima.[29] The possession of the signifier is taken a stage further when Ram becomes 'If-you-like' ['Si-vous-voulez'] (*RS*, 146), these being the words of compliance offered by the dumb native.

'Si-vous-voulez' connects up with the colonizer's desire to convert native passivity into active acceptance of his rule. It recalls indirectly the inscription on the façade of the 'Palais des Colonies' built in Vincennes for the 1931 *Exposition Coloniale* and today housing the Musée des Arts d'Afrique et d'Océanie: 'To her sons who have extended the Empire of her genius and have thus won love and respect for her name overseas, France records her gratitude' ['À ses fils qui ont étendu l'Empire de son génie et fait ainsi aimer son nom au-delà des mers, la France reconnaissante']. The dedication, which adorns a list of illustrious heroes who

have served abroad, runs uninhibitedly from the eleventh-century cru-
sader Godefroy de Bouillon to more recent figures such as Bugeaud,
Jules Ferry, and Charles Mangin. It suggests an empire not of military
might but of national genius and identifies a central element in the colonial dream, to prompt in the oppressed an autonomous, enthusiastic legitimization of French rule. If Auligny is the fictional embodiment of that
dream, the 'Si-vous-voulez' nickname confirms a colonial failure to
convert subjugation into proactive adulation.

While Auligny makes much play of his sexual restraint when with
Ram, the narrator sarcastically points out that the lieutenant's exploitation still services an emotional economy working between colonial
outpost and European centre. His letters back to France and his paperwork as a colonial officer become suffused with the energy associated
with Ram. In the immediate wake of the protagonist's intimate encounter with her, the narrator refers to 'the voluptuousness of the correspondence! . . . the voluptuousness of the report!. . . . What a craving for
paperwork that girl Ram gave him!' ['La volupté de la correspondance!
. . . La volupté du rapport! . . . Quelle fringale de paperasserie cette Ram
lui donnait!'] (*RS*, 147). Montherlant is alert to the recycling of energies,
seeing the high-sounding nationalistic moralism in Auligny's letter to his
mother as the first consequence of his love for a Moroccan minor (*RS*,
148). In this arresting conjunction, paedophilia prompts an excited
restatement of the civilizing mission. For the letter in question parades
the son's ascetic pursuit of duty in the desert wilderness, signalled by the
reading of Racine and books on Moroccan military history. But the
impetus for these rhetorical flourishes, Ram, is erased. In Montherlant's
suggestive concatenation, a picture of edifying colonial austerity is the
outcome of the colonizer's sexual predation.

Writing half a century earlier, Loti too uses the exchange of letters
between France and its colonial margins as a powerful vehicle for height-
ening ideological conflict. The pious letters from the ageing Cevennol
mother of Jean Peyral in *Le Roman d'un spahi* accentuate the taboo surrounding the young soldier's liaison with Fatou, as does the fact that the
meagre savings sent by the parents are spent by his black African concubine to beautify herself. The clear inference is that parental restraint and
thrift sponsor the spahi's sexual licence and African prodigality.

The clash in Loti between domestic repression and unbridled hedonism abroad is replicated in *La Rose de sable*. In both novels, nagging parental preoccupations with filial duty, promotion, and sexual temperance
signal the super ego that weighs heavily on both Auligny and Peyral as

they pursue illicit pleasure. Both texts project what is inadmissible on to Africa, seen as an indivisible, homogenized continent. Persistently labelled as the locus of sadness in *Le Roman d'un spahi* and as sterile desert in *La Rose de sable*, it stands for a newfound sexuality and growing autonomy, although it remains axiomatic that the relationships pursued by both protagonists are based on mastery rather than mutuality. Like Loti's spahi, Montherlant's colonial soldier meets his death in Africa, Eros and Thanatos both being situated at the hub of this exotic primitivism.

The Parisian salons find especially appealing in the young lieutenant's letter the catchphrase that becomes shorthand for his spartan consolations: 'Le désert, et Racine':

The formula became inseparable from the name of Lucien Auligny. Love of the desert signified the love of solitude and of asceticism, love of God – in short, nobility of soul; whereas the cult of Racine meant the whole of French tradition. . . . Everyone agreed that the man who had found this admirable shortcut linking moral and intellectual virtues was indeed, as one lady said . . . a 'living flag'.

[Cette formule devint inséparable du nom de Lucien Auligny. L'amour du désert signifiait l'amour de la solitude, de l'ascétisme, l'amour de Dieu, – toute la hauteur d'âme; tandis que le culte de Racine signifiait toute la tradition française. . . . On tomba d'accord que l'homme qui avait trouvé ce raccourci admirable, mariant les vertus du caractère et celles de l'esprit, était bien, comme le dit une dame . . . un 'drapeau vivant'.] (*RS*, 149)

High society may marvel at the conflation of ascetic and literary instincts but the reader identifies the direct link, invisible to the salon, between moral conscience and the taboo of sexual gratification with an African child-mistress. In the convergence of colonialism, nationhood, and sexuality that the scene accommodates, the super ego of the *mission civilisatrice* parades in the salon, while libidinal desire is enacted in the colony.

From anxious lover to intrepid letter-writer, Auligny works between a *libido dominandi* and a *libido scribendi*, satisfying in the process the domestic appetite for colonial self-sacrifice. Deriding the culture of self-congratulation at work in the talismanic image of Racine, Montherlant intensifies the picture of cultural narcissism, the fingered page-ends of Auligny's Racine edition symbolizing a contraction of horizons in which the dramatist stands fetishistically, in the narrator's ironic formulation, as 'the quintessence of the human mind' ['la quintessence de l'esprit humain'] (*RS*, 121).

The imbrication of remote Sahara and French salon reminds us of the title of Chapter 1 of Said's *Culture and Imperialism*, 'Overlapping

Territories, Intertwined Histories', denoting the hierarchy of spaces that includes metropolitan centre and territory overseas. Said spells out especially an economic dependence, a perfect example of which appears in Jane Austen's *Mansfield Park*, where Thomas Bertram's Antiguan slave plantation underwrites the beauty of Mansfield Park.[30] We find a variant on this in *La Rose de sable*, where a French colonial imaginary thrives on the importation of narratives of heroic endeavour. Thus Auligny's doctored account of service in Morocco, without reference to his sexual exploits and his emerging doubts about the impact of colonization in general, satisfies the salon's desire for cultural self-congratulation (*RS*, 292). Struck by the success that his letters enjoy, Auligny consciously practises a form of literary coquetterie, plying with military propaganda the Auligny circle back in France. The once naive soldier now comes to realize that behind a clichéd Sahara of mirages, sunsets, enchanted oases, and biblical scenes, there lies a colonial politics, or what Montherlant terms an 'ulterior patriotic motive' ['une arrière-pensée patriotique'] (*RS*, 292). The spatial metaphor in *arrière-pensée* captures the sense of being back within the fold of the nation, a form of protected rearguard that nevertheless requires a colonial front line.

In the same way, Montherlant recalls General Drude's propagandistic comparison between the French tricolour and the blue Mediterranean sea, the white of Casablanca, and the red sky at sunset. The crudely transparent aim is to endow the cultural symbol with embeddedness and authenticity. Montherlant reflects lucidly on the link between colonial mentalities and *realpolitik*:

The Saharan imagination seeks to increase the moral value of the land we conquer, to make more readily acceptable the sacrifices of every kind that this conquest costs us. The Saharan imagination is thus part of a politics and this is what Auligny had finally come to realize.

[L'imagination saharienne travaille à augmenter la valeur morale de la terre que nous conquérons, et à faire passer ainsi plus aisément les sacrifices de tout genre que nous coûte cette conquête. L'imagination saharienne joue donc sa partie dans une politique, et c'est de cela qu'Auligny avait fini par prendre conscience.] (*RS*, 292)

Auligny has thus learnt the principles of what Barthes is to call in his *Mythologies* an 'African grammar', the distorted images of a serving officer's life now embellishing his correspondence. As the protagonist abandons his earlier view of colonial service as sacrificial, the narrator concludes tritely that to serve is also to be self-serving (*RS*, 293).

Sexual dealings reflect broader social tensions. For Auligny, Ram is the embodiment of reassurance: 'With Ram, with this little desert plant, what total *security*! So neat . . . so impeccable! And looking at this body, a kind of respect came to him' ['Avec Ram, avec cette petite plante du désert, quelle totale *sécurité*! Si nette . . . si impeccable! Et devant ce corps, une sorte de respect lui venait'] (*RS*, 150; Montherlant's italics). Alongside the predictable native attributes of passivity and acceptance, talk of an inchoate respect clearly exposes the ethnocentricity of a humanist discourse of dignity and an absence of relationality. Montherlant's lieutenant is like Loti's spahi: on the boundaries of colonial culture, both start from a threshold of ethnic denigration and relate to Ram and Fatou with, at best, a patronizing sentimentalism. Yet Auligny claims to experience both a sense of proprietorship and awe in respect of Ram.[31] He requires her compliance and acceptance, preferring her asleep, holding her, the text adds, as a sculptor holds wet clay in his hand. Or again, the unconscious Ram lies on top of him 'like one brick on top of another in the wall' ['comme la brique sur la brique dans le mur'] (*RS*, 176). Auligny wants to signal innocuous, even elegant constructions. These images of Ram recall Foucault's docile bodies, 'subjected, used, transformed, and improved'.[32] Ambiguously, Auligny observes self-critically that his actions represent an abuse, while asserting in another lurid colonial stereotype that Ram is 'a captive in the bed of the victor' ['une captive dans le lit du vainqueur'] (*RS*, 178). Alternatively, he expresses remorse for failing to put advancement before pleasure, and thus for disregarding Mme Auligny's stern prescriptions. Failure in respect of the forbidden native girl, then, matches the inability to observe the prescriptions of the forbidding matriarch. In this way, Montherlant's *ingénu* finds emancipation from colonialist stereotyping as unsustainable as unconditional adherence to it.

For all Montherlant's liberalizing claims – 'in Africa, if there was a duty, it was not to combat "the infidels" but to defend them' ['en Afrique, . . . si devoir il y avait, il n'était pas de pourfendre "les infidèles", mais de les défendre'] – *La Rose de sable* corroborates colonial culture in crucial respects.[33] Indeed what Henri Cartier sees as the perpetuation in the colony of 'the calvary of woman enslaved to man' is evident in Auligny's invitation to Guiscart to join him in the desert outpost at Birbatine and share Ram's sexual favours.[34] Montherlant writes ironically about the pleasure experienced by Auligny when procuring Ram's favours for Guiscart, attributing to the young lieutenant 'that charming soul, full of real and near-maternal altruism, which flowers in you when you act as procurer' ['cette âme charmante, pleine d'altruisme vrai, et presque maternel, qui fleurit en vous quand vous faites l'entremetteur'] (*RS*, 274). The perverted altruism masks Auligny's sexual inhibition and clashes with the reality of procurement. But there are other twists to this story of male predation and complicity. In deciding not to have sex with Auligny's 'desert rose', Guiscart enumerates a string of reasons that reveal the capriciousness of European exploitation: 'the pleasure of not possessing her, having travelled two thousand kilometres to do so, was so much more refined!' ['le plaisir de ne la prendre pas, ayant fait deux mille kilomètres pour la prendre, était tellement plus délicat que l'autre!'] (*RS*, 278). For Auligny, there is the sense of insult that, within a code of parasitical European homosociality, what he has generously offered has been rejected. For Guiscart, there is the perverse pleasure of whim. Nevertheless, it is in a powerfully symbolic way that Guiscart violates Ram. On the portrait of her that he paints emphasizing her beautiful teeth, he inscribes the words 'Ram à dents', a demeaning play on the tradition of Ramadan (*RS*, 279). In this wilful act of inscription on the canvas, Guiscart opts for a technique of control that is discursive rather than corporeal.

Fanon's analysis of power relations in the colony in *Les Damnés de la Terre* establishes the paradigm whereby, as the subject of history, the European acts with impunity on the colonized.[35] Montherlant explores the strains in that hegemonic structure, made tangible in Auligny's vacillation between recrimination and curiosity in respect of Ram. Late in the novel, when Ram, knowing of Auligny's imminent departure, becomes increasingly assertive, he reverts to racist and gender stereotyping, complaining that the situation is increasingly like that with European women. What is being lost, he argues dejectedly, is not a woman but 'a great illusion' ['une grande illusion']. In the oscillation between idealization and contempt, a deep-seated prejudice reasserts itself: 'Orient! Orient! father of treason. . . . For him, everything that sustained Africa was withdrawn. Now, what aridity!' ['Orient! Orient! père de la trahison. . . . Tout ce qui, pour lui, soutenait l'Afrique, était retiré. Maintenant, quelle aridité!'] (*RS*, 493). Unable to secure sexual pleasure, Auligny resumes the role of demagogue, his assertions of ethnic superiority becoming increasingly authoritarian and gendered. Simultaneously, his recrimination suggests the insufficiency of the Other, a lack that corroborates the familiar view advanced by Loti, Lyautey, and others that Europe would compensate for African incompleteness. Likewise, the concept, so dear to the lieutenant, of a protectorate in Morocco, with its

built-in hierarchy of cultural value, cannot accommodate native autonomy. Yet as Édouard Glissant demonstrates, the relationship between
Self and Other is not the exclusive preoccupation of the European but
rather entails an endlessly relativized series of negotiations. In Glissant's
formulation, 'We are all, simultaneously, the fallow side, the unconscious, the unrecognized (and yet too familiar) part of the Other'.[36]

'CETTE BRUTE, C'EST MOI': BECOMING THE OTHER

Losing Ram's love, Auligny's reverts to narrow nationalism. He likens
himself to the monument to dead legionaries near Birbatine on which
the inscription 'Honour and the Fatherland' ['Honneur et Patrie'] has
become eroded by the desert sand (*RS*, 508). Switching metaphors, he
sees his combination of patriotism and ethnic curiosity as a 'monstrous
duality' ['dualité monstrueuse'] (*RS*, 508). The uneasiness occasioned by
a form of mental miscegenation re-emerges as misogyny. Enlisting the
services of a young Arab male, Boualem, Auligny experiences what the
narrator terms provocatively 'a purification on moving from woman to
the masculine order' ['un assainissement à passer de la femme à l'ordre
masculin'] (*RS*, 512). As with Ram, his instinct is to play up the adolescent's docility, although this is accompanied by a strong disclaimer of
any homosexual interest on Auligny's part. But to this he adds the boy's
chirpiness, his lies and candour, all of these veiled homoerotic features
contrasting with the recrimination directed at what he scathingly labels
a crooked French bourgeois adolescence (*RS*, 521). The vigorous
Francophobia complements the prestige conferred on Boualem: 'how
could this . . . be so perfect?' ['comment ceci . . . pouvait-il être si parfait?]
(*RS*, 521), he wonders. Still, Auligny confesses to being utterly disorien-
tated when Boualem denigrates the Muslim academic Yahia in a blast
of Arabophobia. His confusion is captured metaphorically as 'a state of
eternal trembling, like the anxious, *unsatisfied* waters of the sea' ['un état
de tremblement éternel, comme les eaux inquiètes, *insatisfaites* de la
mer'] (*RS*, 521; my emphasis). The uneasiness has arguably two sources:
firstly, the sense of exhaustion and defeat in the moral debate about colonization and, more importantly, a repressed sexual desire for Boualem.
Inscribed in this literal master/servant bond that straddles dominant
and subordinate cultures, then, is Auligny's ambiguous sexuality.

Homoeroticism, however strenuously Auligny represses it, compli-
cates the tensions between Europe and its colonial Other and confirms
the paradigm whereby the colonial margins act as a conduit for

perceived forms of sexual aberrance. The cases of Gide and Montherlant confirm that North Africa was a playground for those pursuing homosexual pleasure free from European opprobrium.[37] In *À la recherche du temps perdu*, Proust shunts a prohibited homosexuality into the colonial spaces and improvises the crude category of the *homme-femme* to denote the male homosexual. Gauguin's heterosexual promiscuity in Polynesia confirms the equation that links sexual licence and the exotic, while the cult of androgyny in *Noa Noa* spells a disturbance of gender boundaries. Likewise, the homoerotic encounter between Gauguin and Jotéfa recalls the erotic adventure in *Aziyadé*, in which the protagonist Loti, while waiting for Aziyadé, huddles up against his faithful manservant Samuel. The latter panics at what is for him a sexually ambiguous moment and can only wonder what his master has in mind. His anxious question: 'What do you want from me' ['Che volete mî?'] (*Az*, 53) captures the uncertainty also present in the narrator's assertion that 'in the old Orient, everything is possible!' ['dans le vieil Orient tout est possible!' (*Az*, 53)]. These scenes of dislocation demonstrate how exotic spaces regularly compensate for a domestic, heterosexist conformity. For the discontents of civilization, the transcending of sexual norms beyond Europe merges with forms of engagement with otherness. The perennial outcome, then, is that the Other becomes a mere adjunct in a debate about European psychosexuality.

The repressed authoritarianism of militarism returns in the episode involving the twelve-year-old Bedouin prostitute whom Aulighy comes across in the desert. With hindsight, his brutal possession of her, followed by his violent threat to destroy the tents of her tribespeople, shocks him morally, forcing him to reflect ruefully on the colonizer's omnipotence:

the feeling that he could do anything with impunity, because he was French and an officer, that feeling that had released so many others, caused him horror. '. . . I am a leader, and I have been brought up in a milieu and with ideas and among people that are morally the best. What will become of the others! How can I now accuse anyone? . . . I'm that brute. And yet I am neither bad nor base.'

[cette sensation qu'il pouvait tout, impunément, parce que Français et parce qu'officier, cette sensation, qui en avait débridé tant d'autres, lui faisait horreur. '. . . Et je suis un chef, et j'ai été élevé dans un milieu, dans des idées, parmi des êtres qui sont moralement ce qu'il y a de mieux. Que sera-ce alors des autres! Comment pourrai-je maintenant accuser qui que ce soit? . . . cette brute, c'est moi. Et cependant je ne suis ni mauvais ni bas.'] (*RS*, 299)

The experience of the perverse awakens both self-incriminatory acceptance of the transgression as his own and frantic disavowal.[38] The appeal

to redemptive notions of pedigree signals a displacement of the aberrant on to the North African girl. Likewise, in reconstructing the
moment when he possesses the young Bedouin, he stubbornly appeals
to *her* abjection and *his* value. The encounter typifies what Jonathan
Dollimore calls transgressive reinscription, whereby the repressed or the
suppressed or the displaced returns via what is 'proximate':[39]

In his mind, Auligny tried to repel this little bundle of filth, and at the same time,
because she seemed to him to be a monster, *because* she was ugly, *because* she smelt,
because she had the contemptible body of a frog, as yet untouched by puberty,
Auligny, a normal man, with the most unambiguous sexuality, felt within
himself a desire the like of which he had not experienced.

[L'esprit d'Auligny repoussait de toutes ses forces cette petite ordure, et en
même temps, *parce qu'*elle lui paraissait un monstre, *parce qu'*elle était laide, *parce
qu'*elle sentait fort, *parce qu'*elle avait un misérable corps de grenouille, que la
puberté n'effleurait pas encore, Auligny, homme normal, de la sexualité la plus
claire, sentait en lui un désir tel qu'il n'en avait pas senti.] (*RS*, 297;
Montherlant's emphasis)

Both literally and metaphorically, Auligny is here policing a frontier, with
its boundaries of colonial hierarchy, race, age, and gender. While reinforcing the conjunction of misogyny and colonial racism, the highly provocative use of italics forges a claimed logic of sexual perversion to
explain and even justify Auligny's behaviour. While the return of the
repressed and the abject is via the figure of the prostitute, the *homme
normal* label, intended to exonerate Auligny, in fact criminalizes the
European male unconscious. Sexual taboo masquerading as a brutally
normative impulse underscores Dollimore's notion of the proximate as
a vehicle for transgression and deviance.

In other respects, Auligny's traces of contrition keep alive an awareness of the Moroccan Other. Lying awake in the camp at night, he sees
in his mind's eye a procession of figures including Ram, the Bedouin girl
prostitute, young Boualem, the old *caïd* whom Auligny meets on first
arriving at the encampment of Birbatine, and Guiscart lamenting this
'dying race, whom we are killing off' ['race moribonde, que notre contact
achève'] (*RS*, 318). These perceived moments of generous contact with
the ethnic Other are marked by their violence, their intensity, or their
macabre sentimentalism. When Auligny finally consummates his relationship with Ram (after the scene involving the young Bedouin prostitute in the desert), his embrace is referred to as 'that paternal and almost
maternal deed' ['ce geste paternel, et presque maternel'] (*RS*, 310). A
parental authority thus marks the colonizer's possession of the colonized,

the hierarchy of emotional ties feeding into what Montherlant patronizingly conceptualizes as a 'system of pity' ['système de pitié'] (*RS*, 312). The author is unable to think outside the parent/child template to articulate his claimed anticolonialism.

Colonial authority is nevertheless ambiguously gendered. Looking within the boundaries of his own body, Auligny finds traces of the relationship with Ram:

> Just as our gaze, when staring at a star, sometimes imagines that it can see beside it the reflection of a star, he could see on his naked chest, beside his nipples, the less distinct marks of two nipples, like reflections of his own, where Ram's breasts had pressed against him. Then he looked up, and . . . various thoughts came to him. He thought: 'In what I give her, I *compensate* for the kindness that people do not show the rest of her race.' He thought: 'I don't give a damn about her body. There are millions of other bodies as beautiful as hers. I want the gift of her soul and I possess it.'

> [Comme notre regard, quelquefois, quand il a fixé une étoile, croit voir à côté d'elle un reflet d'étoile, il voyait sur sa poitrine nue, à côté de ses mamelons, deux marques de mamelons, moins distinctes, comme les reflets des siens, là où les seins de Ram s'étaient enfoncés. Puis il leva les yeux, et . . . il eut diverses pensées. Il pensa: 'Je *compense*, avec ce que je lui donne, tout ce qu'on ne donne pas de douceur aux autres de sa race.' Il pensa: 'Je me fous de son corps. Des millions de corps sont aussi beaux que le sien. Je veux le don de son âme, et je l'ai.'] (*RS*, 312; Montherlant's italics)

If the text makes explicit this specular relationship in which the white European sees the Other as a reflected image of himself, so the imperious 'Je veux . . . et je l'ai' completes a vicious and self-deluding containment. Bestowal and appropriation thus remain key colonial reflexes. In the coalescing of *seins* [breasts] and the possessive *siens* [his], what is hailed as a compensatory European eroticism finds its analogue in the figure of the androgyne. In this provocative conjunction of colonialism, race, and sexuality, a significant blurring of boundaries again prevails. And with Montherlant claiming to transform the colonial paradigm in *La Rose de sable*, transracial romance ostensibly offers release from both racial supremacism and an authoritarian conception of gender.

Other forms of mythopoeic association derive from Auligny's authority as head of the *bordj*. At the palm-grove where a young girl begs from him, he remembers the episode in the Gospel when Mary Magdalen mistakes the risen Christ for the gardener: 'but he called her by her name, and she, recognizing him, spoke only a single word: "Rabbi"' ['mais il l'appela par son nom, et elle, le reconnaissant, lui dit ce seul mot:

"Rabbi"'] (*RS*, 348). This story of delayed recognition flatters an enchanted Auligny, whose craving for confirmation from the indigenous population becomes a form of megalomania.

La Rose de sable claims to enact the initial, slow abandonment of the mindset of demeaning colonialism while largely failing to shed the language of domination that served such oppression. In its lexis, metaphors, and analogies, the novel confirms European moral, cultural, and discursive supremacy. But in a significant movement in Auligny's perception at the end of Part I of the novel, the place he occupies in southern Morocco loses its air of Orientalist difference, and he dreams of 'the new mental order of tomorrow' ['la pensée de demain']: 'One individual, Ram, has triggered within him this great beginning' ['Un être, Ram, a ébranlé ce grand commencement qui se fait en lui'] (*RS*, 317).

In a form of 'oneirography', Auligny expresses a lament for Islamic culture, conceived of predictably as lack and absence, the only vocabulary that Europe can muster in its encomium to the Other:[40]

something poor . . . penetrates Auligny's heart. It is the poverty of Islam, its lack of value, its lack of talent, its aborted soul . . ., it is indeed 'the poor, vanquished race'. It seems to him that Islam lies dormant and complains in its dreams. . . . A moribund race . . . laments in silence . . . the misfortunes of its homeland on a reed we do not hear.

[quelque chose de pauvre . . . pénètre dans le coeur d'Auligny: c'est bien la misère de l'Islam, son manque de valeur, son manque de talent, son âme avortée . . ., c'est bien la 'pauvre race vaincue'. Il lui semble que l'Islam sommeille, et se plaint dans ses rêves. . . . Une race moribonde . . . pleure sans bruit . . . sur un roseau qu'on n'entend pas, les malheurs de sa patrie.] (*RS*, 318)

Inaudible, moribund, occupying the space of dream, Islam impacts on no one and contends with a pathogenic Occident. The image of a voiceless Other anticipates, however inchoately, the cultural claims of postcolonialism. Montherlant's ingenuous hero boasts of stealing a march on his military superiors in the direction of liberation. He rejects the publicly vaunted objectives of the colonial 'adventure', asserting that the real motives are enrichment, the pursuit of sexual gratification beyond the law, and the sadistic desire to dominate (*RS*, 320–1). Thinking contritely of the Bedouin girl prostitute, he incriminates himself: 'with his young conqueror's hand, he seizes hold of a truth greater than [that possessed by his superiors]' ['[il] met la main, en jeune conquérant, sur une vérité plus vraie que la leur'] (*RS*, 319). Even in this moment of claimed emancipation and epistemological privilege, the Other remains an object of knowledge that is militaristically appropriated.

In the narrator's provocative explanation of Auligny's evolution, it is the heart and the soul, seen as specifically feminine, that awaken his intelligence. In this disruption of male domination, a string of tidy analogies reflect the consequences of Auligny's mental conversion:

What is an intelligent priest? He will lose his faith. What is a judge who knows life only too well? He can only acquit. What is a clear-sighted officer? One ready to disobey.

[Qu'est-ce qu'un prêtre intelligent? Il perdra la foi. Qu'est-ce qu'un juge qui comprend trop la vie? Il ne pourra plus qu'acquitter. Et qu'est-ce qu'un officier trop lucide? Un officier prêt à désobéir.] (*RS*, 321)

Montherlant's list of wayward custodians of authority spells the demise of a social order. Nevertheless, like the privilege of enlightenment and far-sightedness, cultural authority remains the preserve of the West, with native Moroccans serving as passive adjuncts to a solitary European's crisis of identity. In this way, 'the structure of attitude and reference' that is integral to colonial authority is preserved.[41]

CONTAINING DIFFERENCE

The contradictions inherent in Auligny's conversion emerge strongly in Part Two, *Mission Providentielle*. Seeing a Frenchman spitting at a Moroccan fellow-soldier, Auligny reflects in a disabused way on this recruit from the land of the Rights of Man, this son of Paris, 'the City of Light' ['la Ville-Lumière'] (*RS*, 336–7). But however hypocritical he finds the vocabulary of cultural superiority, Auligny resists instinctively the North African's attempt to assert his independence. Throughout *La Rose de sable*, attitudinizing remains a European prerogative. Auligny's reflex response is thus to censure expressions of native subjectivity and emotional autonomy, disaffection remaining as much the preserve of the European as the bad colonial record that triggers it.

The discourse of primitivism contains the native population. Idealizing the young girls as emblems of purity and compliance, Auligny appeals to the notion of an arrested evolution in a manner that recalls Gauguin's savages or Proust's bird-like *jeunes filles en fleurs*, who form a race apart on the Balbec beach:

they were like a race that was not yet fully human, that still displayed so many animal characteristics. They were simultaneously women, children, and animals, so natural, so light . . . *these* were the people to love . . . . Viewed from this angle, women, especially European women, women as *legal subjects*, seemed

to Auligny to be quite imposing objects, occupying so much space, so complicated, demanding so much time and attention . . . with the wood gatherers,
everything was light and ethereal, as love might have been at the beginning of
time.

[elles suggéraient une race pas encore tout à fait humaine, toute pleine encore
du génie des bêtes. À la fois femmes, enfants et bêtes, si naturelles, si légères . . .
c'était *cela* qu'il fallait aimer. . . . Vues d'ici, les femmes, les Européennes surtout,
les femmes *personnes légales*, faisaient l'effet à Auligny d'objets assez redoutables,
prenant terriblement de la place, terriblement compliquées, exigeant terriblement de temps, d'attention . . . avec les cueilleuses de branches tout était aérien
et facile, tel que pouvait être l'amour aux temps de la fraîcheur du monde.] (*RS*,
348–9; Montherlant's emphases)

Splicing misogyny and colonialist supremacy, Montherlant infers that
the locus of the human is adult, male, and European. But he
camouflages this brutal exclusiveness with appeals to a commodified
native beauty, referring to 'these little miracles of purity' ['ces petits miracles de pureté'] (*RS*, 348). Auligny aggressively campaigns beyond
history and the law for a new consensus, grounded in primitivist love as
experienced in an originary state.

Like Proust, Loti, and Gauguin before him, Montherlant eschews the
contemporary, assigning the native population to a prelapsarian world.
Johannes Fabian, for whom the link between chronology and the Other
is central, complains that

anthropology emerged and established itself as an allochronic discourse; it is a
science of other men in another Time . . . a discourse whose referent has been
removed from the present of the speaking/writing subject. This 'petrified relation' is a scandal. Anthropology's Other is, ultimately, other people who are our
contemporaries.[42]

Fabian's misgivings apply to literary representations of the non-
European. Auligny may protest his enlightenment about race and sexuality, yet his evocation of the Moroccan girls epitomizes the temporal
corralling Fabian signals. In spite of protestations of innocent hedonism,
the reifying depiction involves a miniaturization of their needs and sub-
jectivities. Native women become ever available commodities, condemned to the allochronic prison. They represent an absence of
difference, an atrophied alterity, unlike European women and the
demanding, overdetermined otherness that Auligny attributes to them.
In lieu of burdensome negotiation with autonomous beings, Auligny
opts for what he euphemistically labels the porosity and lightness of
Moroccan women. We can contrast this with Fabian's insistence that

anthropology must draw difference into the area of dialectical contradiction.[43] For Auligny, the burden of cultural difference is signposted lin-
guistically in the triple use of *terriblement* in the above quotation: it is
precisely negotiation that he is rejecting, laying claim to an illusory
freedom outside history.

Auligny's relationship with Ram provokes often bizarre rationaliza-
tions and special pleading. Montherlant warns readers of traditional
romance that, in respect of this couple, there will be no dialogues to
relate and nothing of the see-saw emotions of unswerving love and blind
hate – not unlike the situation in *Madame Chrysanthème*, where Loti's brief
marriage to a Japanese spouse is deemed insufficiently serious for the
tragic genre. Shelving the genre equates to rejecting the Other. Yet it is
a mark of Auligny's *honour*, the text protests aggressively (*RS*, 360), that
the relationship should be free of excessive emotion.[44] Auligny sees
himself as occupying a dual role *vis-à-vis* Ram, that of lover and father;
and he infers from this a link with what he arbitrarily elevates into an
Oriental art of love: 'Childhood is for them a third sex, and it is that sex
that [Easterners] love' ['L'enfance est pour eux un troisième sexe, et c'est
ce sexe-là qu'ils [les Orientaux] aiment'] (*RS*, 360). The corollary is that
the physical childhood of the young Muslim bride matches her moral
infancy as subservient partner. While the perverse rhetoric of wardship
stands as a variant on Fabian's allochronism, Montherlant's random
periodization of Islamic sexuality is wholly cynical. Ironically, a theory
of paedophilia attributed to Islamic culture reflects more accurately the
practices of Western sexual tourism. Thus Europe, through the bogus
sociological category of the third sex, projects on to the colonized its own
taboos.

In other respects, Montherlant's novel begins to unsettle Western
ideological positions. Admittedly, Auligny functions as the self-deluding
European, seduced by philanthropic moralism. He fails to see appeals
to high-sounding humanist values as self-congratulatory, or as discursive tools in a process of social control. At the same time, he dissents
from the doxa of 1930 which sees identification with the colonized
Other not as impossible, but rather undesirable, and worse still, criminal folly: 'in the colonies, someone wanting justice is a delinquent' ['aux
colonies, quelqu'un qui veut la justice est un délinquant'] (*RS*, 406).
Hence, 'our exploited Moroccans' ['nos exploités marocains'] (*RS*, 408)
awaken an emotional and moral concern that Auligny, in his ideological narrow-mindedness, remains ill-equipped to remedy. Alongside
these stirrings of often crudely formulated ethical preoccupations, there

are more eloquent voices. The soldier Pierrotey, whose ethical outlook impresses Auligny, distinguishes between military success and moral failure in the colonies. In his bouts of intolerance and exhaustion, however, Auligny fantasizes about a clinical excision of moral preoccupation: 'Could one burn one's conscience as one burns a cancer?' ['Pouvait-on brûler la conscience comme on brûle un cancer?'] (*RS*, 440).

He devises other escape routes from conscience. In Arabophilic lines worthy of Loti or of Genet's *Un captif amoureux*, he is seduced by the playful banter of native Muslim soldiers in the camp, seeing their sensibility, imagination, and intuition as feminine attributes: 'the extravagance of the harem is in everything they do' ['l'extravagance du harem est dans tout ce qu'ils font'] (*RS*, 472). While the feminizing of the ethnic Other presupposes a European virility, the novel also proposes loose forms of fraternity between Latins and Arabs. Both groups, the narrator asserts, are passionate, disorganized, and erotic. Repelling doubts about coercive French rule, Auligny improvises a string of clichéd similarities that stem the process of domination, North African culture washing menacingly over the French, who become indulgent and complicitous (*RS*, 473).

Dismantling colonial guilt, Auligny wonders if he is not 'one of those Frenchmen who, whilst they are fundamentally patriotic, experience a form of sadistic pleasure in systematically taking sides against France' ['un de ces Français qui ressentent comme une volupté sadique à prendre systématiquement parti contre la France, tandis qu'ils sont patriotes dans le fond'] (*RS*, 476). Questioning colonialism, then, becomes a wilful desecration of national honour. The converse of colonial self-doubt would be vigorous acceptance of military service to the nation, as urged by his domineering mother.

In this array of contradictory responses, Auligny feminizes the Other, sees the Other as assimilating the French, dismisses as fantasy the realities of colonization, and accuses himself of perversely denigrating the civilizing mission. This always superficial engagement with otherness repeatedly eases his moral doubts. Finding intolerable the prospect of a new offensive against the local population, he succeeds, on health grounds, in withdrawing from Birbatine and the frontline to what he believes will be the safety of Fez. The irony is that his relief at being *'on the other side'* [*'de l'autre côté'*] (*RS*, 462; Montherlant's emphasis) provides no immunity from risk, and he dies at the hands of Moroccan rebels.

'LE RÊVE COLONIAL' AND THE CULT OF WHIM

The maverick figure of Guiscart proposes three categories of response for living in North Africa: 'Either the "French" dream: reduce, govern, exploit. Or the "artistic" dream: dancing girls, jasmine, young boys. Or the "human" dream: assimilation, fraternity, justice. You've chosen dream number three' ['Soit le rêve "français": réduire, gouverner, exploiter. Soit le rêve "artiste": danseuses, jasmins, petits garçons. Soit le rêve "humain": assimilation, fraternité, justice. Tu as choisi le rêve numéro 3'] (*RS*, 541). In Guiscart's crude taxonomy, which sees history as commodifiable objects of knowledge, colonialist dominance colours even the third option, which purports to be ethical and yet remains assimilationist.

Reading life beyond Europe oneirographically is an exoticist leitmotif. Gauguin writes in *Noa Noa* of the dream of Tahiti that he conveys through his painting: 'Here is the REAL Tahiti; that is to say FAITHFULLY IMAGINED' ['Voici Tahiti VRAIE; c'est-à-dire FIDÈLEMENT IMAGINÉE'] (*NN*, 24; Gauguin's capitalization). A century later, Genet voices his discomfort at the thought that his campaigning on behalf of marginalized groups such as the Palestinians and the Black Panthers will paradoxically consign them to a dream that does not impinge on reality (*PL*, 149; *CA*, 248). No such scruples affect Guiscart, for whom dreaming the Other is a comfortable *modus vivendi*. Lyautey, too, freely engages in the reverie that comes with empire. This is his Lotiesque description of the grandeur of his installation in Marrakesh in 1912 as he delights in the reception given to him by the *caïds*:

I have been living in a *fairy-tale land* for the last ten days; there is no oriental picture which could portray what I have seen since my arrival at Marrakesh, on that sunny morning. The Arab multitudes, the colourful horsemen, the large military standards, the continuous parades, the joyous fanfares of our troops, the perfume and liveliness of victory, the backdrop of the snow-covered High Atlas Mountains, and the encampment of the victorious column in the Sultan's gardens; the reception of the officers in a palace drowned in verdure.[45]

If Lyautey is entranced by the cocktail of exoticism and military power, the experiences of Guiscart confirm the status of the colony as European playground, adrift from reality. Free from the moral misgivings that complicate Auligny's outlook, he is scathing about the requirements of career and unsettles the lieutenant's belief in the figure of the noble, self-sacrificing artist. A hedonist with no psychological understanding of women, his multiple homes and families show him to be an enemy of prudence and bourgeois conformity. He speaks anarchically about 'a vast human matter, delightful undoubtedly, but in which everything is interchangeable' ['une vaste matière humaine, délicieuse certes, mais où tout est interchangeable'] (*RS*, 240). Whereas Auligny secretly feels guilt about his furtive sexual behaviour with the sleeping Ram, Guiscart brazenly defends such unilateral pleasure, enjoyed, he says, in the absence of her soul (*RS*, 240).[46]

Yet Guiscart's impulsive hedonism extends to a whimsical defence of the Arabic-speaking population. The sight of the adolescent boy Boualem showing signs of premature ageing awakens his compassion (*RS*, 247). Unlike the morally rigid Auligny, he can cope with Boualem's lying, which he sees as the only weapon of a vanquished race (*RS*, 248). His unconventionality thus extends to this desultory engagement with the mindset of the native population. Stung by a sentence once read in a book, 'There is little love in Islam' ['Il n'y a pas beaucoup d'amour dans l'Islam'], he reminds Auligny of the pleasures of nightfall in Algiers, speaking lyrically of a form of local renewal:

'often the vibration of the flute . . . hangs over the city as it sleeps. . . . It is as if Islam, trampled underfoot during the day, repossesses the city, no longer able to express itself except at night, like those prisoners who wait until all is still before communicating with each other by tapping on the wall. Of course the word purity is in no sense applicable to the Muslim world. And yet, after the din of the day, that nocturnal flute brings a breath of pure air. It seems that with it something spiritual returns to the world, washing away eighteen hours of vulgarity and barbarity. You feel that all is not lost.'

['souvent la vibration de la flûte . . . plane sur la ville endormie. . . . On dirait que l'Islam, piétiné durant le jour, reprend possession de la ville, ne pouvant plus s'exprimer que la nuit, comme ces prisonniers qui attendent que tout repose pour correspondre entre eux en frappant sur la muraille. Et je sais bien que, dans aucun de ses sens, le mot de pureté ne saurait convenir au monde musulman. Et pourtant c'est une haleine pure que celle de cette flûte nocturne après le vacarme du jour. Il semble qu'avec elle quelque chose de spirituel renaisse enfin sur le monde, nous lave de ces dix-huit heures de vulgarité et de barbarie. On a l'impression que tout n'est pas perdu.'] (*RS*, 250)

By underscoring Guiscart's detachment from European self-satisfaction, Montherlant rekindles the debate that dominates the 1967 *Avant-propos* to the novel. The contradictions in this romanticized account are symptomatic of the would-be benign Western viewpoint: the reluctance to apply the epithet pure; the grudging, cliché-ridden encomium, with its stereotypes of seductive music, the company of felons, and the nocturnal muse; and the exclusion of daytime, a variant on Fabian's allochronism to which Islam is consigned. The European philanderer who rejects the conventions of career and monogamy piously attempts to restore to Islam its legacy of love which, he protests, the West has attempted to erase. But the indelible myth-making in Guiscart's opportunistic Arabophilia runs counter to Clifford's reminder that 'identity is conjunctural, not essential'.[47] In *La Rose de sable*, there is no developed interethnic encounter.

Guiscart's disaffection thus has clear limits. He may gesture towards an inversion of the civilization/barbarism opposition, but provides only flimsy anecdotal evidence drawn from street life: the Kabyle docker offering his employer mimosa; a child uninhibitedly suckling a she-goat; the beggar-amputee who addresses passers-by not self-pityingly but with a hearty greeting (*RS*, 251). The constructed polarities, then, are European dourness and calculation and North African charm, colour, and spontaneity. By contrast, Auligny argues high-mindedly that the indigenous population enjoys the advantages of the French protectorate, which one contemporary likens to full marriage to France.[48] Unimpressed by this paternalist rhetoric, Guiscart reminds Auligny of a mendacious poster in the centenary *Exposition Coloniale* in which a colonizer puts his arm fraternally around the shoulders of an ageing native (*RS*, 255). Yet Auligny's protests that no other colonizing nation has acted with as much 'true cordiality' ['cordialité vraie'] (*RS*, 256) show that, however much they voice dissidence, the novel's authoritative observers merely flirt with the perspectives of the subjugated. Guiscart especially is reluctant to look beyond anecdote. As a painter, he can only contrast the features of the naked Ram with those of his European models, even wondering if they are of the same sex. He constructs an uncomplicated opposition between the natural and the contrived, privileging, stereotypically, North African grace and poise over Parisian restriction:

In civilized Europe, woman had been subjected to vandalism in the most obvious areas of her beauty: her feet and breasts were deformed by all that is arbitrary in fashion, as were her shoulders, through lack of physical exercise. How was one to desire – in other words . . . cherish with tenderness – a woman without beautiful shoulders? How could love survive the massacre of innocent breasts?

[Dans l'Europe civilisée, la femme avait été comme livrée au vandalisme dans les éléments les plus certains de sa beauté: le pied et les seins déformés par l'arbitraire de la mode; les épaules, par le manque de vie physique. Et comment pouvoir désirer – c'est à dire . . . chérir avec tendresse – une femme qui n'avait pas de belles épaules? Comment l'amour pouvait-il survivre à ce massacre des seins innocents?] (*RS*, 266)

The penchant for the broad-shouldered native woman is a carbon-copy of Gauguin's diagnosis of Western atrophy. Perversely, European brutalization functions in the metropolis, the language of aggression – *vandalisme, déformation, massacre* – being displaced on to a Parisian stage, away from the colony to which it is historically more applicable.

Guiscart's observations are based on his myriad sexual encounters, all of which he single-mindedly logs (*RS*, 260). Thus a rigorous, classificatory eroticism contrasts markedly with unsystematic observations on colonial life. Guiscart reinforces the logic of the civilizing mission, arguing ingenuously that France should only send to the colony what is best in order to 'have men love France when they do not know her' ['faire aimer la France à des hommes qui ne la connaissent pas'] (*RS*, 258). But while conceding that the colonies are the dumping ground of France, he prays for sensations, not conscience. This recourse to whim confirms the failure of ethical debate in the novel. Similarly, faced with Auligny experiencing acutely the loss of Ram, he counsels superficiality. His dictum, 'The pleasurable journey consists in working from depth to surface!' ['Aller de la profondeur à la surface, le beau voyage!'] (*RS*, 537) is intended to neutralize Auligny's anguished, homespun theorizing on the ethnic Other. The provocative cultivation of surfaces already seen in Loti and Proust confirms the departure from moral self-incrimination.

The concrete embodiment of Guiscart's hedonism is his love-nest in Fez where, in the penultimate chapter of the novel, he and Auligny take shelter from the gunfire outside. Guiscart's vacuous posturing about emotional attachments and social duties, before he unceremoniously escapes, provides the foil to Auligny's altogether more complex response to the crisis. For reasons of conscience, Auligny will not kill local insurrectionaries, whose struggle he considers justified. In another of his Arabophile outbursts, he identifies a collection of indigenous faces and voices (plaintive, indulgent, supplicating) and experiences a combination of trust and resigned weariness. This French 'hero of the desert' is frustrated with the irreducibility of the Other, 'the groping through *the night of others*, and through his own night' ['les tâtonnements à travers *la nuit des autres*, et à travers la sienne propre'] (*RS*, 563; my emphasis). His belief that he is immune from harm at the hands of the colonial Other explains the naive generosity of his gesture as he opens the door: '"Here we are friends of the Arabs"' ['"Nous sommes ici des amis des Arabes"']

(*RS*, 564). The chapter thus ends with the *colon* declaring in resoundingly
fraternal terms – and in Arabic – his affection for those who end up
killing him.

The melodramatic finale to Auligny's life in Morocco trivializes discussion of the colonial question – the door through which he and
Guiscart might have escaped, they discover belatedly, opens in and not
out! Still, the denouement carries its cultural symbolism, in that it collapses the ethical debate in a pointedly lurid fashion, casting Auligny as
a sacrificial, Arabophile figure, and the Moroccan insurrectionaries as
rejecting reason and the fraternal embrace of the European.[49]

THE OTHER WITHIN: THE CANNIBALISM OF 'LA PATRIE'

Melodrama in *la France extérieure* is indissociable from a crisis at the centre.
For Auligny faces a different 'night of the Other', that represented by his
mother and her morbid ambitions for him. Thus, opening the door to
the rebels in Fez not only appeases a local desire for vengeance but also
placates Mme Auligny's lust for her son's death and posthumous military
decoration. The malevolent figure of the matriarch dominates the final
chapter of the novel. Looking enormous in her black mourning dress,
she is likened to larger-than-life figures in mourning, including
Volumnia in Shakespeare's *Coriolanus* and the Ancient Roman mother
who breeds children to be sacrificed in defence of the city (*RS*, 580–1).
She is also cast as one of 'those idols from the beginning of time who
gave birth and devoured their children, in a supreme act of unfathom-
able madness' ['ces idoles des premiers âges qui enfantaient et dévo-
raient leurs enfants, dans un divin abîme d'inconscience'] (*RS*, 578). In
the colonialist mindset, cannibalism is a stock emblem of the radical cultural difference of the Other. Moerenhout, Loti, Gauguin, and Segalen
all use it, as we have seen. In Montherlant's account, by contrast, it lurks
in the metropolitan centre, thereby unsettling the dichotomy between
civilized and savage. Faced with the twin forces of matriarchy and *la
patrie*, Auligny experiences crippling inferiority. A vocabulary of ecstasy
– *frisson, sublime, exaltée, idéalisme* (*RS*, 50–1) – captures the mother's
glorification of military rank and national recognition. But as Kristeva
insists, the purity of implacable patriotism is also its perversity.[50] The
son's inhibition is a direct consequence of this potent super ego: 'As for
any religious, emotional or sexual crisis, he had been spared all that'
['Crise religieuse, crise sentimentale, crise sexuelle, tout cela lui avait été
épargné'] (*RS*, 61–2). Only in the colony may the repressed return.

That the influence of the homeland should be sadistic is taken up in the postface where Montherlant, wanting to ground the matriarch's pathological patriotism in historical reality, quotes from the diary of Robert Dubarle, a French captain in the First World War:

Your children, O Fatherland, take them, break them, slay them. Accept the trembling gift of their lives.
I kneel before you. Trample on my body, it is yours, take my abode, send to their death those I love, and may I never return to the beloved homestead. . . . The more I suffer for you, the more I shall love you.

[Tes enfants, ô patrie, prends-les, brise-les, immole-les. Accepte le don frémissant de leur vie.
Je m'agenouille devant toi. Piétine mon corps, il est à toi, prends ma demeure, envoie à la mort ceux que j'aime, que jamais je ne revienne vers le doux foyer. . . . Plus je souffrirai pour toi, plus je t'aimerai.] (*RS*, 591)[51]

La Rose de sable thus ends with this shocking picture of sado-masochistic sacrifice and abjection. In the domestic spaces of French national life, far from the colonial borders and the daily confrontation with ethnic difference, a punitive fanaticism becomes a Goyaesque cannibalism, enacted in the name of France. To the extent that, as a perverting super ego, Mme Auligny represents a pathological ideal, her diseased patriotism becomes France's barbarism within.[52]

For Auligny, patriotism offers ambiguous comfort and security. Seeing the national flag is a sacred moment (*RS*, 88), even if Montherlant sees its arbitrary symbolism. Similarly, in moments of moral doubt, the patriotic instinct steadies him: 'How much easier it was to observe the rule: "Country first"' ['Comme la règle: "Patrie d'abord" était plus facile à observer . . .'] (*RS*, 373). In crucial ways, the spectre of *la patrie*, like the misgivings about colonialism, inhibits pleasure-taking. This alienation from one's desire informs the important epigraph taken from Georges Bourdon's *Les Journées de Casablanca*: 'How many times have I heard that revealing line these past two days: "No need to put yourself out for [the Arabs]"? Very well. But what if we put ourselves out a bit for our own good?' ['Depuis deux jours, combien de fois ai-je entendu ce mot révélateur: "Il n'y a pas à se gêner pour eux [les Arabes]"? Soit. Mais si on se gênait un peu pour soi-même?'] (*RS*, 86). The risk is that Self, by failing to recognize and negotiate with the Other, becomes alienated. Auligny resists the demands of the nation when he resents his mother's greedy anticipation of his military decoration. Expressing disgust at her abbreviation of 'la C.' (*RS*, 430) used to denote the Cross of the Legion of Honour, the son likens this to an unspeakable obscenity. The uncomfortable overlap of taboo and national distinction demonstrates that behind the unswerving pursuit of the ideal lurks perversion. The failure to engage with North African difference is compounded in the national context, where a warped patriotism further alienates him.

Auligny nevertheless colludes with the myth-making peddled by his overbearing mother. In his last letter home, he distorts the details of his transfer to Fez by omitting all reference to his disaffection, a censorship that preserves his heroic status (*RS*, 584). Guiscart's obituary is similarly misleading. Mythopoeia thus surrounds Auligny's death: his burial in Morocco symbolizes a defence of that corner of French influence; the fallen victim is attributed an uncompromising Catholicism, strained comparisons being made with the figure of Christ; and the providential final letter arrives posthumously. As the narrator concludes laconically, Guiscart is not the only one living in a fairytale world (*RS*, 584). Unreality, distortion, and magic are the by-products of patriotism in *La Rose de sable*.

*

For Johannes Fabian, the desired outcome of anthropology is 'to meet the Other on the same ground, in the same Time'.[53] In Montherlant's Moroccan novel, which would, its author claims, destabilize French colonialist attitudes, Auligny sees the Other. But the power relations acting at a discursive and imaginative level guarantee his failure to engage with alterity in any dialectical sense. The interaction with Ram remains petrified, as much in his sense of wonder as in his commodification of her.

The motif of relationship as chimerical governs the oneirographic encounters of *La Rose de sable*: Auligny's dealings with Ram, the matriarchal Madame Auligny *vis-à-vis* her son, and European perceptions of North Africans. To this we can add Auligny's complicity with colonial myth-making as he placates an expectant metropolitan centre. In relations of cultural power, an important symmetry emerges: externally, the ideal of the civilizing mission neither accommodates nor recognizes the alterity of the colonized; and internally, the representation of the *patrie* as devouring matriarch means denying the autonomy of its subjects. In these two situations, Ram and Auligny respectively are alienated victims, although predictably the text highlights the plight of the uniformed soldier and barely signals the victimization of the young Bedouin.

With Auligny actively conniving in his own oppression by internalizing his mother's pathological ambitions, the novel surveys as much the colonial centre as the cultural periphery. The interdependence of the two is crucial: Mme Auligny's frenetic intervention to have her son posted abroad demonstrates that the centre calls to and needs its periphery, that France calls to its soldier-warrior on the colonial border; the matriarch needs the sacrificial son, just as discursive power needs the depotentiated subject. For Mme Auligny, the crowning national glory, 'la C.' of the Legion of Honour – the recognition, at and by the centre, that dare not speak its name – depends crucially on deeds performed on the frontier. It is this periphery that shapes and writes the centre. Moreover, the extremeness of situations described (a perverted transracialism, rape, insurrection, death, and the pathology of visceral nationalism) captures in exemplary fashion the strains of colonial identity.[54]

CHAPTER FOUR

Camus and the resistance to history

Salzburg would be peaceful without Mozart. [Salzbourg serait paisible sans Mozart.]

(Camus)

The *metropolis* . . . strange, fantastic, phantom-like.

(Derrida)[1]

The phenomenon of cultural marginality finds a very particular focus in the work of Albert Camus, France's French Algerian Prix Nobel, whose position was regularly at odds with that of the metropolis. In 1939, in a decade when French public opinion was as ill-informed about life in the colonies as Montherlant's *La Rose de sable* demonstrates, Camus exposed the appalling living conditions in Kabylia in journalism designed to inform France of its responsibilities in relation to the destitute of colonization.[2] Rejecting criticism that it was unpatriotic to campaign in this way, Camus insisted that France's reputation was best served through directly addressing issues of human justice in what he contentiously calls a French country (*Ess.*, 936–7). Twenty years later, with colonial rule in crisis, the French left-wing intelligentsia hounded him for his failure to speak out against atrocities inflicted on the indigenous population in the course of the Algerian War. This silence, together with his earlier campaigning zeal in highlighting Kabyle dispossession, captures the sense of contradiction that his culturally marginal position generated.

Exploring what from a Parisian viewpoint were the Algerian margins, this chapter considers the author's early lyrical essays, with their occlusion of colonial actuality and cultivation of a socially isolating innocence; *Le Renégat*, where Camus engages with cultural conflict in Africa through melodrama and hyperbole; *La Chute*, set in Amsterdam and yet conveying a North African subtext; and finally, his last work, *Le Premier Homme*, written in 1959 and published posthumously in 1994, with its uninhibited defence of the *petits colons* or working-class colonial

Europeans. With the exception of the early essays, Camus was working on these texts in the 1950s, when the claims and legacy of the French Algerians and the culture of colonialism generally were being contested both in Algeria and metropolitan France.

Thanking the Nobel Committee in Stockholm in 1957, Camus insists on his status as a French Algerian: "'I am . . . grateful to the Nobel Committee for having decided to honour a French Algerian writer. . . . All my thoughts go to [the land of my birth] and to the calamity facing her.'" ["'Je suis . . . reconnaissant au Comité Nobel d'avoir voulu distinguer un écrivain français d'Algérie. . . . C'est à elle [la terre où je suis né], et à son malheur, que vont toutes mes pensées'"] (*Ess.*, 1892). In this self-authenticating statement, coming in the middle of the Algerian War, Camus infers the innocence and peripherality of the French Algerians, caught between metropolitan French hostility and Algerian nationalist militancy.

THE BURDEN OF A CULTURAL LEGACY

Long before Stockholm, Camus was busy defending the *petits colons* of Algeria. The early collection of essays *Noces*, published in 1939, earned him the reputation of being a writer imbued with what he claimed to be his native North African landscape. With the ecstatic evocation of the ruins of Djemila in 'The Wind at Djemila' ['Le Vent à Djémila'], he marvels at how the desert has gradually reclaimed this site of ancient Roman settlement. Motioning towards the columns and triumphal arch now absorbed by nature, he asserts in a conceptually simplified way the impermanence of history: 'In the end, the geophysical world always conquers history' ['Le monde finit toujours par vaincre l'histoire'] (*Ess.*, 65). The wedding signalled in the title *Noces* involves the individual human subject enjoying unmediated contact with nature. Man becomes divorced from the nightmare of history, communing with the desert in celebratory and erotic fashion. The spectacle of the ruins thus provides Camus with the space in which to detach radically from the burden of past events:

Successive waves of men and societies have been here; the country bears the marks of the civilization bequeathed by conquering non-commissioned officers. Their idea of greatness was crude and stupid and they measured their empire by the extent of their territorial conquest. The miracle is that the ruins of their civilization are the very denial of their ideal.

[Des hommes et des sociétés se sont succédé là; des conquérants ont marqué ce pays avec leur civilisation de sous-officiers. Ils se faisaient une idée basse et ridicule de la grandeur et mesuraient celle de leur Empire à la surface qu'il couvrait. Le miracle, c'est que les ruines de leur civilisation soient la négation même de leur idéal.] (*Ess.*, 65)

Ironically, while Camus savours the demise of an ancient empire, the context in which he is writing is also one of imperial occupation. But his wholly transparent aim is to eradicate contemporaneity, preferring instead the lyrical depiction of North African landscapes from which man has been removed. Straightaway, then, the aesthetic constructed around the ruins of Djemila occludes contemporary politics.

The arrogant dismissal of history extends to 'The Minotaur' ['Le Minotaure'], an essay Camus was working on in 1939 and again in 1941, in which he writes of the clamour of great events to which Europe resounds. The text is in part a celebration of the Algerian town of Oran, from which vantage-point Camus complains of the weight of Europe's past, preferring what he insists is the anonymity of the desert:

The cities of Europe are too resonant with the sounds of the past. . . . You can feel the dizzying weight of the centuries, of revolution and glory. You remember there that the West came into being in a great clamour. There's not enough silence there.

[Les villes que l'Europe nous offre sont trop pleines des rumeurs du passé. . . . On y sent le vertige des siècles, des révolutions, de la gloire. On s'y souvient que l'Occident s'est forgé dans les clameurs. Cela ne fait pas assez de silence.] (*Ess.*, 813)

If, in Camus's scenario, the noise of Europe's tempestuous past persists, it does so in the most generalized and travestied of forms. Even more unrecognizable is the colonial present, which lies as oddly silent as North Africa's distant troubled history. The landscape, then, is offered as a happy retreat from the world, by which Camus wishes us to understand Europe, when in reality it is contemporary colonial history that is more likely to impinge. The leitmotif of silence is the adjunct of a constructed world of ahistorical innocence. Yet as Barthes observes, the 'privation of history' is an aggressively political act and one which, in Camus's case, is axiomatic for our understanding of the colonial mindset.[3]

The culture evoked in 'Le Minotaure' is unapologetically imperialist: Florence and Athens, Camus comments, have moulded the mentalities of so many Europeans:

In a way, they appease that part of the soul hungering after memory. But how does one feel moved about a town [like Oran] where nothing appeals to the mind, where ugliness itself is anonymous, where the past is reduced to nothing?

[Elles apaisent une certaine faim de l'âme dont l'aliment est le souvenir. Mais comment s'attendrir sur une ville [comme Oran] où rien ne sollicite l'esprit, où la laideur même est anonyme, où le passé est réduit à rien?] (*Ess.*, 820)

Camus randomly cites Descartes, who searches for his figurative desert in Amsterdam, one of the great commercial cities of his day. But in this idealized reading, the feverish pursuit of commerce effectively dehistoricizes the seventeenth-century city. Camus's idiosyncratic history is unashamedly European, what Édouard Glissant calls *Histoire* with a capital H.[4] But the erasure of the non-European is precisely the exclusion Glissant has in mind when he reflects that the histories that Europeans are unaware of or have not made are inevitably discarded.

Camus's travelogue provides clichéd tourist fare: Paris echoes to the sound of revolution, Salzburg to the cries of Mozart's Don Juan, while Vienna stands at a crossroads in her imperial past. In contrast, North Africa, with its neglected history, lower-case h, is occluded, and its 'lands of innocence' ['terres de l'innocence'] (*Ess.*, 829) spared the cacophony of Europe.

The symbolic geography of Camus's early essays is also eroticized. In an impressionistic description of life in Algiers in a text of 1947 significantly entitled 'A short guide for towns without a past' ['Petit guide pour des villes sans passé'], he writes coyly of his attitude to Algeria:[5]

Having been born in this desert, I'm incapable of talking about it like a visitor. Do we list the charms of a woman we greatly love? . . . My links with Algeria . . . go way back and no doubt will never end, and that prevents me from being totally lucid about her.

[Étant né dans ce désert, je ne puis songer en tout cas à en parler comme un visiteur. Est-ce qu'on fait la nomenclature des charmes d'une femme très aimée? . . . J'ai . . . avec l'Algérie une longue liaison qui sans doute n'en finira jamais, et qui m'empêche d'être tout à fait clairvoyant à son égard.] (*Ess.*, 848)

Erotic flirtation thus supplants sociopolitical seriousness and any preoccupation with colonial guilt. Coquetry, not colonization, energizes Camus's mini-guide, which simultaneously feminizes and dehistoricizes Algeria. A vague, pre-colonial European history is adumbrated, while North African actuality is ignored. In this construction of myth, Barthes's diagnosis is confirmed, the removal of 'all soiling trace of origin or choice' spelling 'the miraculous evaporation of history'.[6]

In *Misères de la Kabylie*, the chronicles of contemporary Algerian life reveal a direct and sympathetic engagement with the plight of the indigenous population. But in Camus's fictional writing, *petit colon* loyalism translates into a catalogue of manipulations and exclusions. While shadowy North African figures flit in and out of the narratives, colonials enjoy the limelight: Meursault is promoted as universal, angst-ridden hero, becoming the *victim* of the judicial system in *L'Étranger*; the ethnocentrism of *La Peste* ensures that the plague victims of Oran are invariably European; and in *L'Exil et le Royaume*, French Algerians are the autonomous subjects who wrestle with cultural difference.[7] The crude nature-versus-history paradigm of the early essays masks a more troubling opposition between a French Algerian legacy that is legitimized and celebrated and neglected native histories.

IN DENIAL OF HISTORY: 'ANONYMAT GÉOLOGIQUE'

The opening lines of *Le Premier Homme* contain a dedication to the author's illiterate mother, 'To you who will never be able to read this book' ['À toi qui ne pourras jamais lire ce livre'], and the note: 'add geological anonymity. Land and sea' (*FM*, 3) ['ajouter anonymat géologique. Terre et mer'] (*PH*, 11). This picks up on the lure of petrification in the early essays: 'These are the lands of innocence. But innocence requires sand and stone. And man has forgotten how to live there' ['Ce sont ici les terres de l'innocence. Mais l'innocence a besoin du sable et des pierres. Et l'homme a désappris d'y vivre'] (*Ess.*, 829–30). The attempt is to forge a depoliticized naivety from material, physical realities, the desert standing as a utopian space, a buffer against contemporaneity. In this *locus amœnus* of cultural amnesia, North Africa offers the harsh lessons of an often hostile nature. Oran is

Capital of boredom, besieged by innocence and beauty; the encircling army has as many soldiers as stones. At certain times in the town, however, how tempting to go over to the enemy! to identify with the stones, to merge with this impassive, burning world that defies the upheavals of history!

[Capitale de l'ennui, assiégée par l'innocence et la beauté, l'armée qui l'enserre a autant de soldats que de pierres. Dans la ville, et à certaines heures, pourtant, quelle tentation de passer à l'ennemi! quelle tentation de s'identifier à ces pierres, de se confondre avec cet univers brûlant et impossible qui défie l'histoire et ses agitations!] (*Ess.*, 830)

While the language of virility, violence, sieges, and treachery signals the mindset of militarism, highly revealing displacements are in operation. The encircling enemy comprises soldiers and stones, but it is tempting to side with the stones alone. A lyricism of the desert thus screens off a besieging – presumably native – army, a defiant nature barely concealing a politics of occupation.

The same identification with stone persists in *Le Minotaure*, where, reporting on a giant construction site on the outskirts of Oran, Camus describes a cliff face being demolished. Along a jetty occupied by men and machines, earth-moving equipment transfers fragments of the cliff into the bay (*Ess.*, 827). While rejecting what are labelled the agitations of history, this literal description of a land reclamation project provides an archetypal image of colonial development. The struggle and aggression marking this territorial expansion involve man and nature, as workers drill frenetically into the rock. Mother Earth is munificent, indeed self-sacrificing in her provision of building material. The maternalization of the mining scene is reinforced in the umbilical-cord-like connections that tie cliff and workers together: 'Suspended on the same rope against the cliff face, the bodies of dozens of men, with their bellies pressed against the handles of their automatic drills, vibrate in mid-air for days on end' ['Pendus le long d'une même corde contre le flanc de la falaise, des dizaines d'hommes, le ventre appuyé aux poignées des défonceuses automatiques, tressaillent dans le vide à longueur de journées'] (*Ess.*, 827).

The land, far from being innocent, becomes the impetus for violent, frenzied activity. Camus briefly addresses the question of exploitation and aggression:

In the midst of this building site, man attacks the rock head on. And were it possible to forget, at least for a moment, the harsh slavery that makes this work possible, one would have to feel admiration. Torn from the mountain, these stones serve man in his designs.

[L'homme, au milieu de ce chantier, attaque la pierre de front. Et si l'on pouvait oublier, un instant au moins, le dur esclavage qui rend possible ce travail, il faudrait admirer. Ces pierres, arrachées à la montagne, servent l'homme dans ses desseins.] (*Ess.*, 827)

If the reclamation project relies on North African labour, these dangling figures are the uprooted slaves of colonization, working in the service of would-be universal man, alias the European colonizer. Toying with ethical irresponsibility, Camus blanks out colonial servitude, the memory-loss enhancing the aestheticization that can only function with the privation of actuality. The drift away from contemporaneity continues when he likens the scene to Dutch master-drawings of the Tower of Babel, in which a teeming mass of humanity, beasts, and machines highlights the superhuman scale of the project (*Ess.*, 826). Re-routed through European art history, the original land reclamation scheme becomes essentially depoliticized, Babel displacing contemporary Algeria and universal man being projected as microcosmic and innocuous.[8]

Dispersing colonial traces in his depiction of Oran, Camus appeals to other cultural markers, most notably the figure of the Buddha Sakyamuni, the exemplary contemplative who sits motionless in the desert for years. While symbolizing the search for emotional quietude, the Buddha's appearance in *Le Minotaure* renews the tension between private mythologizing and public politics. The effusive portrait of the great ascetic embracing his 'destiny of stone' ['destin de pierre'] and shunning a life of desire takes us back to geology: 'Yes, let us yield to stone when necessary' ['Oui, consentons à la pierre quand il le faut'] (*Ess.*, 830). In attempting to break what he calls the chain of desires, Camus prevents a connection back into colonial society and advocates uncompromisingly the death of the self: '"To be nothing!" For thousands of years, that great cry has inspired millions of men in revolt against desire and suffering' ['"N'être rien!" Pendant des millénaires, ce grand cri a soulevé des millions d'hommes en révolte contre le désir et la douleur'] (*Ess.*, 830). Such Buddhist-inspired quietism assumes provocative new meaning in the Algerian context in which Camus is writing.

R. D. Laing's theory of human engulfment developed in *The Divided Self* is wholly germane to *Le Minotaure*, in particular his observations on the use of isolation as a manoeuvre to stave off loss of identity:

Thus, instead of the polarities of separateness and relatedness based on individual autonomy, there is the antithesis between loss of being by absorption into the other person (engulfment), and complete aloneness (isolation).[9]

The dread of engulfment energizes the search for emotional quietism in *Le Minotaure*, a politics of isolationism being the antidote to colonial imbroglio. The psychology of colonial oppression is also relevant here. In his preface to Memmi's *Portrait du colonisé*, Sartre describes how the dehumanization heaped on the colonized is inverted, becoming the alienation of the oppressor,

who reawakens, with his every gesture, the humanity that he wishes to destroy. . . . To escape from this, he must convert himself into mineral form, give himself the opaque consistency and impermeability of rock, in short, he in turn must 'dehumanize' himself.[10]

It is precisely self-petrification that we find in *Noces*, where Camus writes of being 'a stone among stones, the solitude of a column' ['pierre parmi les pierres, la solitude d'une colonne'] (*Ess.*, 62).[11]

Sartre and Laing thus enable us to politicize Camus's reverie as a form of radical social isolationism. Moreover, seen in the light of Barthes's observations on myth as depoliticized speech, Camus's stone-like self stands as an attempt to inject into reality an essence that would prevent, in Barthes's words, 'its flight towards other forms of existence'.[12] Indeed, revisiting the persistently dehistoricized tale of Sisyphus, we find a model of immurement and colonial disengagement: 'A face that labours so close to stones is already a stone itself!' ['Un visage qui peine si près des pierres est déjà pierre lui-même!'].[13] The tautology here and elsewhere in Camus's mythologized account of colonial life reminds us of the observation in *Mythologies* that we take refuge in repetition when we are at a loss for an explanation. In Barthes's memorable formulation: 'Tautology is a faint at the right moment, a saving aphasia . . . the indignant "representation" of the *rights* of reality over and above language'.[14] The topoi of Camus's desert (the silence, the Buddhist self-containment, the human petrification) thus signal the postulation of an immutable truth requiring no justification.

A ludic variant on the logic of identification with the landscape occurs when, in a flamboyant, delusional scenario, Camus launches the mountains on to the open sea:

all the capes along the coastline look like a flotilla setting sail. These stout galleons of stone and light tremble on their keels, as though they were getting ready to head for islands in the sun. . . . As the whole coast prepares to leave, a ripple of adventure runs along it. Tomorrow, perhaps, we'll leave together.

[tous les caps de la côte ont l'air d'une flotille en partance. Ces lourds galions de roc et de lumière tremblent sur leurs quilles, comme s'ils se préparaient à cingler vers des îles de soleil. . . . La côte entière est prête au départ, un frémissement d'aventure le parcourt. Demain, peut-être, nous partirons ensemble.] (*Ess.*, 831–2)

What more political, we might ask, adapting Barthes, than this image of a coastline adrift?[15] Camus's fantasia, with its anachronistic galleons, marks a grand departure from the locus of contemporary conflict. Under cover of a romanticized description, the desire to possess the land finds its most radical expression as the very coastline is pirated away.

The moot question of provenance which has perennial significance in the culture of the colonial margins emerges in various ways. Stone provides a point of initiation in the retreat from human agency. Moreover, the minotaur entails a fantasticated account of origins. By opting for this half-animal, half-human figure, Camus proposes beginnings that are simultaneously hyper-present and unreal, displacing any more mundane demographic enquiry. Mythology, then, supplants sociology and becomes a style of self-representation for a culture that is historically punitive.

Le Minotaure offers an idiosyncratic travelogue in which Camus's seductive 'towns without a past' are juxtaposed with their European equivalents, heavy with history. But the travelogue, in which an anthropomorphic nature delivers socio-cultural naivety, facilitates what is unquestionably 'a politics of identity'.[16] Arrogance and bravado also mark Camus's self-isolation:

these shorelines . . . welcome higgledy-piggledy and without taking any notice of them the monk, the functionary, and the conqueror. There were days when I was expecting to meet Descartes or Cesar Borgia in the streets of Oran.

[ces rivages . . . accueillent pêle-mêle, et sans les regarder, le moine, le fonctionnaire ou le conquérant. Il y a des jours où j'attendais de rencontrer, dans les rues d'Oran, Descartes ou César Borgia.] (*Ess.*, 831)

However much Camus's shoreline remains stubbornly impassive to the agents of colonization, nostalgic emblems of European grandeur persist.

In spatial terms, *Le Minotaure* skirts along a littoral, with no promise of a hinterland, thus confirming the colonizer's toehold position in North Africa. Just as the appeal of Salzburg, cited in the epigraph that opens this chapter, is enhanced with the absence of its most famous cultural icon, so Camus works to perfect a tranquillized North Africa, rid of the clamour of contemporary history.

LE RENÉGAT OU UN ESPRIT CONFUS: CAMUS'S 'CONSTELLATION OF DELIRIUM'[17]

> Each tribe that . . . we disparage separates us from harmony.
>
> (Glissant)[18]

Nightmare, not idyll, dominates in *Le Renégat ou Un esprit confus*.[19] The story is one of six *nouvelles* that make up *L'Exil et le Royaume*, which was published in 1957 during the Algerian War. It reconstructs a Catholic missionary's state of derangement, his unconscious unleashing violent projections about African and European identity.[20] *Le Renégat* thus confronts its reader with strident expressions of religious and ethnic allegiance, unfolding against an ominous colonial backdrop.

The setting for this identitarian conflict is the southern Algerian desert. The young French missionary, hailing from what in context is the suggestively named Massif Central, zealously leaves the seminary in Algiers, intent on converting a 'savage' tribe 'on the confines of the white country and the land of the blacks' (*EK*, 34) ['à la frontière de la terre des noirs et du pays blanc'] (*TRN*, 1582). He is, to borrow from Clifford, a white man on the frontier, occupying '[a point] of danger and disintegration'.[21] In this menacing interstitial space, they torture him, cutting out his tongue, and he converts to their religion and the cult of evil. While desperate to safeguard the rule of the 'barbarians', he learns that they have agreed to accept a small colonial garrison and in order to frustrate this cooperation, he determines to kill the replacement missionary and thus sow discord between desert-dwellers and Europeans.

A dichotomous logic of strident Christian good and implacable pagan evil thus perverts the renegade missionary. His castigated body marks a literal incarnation of ideological conflict. Commenting on this brutalization, Said stresses the logic whereby the only way of going native is through being mutilated.[22] In the renegade's troubling self-portrait, layers of confused psychical identity compete with one another:

Since they cut out my tongue, *another tongue*, it seems, has been wagging somewhere in my skull. . . . Order and method, the tongue says, and then goes on talking of other matters simultaneously – yes, I always longed for order. (*EK*, 30)

[Depuis qu'ils m'ont coupé la langue, *une autre langue*, je ne sais pas, marche sans arrêt dans mon crâne. . . . De l'ordre, un ordre, dit la langue, et elle parle d'autre chose en même temps, oui j'ai toujours désiré l'ordre.] (*TRN*, 1579; my emphasis)

The opposition between a deranged search for order and images of mutilation finds an echo in Sander Gilman's work on the recurring configuration in colonial literature of difference and disease:

The concept of difference is needed to distinguish the healer from the patient as well as the 'healthy' from the 'sick'. Order and control are the antithesis of 'pathology'. 'Pathology' is disorder and the loss of control, the giving over of the self to the forces that lie beyond the self. It is because these forces actually lie within and are projected outside the self that the different is so readily defined as pathological.[23]

The renegade's sickness is both physical, in the lurid form of his mutilation, and mental. Yet the consequence of his defection is that the stereotypical division between European health and African disease collapses, and a cultural supremacism falters. His desire for control is repeatedly frustrated:

something has been talking, or someone, that suddenly falls silent and then it all begins again – oh, I hear too many things I never utter, what a jumble, and if I open my mouth it's like pebbles rattling together. (*EK*, 30)

[quelque chose parle, ou quelqu'un qui se tait soudain et puis tout recommence, ô j'entends trop de choses que je ne dis pourtant pas, quelle bouillie, et si j'ouvre la bouche, c'est comme un bruit de cailloux remués.] (*TRN*, 1579)

The drama of *Le Renégat* is thus one of projection. For the renegade externalizes inner anxieties, casting as other voices what are, in reality, his own.[24] The exaggeration of his position is the guarantee of its exemplarity: 'I groused at the normal, in short I too wanted to be an example in order to be noticed' (*EK*, 32) ['Je rognais sur l'ordinaire, enfin je voulais être un exemple, moi aussi, pour qu'on me voie'] (*TRN*, 1580). As with Proust's Charlus and Montherlant's Madame Auligny, extremes of sectarian attitude serve to mirror forms of ethnic and religious prejudice that are normative and widespread.

In the overdetermination that characterizes *Le Renégat*, what Freud calls the 'pathology of cultural communities' finds melodramatic expression.[25] For Camus's *nouvelle* constructs a symptomatology of the European colonial imagination. From being a model seminarian, the missionary becomes a model, that is to say, zealous and intolerant colonizer. The melodramatic projection on to the Other of cruelty is transparently confirmed at the seminary, where the lessons in the old priest's account continue to have influence:

I had been dreaming about his tale, about the fire of the salt and the sky, about the House of the Fetish and his slaves, could anything more barbarous, more exciting be imagined, yes, that was my mission and I had to go and reveal to them my Lord. (*EK*, 33)

[je rêvais sur son récit, au feu du sel et du ciel, à la maison du fétiche et à ses esclaves, pouvait-on trouver plus barbare, plus excitant, oui, là était ma mission, et je devais aller leur montrer mon Seigneur.] (*TRN*, 1581)

By demonizing the Other, the protagonist and his mentor savour an exoticism built around sado-masochistic fantasy. But what feeds the renegade's insanity is that the mythopoeic solutions to identitarian conflict that he envisages are predicated on the unshakeable opposition of Christian and pagan. Indeed talk of medical aid for the tribe of Taghâsa leaves him fearing the end of the brutal polarization that defines him. He entertains two scenarios, both of which share colonialism's logic of polarization: total victory for the Christians or the barbarian invasion of Europe. Willing the continued impossibility of negotiation across ethnic borders, the narrator speaks automatically of African and European as hermetically sealed, mutually antagonistic categories. Thus, the diegesis of *Le Renégat* confirms the struggle to preserve ethnic homogenization, an essential feature of the epistemology of imperialism.[26]

In these mutually exclusive styles and value systems, the incontrovertible grammar that rules pagan and Christian cultures alike excludes relationship. Hence the concatenation of hegemonies in the text: the renegade's indoctrination in the seminary, the Christian colonization of the southern Algerian desert, Taghâsa's revenge, and the nightmare scenario of an African march on Europe. The oscillation between megalomania and imagined persecution mirrors Said's ironic perception that deconsecrating Eurocentrism means instating Afrocentrism.[27]

Dementia is the outcome of this pathological belief in an essentialized difference, and the text re-enacts what Bhabha in a related context refers to as complex psychic projections in the pathological spaces of colonial relation ('Foreword' to *Black Skin, White Masks*, p. xx). Enmeshed in the workings of a diseased imperialist logic, the deranged monologue flags menacing cultural encroachment. To that extent, *Le Renégat* dramatizes the porosity of the colonizing subject, as the tribe that he views antagonistically eventually engulfs him. Bhabha's incisive remarks on the drama of identity in *Black Skin, White Masks* highlight what the critic sees as the perversion at the core of these relations:

the shadow of the colonized man, that splits [the colonizer's] presence, distorts his outline, breaches his boundaries, repeats his action at a distance, disturbs and divides the very time of his being. This ambivalent identification of the racist world – moving on two planes without being the least embarrassed by it . . . – turns on the idea of Man *as* his alienated image, not Self and Other but the 'Otherness' of the Self inscribed in the perverse palimpsest of colonial identity. ('Foreword', pp. xiv–xv; Bhabha's italics).

While Bhabha signals the ineradicable otherness within the colonizer, the renegade's folly is to believe that the Other is always the enemy without. As a marginal, he helps give coherence to the groups from which he is excluded: his treachery confirms the missionaries in their religious conformity; and his foreign discourse of Christian mercy provides social cohesion for the pagans of Taghâsa. He is, then, the scapegoat. There are suggestions that the renegade is a Christ-like figure.[28] But in his reworking of the Christian story, the template of the outsider ransomed to placate the tribe is significantly reconfigured to include the ethnic tensions in which *Le Renégat* is grounded. Or to reformulate the point, the perverted simulacrum of Christ that we find in the renegade is a figure who carries the additional burden of colonial history.

Fanon talks of 'the amputation of the [black man's] being', a deformity that is corrected as he boards ship for France, in other words as he leaves the colony and moves towards 'the Tabernacle' or would-be restorative cultural centre.[29] For Camus, the same logic is perversely re-enacted, in that, having undertaken the reverse journey from seminary to colonial outpost, the renegade suffers mutilation in his contact with what is dramatically represented as demonic cultural difference. As though by a process of contagion and diminution, the missionary experiences degradation in contact with the African. Wholeness is a European prerogative, and incompletion, as Fanon notes uncomfortably and writers of the exotic affirm unproblematically, is the dubious attribute of the Other. But unlike, for example, Loti's protagonists, for whom cultural conversion may be no more onerous than the slipping on of ethnic dress, or Gauguin's self-reinvention, Camus's renegade converts at a somatic cost, as difference is literally etched on to his body. Violent cohabitation in North Africa in the 1950s clearly provides an extreme cultural context that is mirrored in the colonial imaginary at work in *Le Renégat*.

Writing about war in Europe, Freud laments the erasure of individual moral formations caused by militant nationalism. He argues that, in mass conflict, 'only the most primitive, the oldest, the crudest mental attitudes are left'.[30] The psychosocial world of *Le Renégat* is similarly rebarbative, colonial Algeria conveying a powerful collective sickness. Cultural intolerance is endemic as the missionary envisages imposing conformism militaristically. Denigrating the puny efforts of his elders in the seminary to influence pagan Africa, he harbours totalitarian fantasies in relation to the tribe of Taghâsa:

> to fling them on their knees and make them say: 'O Lord, here is thy victory', to rule in short by the sheer force of words over an army of the wicked. Oh I was sure of reasoning logically on that subject, never quite sure of myself otherwise, but once I get an idea I don't let go of it, that's my strong point, yes the strong point of the fellow they all pitied! (*EK*, 33–4)

> [les jeter à genoux et leur faire dire: 'Seigneur, voici ta victoire', régner enfin par la seule parole sur une armée de méchants. Ah! j'étais certain de bien raisonner là-dessus, jamais très sûr de moi autrement, mais mon idée quand je l'ai, je ne la lâche plus, c'est ma force, oui, ma force à moi dont ils avaient tous pitié!] (*TRN*, 1582)

Hegemonic control, be it that of the African or of the European missionary, thus comes with an authority vested in language itself. Cultural superiority also works sadistically, the renegade linking his mutilated mouth to the sun, 'a mouth voluble as mine, constantly vomiting rivers of flame over the colourless desert' (*EK*, 40) ['bouche comme la mienne volubile, et qui vomit sans trêve des fleuves de flammes au-dessus du désert sans couleur'] (*TRN*, 1587). A symbol of destructive intensity, then, the sun connotes cultural absolutism. Beyond the triumphalist equation, 'Catholicism is the sun' ['le catholicisme c'est le soleil'], we see the narrator-proselyte's arrival in the seminary described as the victorious sun of Austerlitz (*EK*, 31; *TRN*, 1580). In the colonial imagination, a combination of heliocentrism and patriotic militarism ensures a perverse denial of difference.[31] Rigidity, here the hallmark of missionary zeal, is displaced on to Taghâsa deep in the desert: 'the sterile city carved out of a mountain of salt, divorced from nature . . . the city of order in short, right-angles, square rooms, rigid men' (*EK*, 43) ['la ville stérile sculptée dans une montagne de sel, séparée de la nature . . . la ville de l'ordre enfin, angles droits, chambres carrées, hommes roides'] (*TRN*, 1589). In spatial and architectural terms, this exoticized cityscape, resistant to colonial infiltration, remains devoid of vegetation. It represents in caricatural form a physical embodiment of the kingdom of evil. Once again, its inhabitants' lack of affect is a projection of the renegade, who himself hankers after seamless certainties: 'solely the reign of malice was devoid of defects, I had been misled, truth is square, heavy, thick, it does not admit distinctions' (*EK*, 43) ['seul le règne de la méchanceté était sans fissures, on m'avait trompé, la vérité est carrée, lourde, dense, elle ne supporte pas la nuance'] (*TRN*, 1589).

The quest for an indivisible truth that energizes the missionary is doomed to failure, given that the shadow of the African, as Bhabha reminds us, invades the colonizer's boundaries. There are fleeting, nervous moments of conjunction between cultures. Describing how the inhabitants of Taghâsa respond to the severe night-time cold, the narrator observes:

without transition the cold of the night congeals them individually in their rock-salt shells, nocturnal dwellers in a dried-up icefloe, black Eskimos suddenly shivering in their cubical igloos. Black because they wear long black garments, and the salt that collects even under their nails, that they continue tasting bitterly and swallowing during the sleep of those polar nights . . . often spots their dark garments with something like the trail of snails after rain. (*EK*, 35–6)

[sans transition le froid de la nuit les fige un à un dans leurs coquillages de gemme, habitants nocturnes d'une banquise sèche, esquimaux noirs grelottant tout d'un coup dans leurs igloos cubiques. Noirs oui, car ils sont habillés de longues étoffes noires et le sel qui envahit jusqu'aux ongles, qu'on remâche amèrement dans le sommeil polaire des nuits . . . laisse parfois sur leurs robes sombres des traces semblables aux traînées des escargots après la pluie.] (*TRN*, 1583)

In a magical conflation of reified Eskimos and Saharan dwellers, the missionary offers a stubbornly literal reflection on the colours black and white, the ingestion of the ubiquitous salt arguably connoting Black Africa's absorption of the white man's corrosive influence. The stark monochrome of Arctic and African metaphorically reproduces the dichotomous logic governing racial typecasting.

The schism assumes its most vigorous expression in the invasion scenario sketched by the renegade. Here, he speculates that, by killing the missionary sent to replace him, he may precipitate a war in which the leaders of Taghâsa will exact vengeance:

O my masters, they will conquer the soldiers, they'll conquer the world and love, they'll spread over the deserts, cross the seas, fill the light of Europe with their black veils – strike the belly, yes, strike the eyes – sow their salt on the continent, all vegetation, all youth will die out, and dumb crowds with shackled feet will plod beside me in the world-wide desert under the cruel sun of the true faith, I'll not be alone. (*EK*, 47)

[Ô mes maîtres, ils vaincront ensuite les soldats, ils vaincront la parole et l'amour, ils remonteront les déserts, passeront les mers, rempliront la lumière d'Europe de leurs voiles noirs, frappez au ventre, oui, frappez aux yeux, sèmeront leur sel sur le continent, toute végétation, toute jeunesse s'éteindra, et des foules muettes aux pieds entravés chemineront à mes côtés dans le désert du monde sous le soleil cruel de la vraie foi, je ne serai plus seul.] (*TRN*, 1592)

At the heart of European cultural paranoia, then, lies the fear that colonial occupation, brutalization, and enslavement will be reciprocated. The colonizer thus finds his simulacrum in the African invader. In this visceral expression of insecurity, the 'dark' continent snuffs out 'the light of Europe' and the censored violence of French *pacification* becomes flagrant African revenge.

Concluding this story of mental pathology, the renegade entertains reconversion to Christianity, inviting an imagined interlocutor to join in the construction of 'the city of mercy' (*EK*, 48) ['la cité de miséricorde] (*TRN*, 1593). True to the schizoid logic of the text, cruelty makes way for Christian charity. Moments earlier, the protagonist laments the absence of the cult of Taghâsa in terms that evoke a Christian cosmology: 'O Fetish, why hast thou forsaken me?' (*EK*, 48) ['ô fétiche pourquoi m'as-tu abandonné?'] (*TRN*, 1593). These words of reproach from the bibli-

cal account of Christ's crucifixion demonstrate the imbrication of allegedly irreconcilable worldviews, as does the corrupt version of the 'Our
Father' addressed to the pagan idol:[32]

O Fetish, my god over yonder, may your power be preserved . . . may hate rule
pitilessly over a world of the damned, may the wicked forever be masters, may
the kingdom come, where in a single city of salt and iron black tyrants will
enslave and possess without pity! (*EK,* 46)

[Ô fétiche, mon dieu là-bas, que ta puissance soit maintenue . . . que la haine
règne sans pardon sur un monde de damnés, que le méchant soit à jamais le
maître, que le royaume enfin arrive où dans une seule ville de sel et de fer de
noirs tyrans asserviront et posséderont sans pitié!] (*TRN,* 1592)

In this delusional world, Camus's protagonist apes his masters, pagan
and Christian alike. As his prayer makes clear, his crossing of the cultural divide is always equivocal. In this way, the invocation of the fetish
provides a sadistic variant on the Christian exemplum and shares its
structure. Africa thus becomes Europe's negative. That the renegade
missionary should embody good and evil in a rigid sequential manner
confirms the point that, within the pathological relations of *Le Renégat,*
dialectical engagement with the Other becomes impossible, as the
violent juxtaposition of rival hegemonies confirms.

The body of Camus's narrator thus becomes, adapting a model used
by Peter Brooks, the site on which the aspirations, anxieties, and contradictions of French Algeria are played out.[33] The perversions of colonialism are reflected in the renegade's religious delusion. Christ's doctrine of
charity is judged no less implacable a message than that of the pagan cult
of Taghâsa – as the renegade argues, they cut out Christ's tongue so that
his message would not deceive the world (*EK,* 44; *TRN,* 1590). Thus the
uncompromising discourse of moral good is flawed and inapplicable.
Camus generalizes the predicament of his unnamed missionary – 'and
still millions of men between evil and good, torn, bewildered' (*EK,* 48) ['et
toujours encore des millions d'hommes entre le mal et le bien, déchirés,
interdits'] (*TRN,* 1593). In the absence of relationality, the deranged pred-
icates of pure good and seamless evil ensure that a dichotomous logic fails.

ON EUROPE'S EDGE

La Chute offers a counterpoint to the world of *Le Renégat* and yet simultaneously an unexpected re-statement of its tensions. *Prima facie,*
Clamence's polished linguistic manipulation of his interlocutor

contrasts markedly with the rantings of the renegade. In addition, the setting in *La Chute* is a caricaturally misty Holland – a far cry both from the hostile environment of Taghâsa and the benign desert landscapes of the early essays. Yet *La Chute* and *Le Renégat* express an acute sensitivity to territorial and cultural borders. Conor Cruise O'Brien makes the point that *La Chute*, although not set in Algeria, is the work in which that country is most painfully present. In O'Brien's phrase, Camus was 'all the more intensely French because of the insecurity of the frontier'.[34] Standing on a political and cultural edge, astride cultures in conflict, his protagonists are absorbed by identitarian quests. While Clamence talks of life on the periphery of Europe, he sees himself ironically 'soaring over this whole continent which is under my sway without knowing it' (*TF*, 105) ['planant par la pensée au-dessus de tout ce continent qui m'est soumis sans le savoir'] (*TRN*, 1549). Thus, both Algeria and Amsterdam offer panoptic positions from which to review the centre.[35] The choice of an extreme point on the continent provides a re-statement of Camus's own cultural status, on the territorial margins and yet simultaneously, as Said insists, central to a metropolitan culture that welcomed his work as an endorsement of French Algeria.[36] Indeed for much of the Algerian War, Camus's anti-independence rhetoric, while rejected by opponents of colonization such as Sartre, Francis Jeanson, and Simone de Beauvoir, echoed that of the French government.[37] Such was Camus's influence in the post-war period that, as O'Brien demonstrates, 'the moral capital' of his work was being drawn on by proponents of the Cold War and colonial militarism.[38]

THE CARCERAL SOCIETY

Jean-Baptiste Clamence cries out not in the desert of his New Testament namesake but in the wilderness of the modern European city. If the motif of the desert corroborates O'Brien's reading of Amsterdam as a parable of Algeria, the colonial analogy is reinforced through the text's dense thematic web of control, policing, and containment. The crowded setting of Amsterdam ensures an aggressively social world. Significantly, the isolationism fed by the desert in *L'Été* still lurks in *La Chute*, as Clamence reflects nostalgically on the lofty vantage-points from which he used to contemplate 'the human ants' (*TF*, 20) ['[les] fourmis humaines'] (*TRN*, 1488). Yet that aloofness is now irretrievable and engulfment in actuality ensures that the present is carceral.[39]

   Clamence ingeniously categorizes himself as judge-penitent: 'practise the profession of penitent to be able to end up as a judge' (*TF*, 101) ['faire métier de pénitent pour pouvoir finir en juge'] (*TRN*, 1546) is his formula. This offers an eccentric extension to Foucault's catalogue of judges, the teacher-judge, the doctor-judge, the educator-judge, all of whom enforce 'the universal reign of the normative'.[40] Foucault's reflections on the technology of control over the body find an echo in Camus's fiction generally: *L'Étranger* depicts the regime of the old people's home, Meursault's imprisonment, and the spectre of the guillotine;[41] in *La Peste*, we have quarantine and the isolation of Oran, in *Le Renégat*, the renegade's disfigured body and his incarceration. These instances of the castigated or diseased body signal societal constraint writ large in France's North African margins. Metaphorically, the prison signals insertion in a dysfunctional colonial society.

Clamence goes a stage further, confessing to a perverse curiosity in the most ingenious forms of physical control. The proportions of the medieval *malconfort* or little-ease, he explains, mean that the prisoner is unable either to stand up or stretch out on the ground. In commenting ironically on its proportions, he points to human intelligence in the service of domination and coercion. A modern extension to this is the 'spitting cell' (*TF*, 81) ['la cellule des crachats'] (*TRN*, 1532) where the jailers spit copiously on the prisoner who is wedged into his concrete shell. If bodily torture is connoted by the very name of Jean-Baptiste Clamence, the demise of his New Testament counterpart is echoed in the closing scene of *La Chute*: 'Above the gathered crowd, you would hold up my still warm head, so that they could recognize themselves in it and I could again dominate – an exemplar' (*TF*, 107) ['Au-dessus du peuple assemblé, vous élèveriez alors ma tête encore fraîche, pour qu'ils s'y reconnaissent et qu'à nouveau je les domine, exemplaire'] (*TRN*, 1551). In this pathological scenario, Clamence joins the renegade missionary and Meursault, all three being marginals whose mutilated bodies placate a societal demand for revenge and sacrifice.

How we read this backcloth of physical punishment and social dysfunctionality is conditioned by the colonial situation that Camus knew intimately and that was necessarily sustained by violence. Bizarrely, Camus's victims are European and yet they could all be seen as making amends at an unconscious level for collective European wrong-doing. The context in which *La Chute* was written is wholly relevant. Sensitive to left-wing metropolitan criticism that he was actively defending a regime that was using torture in Algeria, Camus's ploy was to play to his hostile Parisian gallery through an exaggerated assumption of colonial guilt. Hence the proliferation of extreme forms of torture in the text. Allowing Clamence, the ironic author of an 'Apotheosis of the Guillotine' and an 'Ode to the Police' (*TF*, 68; *TRN*, 1522), to linger on such violence, Camus offers a self-incriminating caricature to corroborate his alleged indifference to Algerian suffering.

Beyond this archive of literal physical torture, *La Chute* reflects implicitly on the punitive input of educators and psychologists. Indeed the text constructs a carceral society in microcosm, in which a Foucauldian 'domination-observation' is ironically enacted.[42] Clamence makes his position as judge symbolically impregnable by keeping in his home the 'Just Judges' ['Les Juges intègres'], the stolen panel from Van Eyck's Christian triptych, 'The Adoration of the Lamb' ['L'Agneau mystique'] (*TF*, 94; *TRN*, 1542), while a reproduction of the panel seduces the unsuspecting visitors to the Van Eyck museum. Pursuing O'Brien's Algerian allegory, we see how a metropolitan centre presumes to know, while the probity and authenticity signalled by the panel title are housed in the (colonial) fringes.

In another ironic expression of power, Clamence sees himself ruling over such a world in miniature, when he refers to 'the closed little universe of which I am the king, the Pope, and the judge' (*TF*, 94) ['[le] petit univers bien clos dont je suis le roi, le pape et le juge'] (*TRN*, 1541). The crude accumulation of political, ecclesiastical, and judicial authority reads like a colonizer's charter of the kind already seen in *Le Minotaure* and *Le Renégat*. But in Clamence's burlesque surveillance and punishment, we find Camus acting out exaggeratedly an assumed indifference to a punitive colonial war, the better to dismiss that allegation. Travesty and caricature thus become new weapons in the refutation of settler guilt.

A figure of mock religious authority, 'Pope' Clamence pronounces on the struggle between God and Satan. As he explains, Dante accommodates those angels who are neutral in limbo, 'a sort of vestibule of his Hell. We are in the vestibule, *cher ami*' (*TF*, 62) ['une sorte de vestibule de son enfer. Nous sommes dans le vestibule, cher ami'] (*TRN*, 1518). If the liminality marks the refusal of tidy classification, *La Chute* constructs an ambiguous world, beyond the stark polarities of *Le Renégat* and *Le Minotaure* where Europe has history and North Africa has none. For O'Brien, this limbo captures Camus's position on the war of independence, in which he is vilified by French Algerian loyalists and dismissed by Algerian militants.[43]

If Camus is in the dock, charged with colonialist bad faith, he himself places on parodic trial in *La Chute* European intellectual and moral history. The opening page shows the owner of the Mexico-City bar standing in an uneasy relationship to that tradition, trying, through his inscrutable silence, to resist the weight of actuality:

His dumbness is deafening. It's the silence of primeval forest, heavy with menaces. At times I am amazed by his obstinacy in snubbing civilized languages. (*TF*, 5)

[son mutisme est assourdissant. C'est le silence des forêts primitives, chargé jusqu'à la gueule. Je m'étonne parfois de l'obstination que met notre taciturne ami à bouder les langues civilisées.] (*TRN*, 1477)

In this ironic rewriting of the early lyrical essays, the retreat from utterance finds a corollary in his return to the past, a point made mockingly when the narrator refers to the proprietor as a 'worthy gorilla'. While sailors from all over the world frequent the bar, its owner's linguistic range remains nil: 'Fancy the Cro-Magnon man lodged in the Tower of Babel! He would certainly feel out of his element' (*TF*, 5) ['Imaginez l'homme de Cro-Magnon pensionnaire à la tour de Babel! Il y souffrirait de dépaysement, au moins'] (*TRN*, 1477).

In *Le Minotaure*, Camus compares colonial Algeria's development to a latter-day Babel. The re-emergence of the biblical city in *La Chute* helps forge the link between Amsterdam and Algeria and allows us to revisit this highly suggestive biblical metaphor. For colonial Babel signals cacophony, awakening nostalgia for the monolingual innocence that pre-dates it. It heralds a form of retribution for the presumptuousness of this deluded architectural project, the speech of Noah's descendants becoming fragmented and incomprehensible.[44] Applied in an African context, the Babel myth suggestively conflates French ambition, expansion, guilt, and retribution. Circuitously, it reinscribes colonialism's nostalgia for cultural sameness. But in another context, it is potentially the site for the inclusion of cultural difference and the prelude to social wholeness, symbolizing the movement advocated by Glissant 'from the world-as-solitude to the world-as-relation'.[45]

THE SETTLER'S TALE: *LE PREMIER HOMME*

Clamence's mocking choice of Cro-Magnon as an improbable cultural cradle contrasts with Camus's solemn visitation of nineteenth-century colonial history a few years later in his final, unfinished work, *Le Premier Homme*. If *La Chute* reconstructs the cerebral games that the author's intellectual persecutors goaded him into, *Le Premier Homme* marks a confidently literal and unapologetic return to origins. Its commemoration of working-class French Algerian colonizers takes Camus back, less to 1830, when French forces first arrived in the country, than to the waves of populist immigration following the 1848 revolution and the loss of Alsace-Lorraine in 1871.

Le Premier Homme is substantially autobiographical. It articulates Jacques Cormery's desire to honour his obscure family, especially his father, who was born in Algeria in 1885 and died in a French military hospital in 1914 as a result of wounds received at the Battle of the Marne. The text reflects ironically on the fact that the father, victim of a distant European war, embarks for the first time on the Mediterranean Sea 'for the France he had never seen, on the sea that had never before carried him' (*FM*, 53) ['pour la France qu'il n'avait jamais vue, sur la mer qui ne l'avait jamais porté'] (*PH*, 67). Thus an anonymous, socially underprivileged *colon*, whose homeland is unequivocally Algeria, first sees France in 1914 and is killed almost immediately. Europe is thus the site of History and the hitherto unknown continent that claims the father's innocent life.

A sense of pathos is constructed around the peripheral spaces occupied by the working-class French Algerians, who form the dominant social grouping in the novel. They are restricted to a precarious foothold, the narrator insists, 'nothing but bare empty space; to them it was the end of the world, between the deserted sky and the dangerous land, and then the women cried into the night, from exhaustion, and fear, and disappointment' (*FM*, 146–7) ['rien qu'un espace nu et désert, ce qui était pour eux l'extrémité du monde, entre le ciel désert et la terre dangereuse, et les femmes pleuraient alors dans la nuit, de fatigue, de peur et de déception'] (*PH*, 174). The remoteness of a perceived cultural centre fuels the symbolism of a menacing *finis terræ*. Describing Jacques Cormery's stay as a boy at a summer camp in the Zaccar Mountains, the narrator plays up the child's sensation of engulfment, a vulnerability made all the more poignant by a bugle call from the nearby barracks announcing the evening curfew: 'the child felt a limitless despair rising in him and in silence he cried for the destitute home of his . . . childhood' (*FM*, 114) ['l'enfant sentait monter en lui un désespoir sans bornes et criait en silence après la pauvre maison démunie de tout de son enfance'] (*PH*, 138). This is Camus's unbridled frontier imagination. In the word-picture of colonial melancholia, his sentimentalism remains resolutely partisan: French Algerians are dwarfed by the vastness of the land they have colonized, and the lullaby comes courtesy of a military bugle.

North Africa is imagined as a form of immense island bordered by the Sahara to the south and the sea to the north (*FM*, 3, 151; *PH*, 11, 180). Yet this daunting expanse, while instilling unease in the *colon*, is also his home, unlike France, which Jacques Cormery regularly evokes in terms of its dreariness. The impatient allusion to a flat landscape and ugly houses stretching across northern France (*FM*, 16; *PH*, 25) becomes an outpouring of dread at the prospect of returning to Paris, the suburbs of which Cormery likens to 'an ill-fated cancer [that] reached out its ganglions of poverty and ugliness to absorb this foreign body and take him to the centre of the city' (*FM*, 33) ['un cancer malheureux, étalant ses ganglions de misère et de laideur et qui digérait peu à peu le corps étranger pour le conduire jusqu'au coeur de la ville'] (*PH*, 44). The pattern of pathology traditionally located in colonial spaces is thus reversed, as the *petit colon* experiences dislocation in a diseased metropolitan centre.

By the same token, anticipating the pleasure of returning to Africa in the 1950s, the mature narrator experiences 'a secret exultation' (*FM*, 32) ['une jubilation sourde'] (*PH*, 44). On one level, North Africa is a ludic site. The narrator records the pleasures that Jacques Cormery experiences as a boy: on the beach, where 'the glory of the light filled their young bodies with a joy that made them cry out incessantly' (*FM*, 41) ['la gloire de la lumière emplissait ces jeunes corps d'une joie qui les faisait crier sans arrêt'] (*PH*, 54); in the shabby cellar of the tenement block, where they construct, in a makeshift tent, a form of homeland; or in the same cellar, this time flooded after heavy rain, '[they] would play Robinson Crusoe far from the open sky and the sea breezes, triumphant in their kingdom of poverty' (*FM*, 37) ['ils jouaient aux Robinsons loin du ciel pur et des vents de la mer, triomphants dans leur royaume de misère'] (*PH*, 50–1). The construction, then, of spatial retreats, places of autonomy and redemption, and sites of infantile pleasure, together with the rhetoric of a kingdom for the poor, is central to Camus's cultural self-justification. Tribal pleasure-taking, as when the Cormery family and others picnic on Easter Mondays in the Sidi-Ferruch forest, provides carnival images of the *petits colons* at play along the Algerian coastline (*FM*, 101; *PH*, 124).

The precarious hedonism derives from a sensitivity to spatial parameters that are carefully delineated and vigorously defended. Excursions beyond the streets and outskirts of Algiers acquire an intense affective charge. The occasions when, as a boy, Cormery goes off with his uncle Ernest and others to hunt in the interior are ambiguous moments for the settler community. The narrator spells out the insecurity that underpins the homosocial bonding at work within the party, referring to the hunters as 'uninhibited and in a mood of amused tolerance that is peculiar to men when they have got together . . . for some brief violent pleasure' (*FM*, 84) ['cet abandon et . . . cette tolérance amusée particulière aux hommes quand ils se retrouvent entre eux pour un plaisir court et violent'] (*PH*, 102–3). But once out of the train and confronted with what is insistently represented as the immensity of the interior, the town-dwellers fall silent. To an extent, the high plateau on which the hunting takes place is an enchanted space for Jacques, who enjoys primitive exhilaration in the company of the menfolk. But predictably, the incursion is brief and the day of animal pleasure ends abruptly: 'then it was the brief African twilight, and the night, always disturbing on those wide-open spaces, would fall without transition' (*FM*, 88) ['puis c'était le rapide crépuscule africain, et la nuit, toujours angoissante sur ces grands paysages, commençait sans transition'] (*PH*, 107). Africa, in all its clichéd geophysical grandeur, seduces and threatens the *pieds noirs*. A tribal anxiety marks the settler's exposure to the interior, as the cultural confidence acquired on the shoreline evaporates in this hesitant excursion inland.[46]

EDUCATION AND CULTURAL MEMORY

The images of France made available to Cormery through his schooling fuel a self-congratulatory exoticism. At the point in Camus's manuscript where he evokes the boy's despair and panic in the summer camp in the Zaccar Mountains, he notes the need to sing the praises of secular education (*FM*, 114 n.; *PH*, 138 n.). The republican system provides exposure, through a syllabus common to Algeria and metropolitan France, to an idyllic, almost unreal France. Images of schoolchildren returning home in the snow conjure up for Cormery an Edenic universe and the quintessence of exoticism (FM, 113; *PH*, 137). As a counterpoint to the troubling difference of the 'dark' continent and its ominous twilights, we have then an indulgent, mythical celebration of Francocentrism on the colonial frontier. As Barthes says of exoticism, 'its fundamental justification . . . is to deny any identification by History'.[47]

The school begets a paradise but also a politics. It becomes a protected space, while the schoolteacher, M. Bernard, stands as a benign father-figure instilling in his pupils a thirst for knowledge and discovery: 'they were judged worthy to discover the world' (FM, 114) ['on les jugeait dignes de découvrir le monde'] (*PH*, 138). Pivotal in the institution and nurturing of patriotic memory, education and the development of new horizons provide an uneasy echo of colonial expansion. M. Bernard's references to the then very recent First World War, in which, like Cormery's father, he had fought, confirm the forging of a national identity. The teacher's readings from Dorgelès's hugely popular war novel, *Les Croix de bois*, form an end-of-term ritual that is culturally self-indulgent in the colonial context:

For Jacques, these readings again opened the door to the exotic, but this time an exotic world stalked by fear and misfortune, although he [only ever] made . . . a theoretical connection with the father he never knew. (*FM*, 114–15)

[Pour Jacques, ces lectures lui ouvraient encore les portes de l'exotisme, mais d'un exotisme où la peur et le malheur rôdaient, bien qu'il ne fît jamais de rapprochement, sinon théorique, avec le père qu'il n'avait pas connu.] (*PH*, 139)

The underlying anxiety spills over when, with the death of the hero Daniel, both the teacher and young Cormery are overcome with grief. The Dorgelès provides an oblique dialogue with the absent father-figure, and a conduit for tribal self-recognition. Thus an exoticized France affords the orphan child of colonization an imaginative space in which the work of mourning may be accomplished. Eschewing any ethical examination of colonial responsibility, Cormery's commemoration of the father straddles two sites, then, the battlefield of France (which Cormery's French bourgeois classmate Didier sees as the place of national honour, *FM*, 162; *PH*, 191) and North Africa, the only world that the father has hitherto known.

In the unproblematically benign figure of M. Bernard, French educational culture finds a ringing endorsement. But behind the narrator's protestations about the innocence of the socially obscure (*FM*, 137; *PH*, 163), we need to confront the politics implicit in literacy, an academic meritocracy, and the racial exclusion that blights it. The narrator himself remarks on the paucity of Muslim pupils at the lycée in Algiers. Crucially, Camus converts a specifically secular French tradition into what is virtually a sacred cultural practice. As Abdul JanMohammed observes, literacy produces 'a sense of . . . the human past as an objective reality available to causal analysis, and of history as a broad attempt to determine reality in every area of human concern'.[48]

Evidence of cultural authority in *Le Premier Homme* lies in the appeal to European historical events (1848, the Franco-Prussian War, the Moroccan campaign of 1905, the First World War), which, like the *Les Croix de Bois* intertext, authenticate Jacques Cormery's world view. Local Muslim culture is absent. Camus himself proposes an explicit separation between Europe and North Africa that underscores this division. Europe enjoys historical objectivity. The dates on the father's grave (1885–1914) spell an exactness that is absent in the Algerian context, while the plotting of graves in the same Saint-Brieuc cemetery indicates a meticulous taxonomy and infers a determination of historical reality:

The Mediterranean separates two worlds in me, one where memories and names are preserved in measured spaces, the other where the wind and sand erase all trace of men on the open ranges. (*FM*, 152–3)

[La Méditerranée séparait en moi deux univers, l'un où dans des espaces mesurés les souvenirs et les noms étaient conservés, l'autre où le vent de sable effaçait les traces des hommes sur de grands espaces.] (*PH*, 181)

The corollary to a documented, verifiable European history is perpetuation of the myth of Africa as outside and pre-dating history. Camus works unambiguously between a constructed historical plenum and a perceived cultural vacuum to the south of the Mediterranean. Nevertheless, in longing for anonymity and self-effacement, he simultaneously reinscribes the French Algerians in 'the land of oblivion' (*FM*, 152) ['la terre de l'oubli'] (*PH*, 181) which is paradoxically the place of memory for the *petit colon*.

*

Those dissidents of the 1848 revolution who leave Paris to settle in Algeria go in search of nothing less than an earthly paradise:

And all of them dreaming of the Promised Land. Especially the men. The women, they were afraid of the unknown. Not the men! They hadn't made the revolution for nothing. They were the kind who believe in Santa Claus. And their Santa Claus wore a burnoose. Well, they got some kind of Santa Claus. They left in '49, and the first house was built in '54. (*FM*, 144)

[Et tous rêvaient de la Terre promise. Surtout les hommes. Les femmes, elles avaient peur de l'inconnu. Mais eux! Ils n'avaient pas fait la révolution pour rien. C'était le genre à croire au père Noël. Et le père Noël pour eux avait un burnous. Eh bien, ils l'ont eu leur petit Noël. Ils sont partis en 49, et la première maison construite l'a été en 54.] (*PH*, 172)

Reinforcing the Francocentrism of the colonizers, whose migration is predicated on a wholly domestic political agenda without reference to native Algerians, we have bizarre anecdotal details – Father Christmas in

Arab headdress and the ironically named vessel that transported the settlers across the Mediterranean: "'the *Labrador* to go to the mosquitoes and
the sun'" (*FM*, 145–6) ["'*Le Labrador* pour aller vers les moustiques et le
soleil'"] (*PH*, 173). That the cultural signs are all pointing incongruously
northwards suggests a denial of colonizing zeal and intentionality, and
reflects Camus's desire to rehabilitate the early settlers, who are cast as
mere accidents of history. Crossing the Mediterranean, these unlikely conquerors vomit over one another in their desperate sea-sickness and, once
ashore in Bone, want to lie down and die (*PH*, 173). The nearest we get to
colonial guilt is in reference to the Alsatians, who in 1871 are assigned lands
confiscated by the colonial authorities from the Kabyles, then in open
revolt: 'dissidents taking the places kept warm by insurgents, persecuted-
persecutors from whom his father descended' (*FM*, 149) ['réfractaires
prenant la place chaude des rebelles, persécutés-persécuteurs d'où était né
son père'] (*PH*, 178), a case of losers-become-winners that Camus accepts
fatalistically and without self-incrimination. Appealing to the *force majeure*
of the Franco-Prussian War and its aftermath, he essentially vindicates the
petits colons, sandwiched between European aggressor and local rebel.

Settler guilt is relativized and even erased in this retrospective.
Frequently, the newly arrived, Camus protests, never get the chance to
colonize, two-thirds of them dying before they ever lay hands on a spade
or a plough (*FM*, 148; *PH*, 176). On the basis of this unilateral evidence,
colonization becomes not calculating oppression but a haphazard enter-
prise, more threatening for the colonizers than for the colonized, a direc-
tionless, ingenuous odyssey undertaken by the dispossessed.

BIBLICAL MYTHS, ARCHAIC TIMES

The process of exoneration is already signalled in the novel's title, which
evokes Adam and the Genesis myth. At the diegetic level, Camus rejects
Christian religious practice, stressing that the Cormery family are only
nominally Christian and endorsing a French secular tradition. Yet symbolically, the discourse of exile and persecution, and of finding the
kingdom, presupposes a biblical imaginary. The *first man* is the rootless
innocent, without the burden of cultural baggage, Eden's naive hedonist who only assumes the weight of guilt in his fallen state. But he is also,
in Camus's narrative, incontrovertibly European, 'wandering through
the night of the years in the land of oblivion where each one is the first
man' (*FM*, 152) ['cheminant dans la nuit des années sur la terre de l'oubli
où chacun était le premier homme'] (*PH*, 180–1).

Sander Gilman reminds us of the theological model whereby the Fall, the wellspring of History, signals human degeneration, whereas Christ's crucifixion is the source of human regeneration.[49] It is worth recalling the causes and consequences of the expulsion from the biblical Eden, since the theological template helps shape Camus's partisan history of nineteenth-century settlement. The first man does not know the distinction between good and evil until he and Eve have transgressed. Among the divine punishments incurred, the land becomes accursed, woman suffers pain in childbirth, and man sweats and toils to earn his daily bread, before returning to the dust of the earth.[50] This retribution is echoed in *Le Premier Homme*, where, beyond a prelapsarian innocence in which the young Cormery thrives, the mother's painful confinement in an unknown environment dominates the first chapter, the early settlers struggle to cultivate the inhospitable land of Algeria, and their graves are monuments to social obscurity. To that extent, Camus stresses much less a paradise and more a fallen state, in a tone of often bitter recrimination: for the *petits colons* are all cast adrift, he pleads, and walk in a form of historical limbo. The regenerative power of a Christian cosmology is nevertheless present in key redemptive figures in the novel. Beyond the rapprochement between Madame Cormery and the figure of Christ (*FM*, 239; *PH*, 295), the suggestive initials of Jacques Cormery corroborate the details of the birth narrative in Chapter 1 (the itinerant parents, the straitened circumstances of the birth, and the wondrous signs in the sky all echoing the birth of Christ).[51]

In Camus's colonial landscape, we can therefore identify contrasting configurations of time and space. The Judæo-Christian frame of reference heralds a premodern, Mediterranean-centred order and a mythical time of human fall and subsequent redemption. This intersects with the axis of nineteenth-century colonization that problematically ushers in a modern secular time and ethnic conflict.[52] The resultant sense of disturbance and dislocation is captured at the Saint-Brieuc cemetery, where the adult son bonds with the deceased father and yet realizes that the latter's twenty-nine years of life make him almost a son of Cormery junior: 'and the [order of the years became dislocated] in the great river that flows to its end' (*FM*, 20) ['et les années cessaient de s'ordonner suivant ce grand fleuve qui coule vers sa fin'] (*PH*, 30). Camus's sentimentalism requires this reversal and the cancellation of a teleological continuum. The Hegelian concept of successive ages makes way for a private, mythologized time, ruled by the affective demands of private memory. Archaism is central to Camus's project in *Le Premier Homme*, the strategy being to legitimize the French presence in Algeria by regularly appealing to premodernity.

In this context, young Cormery's uncle Ernest becomes a key father-substitute. Camus promotes this retarded, inarticulate figure as providing access to a mythical past. His dog-like shouts and animal attachment to his mother (Cormery's imposing grandmother) are greedily interpreted by the narrator as proof of an 'Adam-like innocence' (*FM*, 79) ['innocence adamique'] (*PH*, 98). Ernest is 'like a prehistoric beast that wakens each day to a strange and hostile world' (*FM*, 78) ['comme la bête préhistorique qui se réveille chaque jour dans un monde inconnu et hostile'] (*PH*, 96). When hunting, his ability to mimic the movements of the various animals enthrals his audience as he becomes, for a day, leader of the tribe. A form of refined, primitive animality energizes this unlikely role-model. Ernest rules the paradisiacal space of the hunting ground, which is a sealed, precarious, and essentially male site. The catalogue of primitivist poses and attitudes deflects attention away from an unpalatable present moment in history. By appealing to prehistory, Camus rejects contemporaneity. In its place, a sentimentalized account of private eccentricities, handicaps, and scars confirms a family's mythopoeic innocence.

In eschewing a teleological history, Camus purloins the archaic time traditionally ascribed to the African, protecting himself and the *pieds noirs* from the charge of brutal colonization. Stereotypes of the African as a primitive close to the animal kingdom are second nature in the modern colonial imaginary. But whereas for Loti or Montherlant, this is part of a clichéd denigration, *Le Premier Homme* inverts the model. Ernest assumes the role traditionally assigned to the simian Other, dominating the African landscape: 'Ernest . . . always as agile as a monkey and now he was running almost as fast as his dog, baying like him' (*FM*, 86) ['Ernest, toujours adroit comme un singe et qui courait cette fois presque aussi vite que son chien, criant comme lui'] (*PH*, 106). Vignettes such as this are central to the defence of 'the infant people of this country' ['le peuple enfant de ce pays'] and the Nobel Prize winner from working-class Algiers categorically refuses to see his tribe as agents of a punitive colonial exploitation.[53]

UTOPIAN SOLUTIONS

Camus regularly distances himself from a metropolitan French identity. In his last interview, he observes that French critics have focused on his ideas, neglecting the blindspots and opaque instinctual elements in his work. He calls on his public to read him in the Algerian context, just as Faulkner needs to be understood against the backdrop of the deep South.[54] This renewed insistence on atavisms highlights a shunning of bourgeois liberalism. Indeed in some revealing manuscript drafts for *Le Premier Homme*, he appeals for transracial justice for those Algerians who have been materially deprived. In what may have been intended as the ending for his unfinished novel, he envisages a utopian order in which the poor inherit the earth:

The end.
Return the land, the land that belongs to no one. Return the land that is neither to be sold nor to be bought. . . .
And he cried out, looking at his mother, then the others:
'Return the land. Give all the land to the poor, to those who have nothing and who are so poor that they never wanted to have and to possess, to those in the country who are like her [Cormery's mother], the immense herd of the wretched, mostly Arab and a few French, and who live and survive here through stubbornness and endurance, with the only pride that is worth anything in the world, that of the poor, give them the land as one gives what is sacred to those who are sacred, and then I, poor once more and for ever, cast into the worst of exiles at the end of the earth, I will smile and I will die happy, knowing that those I revered, she whom I revered, are at last joined to the land I so loved under the sun where I was born.' (*FM*, 255)

[Fin.
Rendez la terre, la terre qui n'est à personne. Rendez la terre qui n'est ni à vendre ni à acheter. . . .
Et il s'écria, regardant sa mère et puis les autres: 'Rendez la terre. Donnez toute la terre aux pauvres, à ceux qui n'ont rien et qui sont si pauvres qu'ils n'ont même jamais désiré avoir et posséder, à ceux qui sont comme elle [la mère] dans ce pays, l'immense troupe des misérables, la plupart arabes, et quelques-uns français et qui vivent ou survivent ici par obstination et endurance, dans le seul honneur qui vaille au monde, celui des pauvres, donnez-leur la terre comme on donne ce qui est sacré à ceux qui sont sacrés, et moi alors, pauvre à nouveau et enfin jeté dans le pire exil à la pointe du monde, je sourirai et mourrai content, sachant que sont enfin réunis sous le soleil de ma naissance la terre que j'ai tant aimée et ceux et celle que j'ai révérés.'] (*PH*, 320–1)

Camus's emotionally charged appeal, written in the year preceding his sudden death in a car accident, reads uncannily like a last will and testament. The attempt to forge a fraternity across ethnic groupings may be seen as idealized and impractical, worse still as politically manipulative, as though concessions from the French Algerians were finally forthcoming at a late stage in the colonial war.

The extended quotation enables us to identify afresh central elements in Camus's utopian solution: firstly, the intractable problems of Algeria are lived out in a liminal space, a phantasmal end-point on the earth; secondly, the insistence that the land is not to be commodified stands as an indictment both of colonial appropriation and of inferred native claims to ownership; and thirdly, in the special pleading for the mother, Camus reawakens the controversy surrounding his celebrated remark in Stockholm in 1957 that, if forced to choose between his mother and justice, he would choose his mother.[55]

Camus handles grievance on European terms, couching his improbable panacea in transparently biblical tones. The pious discourse of recompense and of an ethnically inclusive community of the dispossessed suggests especially the Christian Beatitude, 'Blessed are the meek, for they shall inherit the earth'.[56] Yet if the concern for social justice becomes an emotional imperative, the risk is that his identification of the meek is culturally naive in failing to address the specificity of an intractable colonial war. The retreat into sentimentalism may be read as a sublimation of colonialist guilt. Nevertheless, Camus's plea, composed in 1959, suggests an author adrift from the colonizing nation, a defection confirmed by his siding with 'the immense herd of the wretched, mostly Arab and a few French'. This eleventh-hour call for a community formed of the dispossessed Algerian majority and the *petits colons* is a fantasy solution that history will not tolerate.

Camus's most direct intervention in the Algerian War came a few years earlier in January 1956, when he appealed unsuccessfully to the warring factions.[57] Calling for a truce for civilians, he alludes idealistically to a community of hope grounded in cultural pluralism:

Reunited on this soil are a million French, who have been settled here for a century, and millions of Muslims, Arabs and Berbers who have been settled here for centuries. . . . These men must live together, at the crossroads of routes and races where history has situated them.

[Sur cette terre sont réunis un million de Français établis depuis un siècle, des millions de musulmans, Arabes et Berbères, installés depuis des siècles. . . . Ces hommes doivent vivre ensemble, à ce carrefour de routes et de races où l'histoire les a placés.] (*Ess.*, 994–5)

The talk of crossroads suggests the potential for a conjunctural identity, yet in Camus there is a repeated failure to sustain engagement with the Other. If his appeal for a truce fails, he persists in his search for ethnic tolerance in *Le Premier Homme*. Still, it is symptomatic of French Algerian immurement that the novel's most substantial evocation of the Other involves not the mainstream Muslim population but one of its minority sects, the Mozabites. Living in the harshest of desert environments, this puritanical sect is the butt of *petit colon* jokes. Having broken away from orthodox Islam, they occupy a desert region, 'as far from the half-civilized world of the coast as a lifeless cratered planet might be from the earth' (*FM*, 91) ['aussi loin du monde à demi civilisé de la côte qu'une planète croûteuse et sans vie peut l'être de la Terre'] (*PH*, 112). They live what the narrator labels a strangely ascetic life: the able-bodied menfolk work in the coastal region to support the isolated communities of the Mzab region and long to retire to their desert retreat, with its religious freedom.

The search for land undertaken by the expelled Parisians of 1848 parallels the Mozabite quest for freedom. In both instances, Camus indulges his quirky predilection for improbable paradises created in the face of adversity. His kingdom of the dispossessed is a Foucauldian space of compensation, a home for the zealous and the passionate, categories exemplified by hardline Parisian revolutionaries of 1848 and Mozabite fundamentalists alike. Camus's overriding aim in *Le Premier Homme* is, he infers, to give a voice to what Claudel calls 'a life that is humble, ignorant, stubborn' (*FM*, 229) ['la vie humble, ignorante, obstinée'] (*PH*, 275). Yet in his evocation of the ascetic Mozabites, his portrayal remains essentialized and their tribal isolation reflects another insularity, that of the French Algerians.

*

Le Premier Homme foregrounds aggressively settler misery. It sends up a smokescreen of sentimentalism to mask the harsh realities of French colonial domination in Algeria. Moreover, the settler's would-be innocent playground can only function to the exclusion of a submerged majority population. But there is also a fitful desire on the part of the mature narrator to transcend tribalism. Camus mourns the death of Muslim Algerians and French Algerians alike in the First World War and calls for the land to be restored to those he indiscriminately labels the underprivileged. In this regard, his 'Give all the land to the poor' (*FM*, 255) ['Donnez toute la terre aux pauvres'] (*PH*, 320) approximates to a form of Christian socialism, a heavenly paradise being converted into an earthly kingdom of the dispossessed. But ultimately, this utopian order must accommodate, however precariously, the *pieds noirs*. Their paradise of the street can rapidly become the site of terrorist violence, while pleasurable day-time sallies into the Algerian interior give way to dread as night falls. Camus's Algeria thus remains the vulnerable haven of those who refuse to countenance colonial guilt.

Le Premier Homme shuttles uneasily between history and memory-loss, commemoration and the erasure of historical traces. More accurately, it enacts the *petit colon*'s amnesic relationship with the colonized, a pre-condition for a self-congratulatory history. When Camus writes with pathos about the possible obliteration of a French Algerian culture, his appeal is resoundingly political. Benjamin Stora, exploring the French concern today to review the legacy of the war in Algeria, refers to the entrapment and blind self-justification of the colonial aggressor. The work of retracing the colonizer's steps, what Stora calls 'revisit[ing] this exile from oneself', entails a rediscovery of Self predicated on the readmission of the Other.[58]

Such a process is adumbrated in the last chapter of Camus's unfinished novel. Entitled 'A Mystery to Himself' ['Obscur à soi-même'], it explores the elusiveness of self-knowledge and the place of the irrational. In a recycling of the geological tropes to be found in *Le Minotaure*, the colonizer is caught between the immensity of the sea and the enveloping mountains and desert: 'yes this mysterious stirring through all those years was well matched to this immense country *around him*; as a small child he had felt its weight and that of the immense sea before him' (*FM*, 216–17) ['oui ce mouvement obscur à travers toutes ces années s'accordait à cet immense pays *autour de lui* dont, tout enfant, il avait senti la pesée avec l'immense mer devant lui'] (*PH*, 257; my italics). The fear of engulfment that permeates the early lyrical essays thus returns:

around him these people, alluring yet disturbing, near and separate, you were around them all day long, and sometimes friendship was born, or camaraderie, and at evening they still withdrew to their closed houses, where you never entered, barricaded also with their women you never saw . . . and they were so numerous . . ., they caused an invisible menace. (*FM*, 217)

[autour de lui ce peuple attirant et inquiétant, proche et séparé, qu'on côtoyait au long des journées, et parfois l'amitié naissait, ou la camaraderie, et, le soir venu, ils se retiraient pourtant dans leurs maisons inconnues, où l'on ne pénétrait jamais, barricadées aussi avec leurs femmes qu'on ne voyait jamais . . . et ils étaient si nombreux . . ., ils faisaient planer une menace invisible] (*PH*, 257–8)

Both the landscape and the ethnic Other envelop and mesmerize Cormery. In the logic of these parallel evocations, the metaphor of obscurity captures both the desire to pursue the shadowy encounter with the Other and the feared loss of cultural identity. The reactions of dread and fascination confirm the colonial mindset. This is the dangerous moment of greatest interethnic proximity in *Le Premier Homme* when, applying Bhabha's words, 'the shadow of the colonized man . . . splits [the colonizer's] presence [. . . and] repeats his action at a distance' ('Foreword', p. xiv). In a reciprocal mirroring, European and Algerian barricade themselves in their homes at night. But while the sense of silent, physical menace intensifies, the tone of longing for these abandoned, nascent friendships and unseen domestic interiors persists. Thus Camus's *petit colon* articulates his alienation and insufficiency, identifying a lack that only dialectical engagement with the Other can remedy.[59]

CHAPTER FIVE

Peripheries, public and private: Genet and dispossession

[the] strong attraction to marginality and its strange ecstasies
[l'appel à la marginalité, à ses extases singulières]

the West, which wants the Arab world to remain a race of shadows
[l'Occident pour qui le monde arabe doit rester un peuple d'om-
bres][1]

REQUIRING THE MARGINS

In his 1971 essay on *Aziyadé*, Barthes wonders what the modern-day
equivalent of Loti's defection from the West might be. The lieutenant's
counterpart a hundred years on, he speculates, could be some young
Arabophile teacher, identifying perhaps in Egypt or Morocco a phantas-
matic Orient. And just as Loti defended a declining Ottoman culture
against imperialist Russia, so Barthes's putative dissident of the 1970s
might campaign against Israeli expansion.[2] In reality, the role came to
be played by an established writer, who was indeed older than Barthes.
For around the time of the appearance of Barthes's *Nouveaux Essais critiques*, Genet was meeting secretly with Yasser Arafat in a camp near
Amman and promising to write in support of the Palestinians.[3] His testimony, *Un captif amoureux* [*Prisoner of Love*], finally appeared in May 1986,
in the month after his death and twenty-five years after the appearance
of his penultimate literary work, *Les Paravents* [*The Screens*].

While Genet exploits caricatural self-images in his earlier works – one
thinks immediately of his imprisonment, his aggressively asserted homosexuality, and his social marginality, all of which fuelled the Genet myth
that Sartre made such play of – he refuses to see social opprobrium as a
necessary condition or guarantee of artistic success. In an interview with
José Monléon in *Triunfo*, he avoids self-satisfaction, arguing that his artistic achievement is not a consequence of his biography, just as the work

of artistic superiors such as Dostoievsky, Kafka, and Proust is not dependent on their bourgeois upbringing.[4] Yet biography is centrally relevant to *Un captif amoureux*, which reflects on Genet's overtly political phase between 1968 and his death in 1986 and especially on his life with the Black Panthers and the Palestinians. As Derrida writes: '[Genet] pops up in all the world's trouble spots'.[5]

Genet delights in subverting images of seemingly impregnable cultural homogeneity. As the title of his journalistic piece on Chartres suggests, 'Chartres Cathedral – "A Cavalier View"' ['Cathédrale de Chartres – "Vue cavalière"'], he plays at reappropriating the cathedral, the legacy, he argues seditiously, of travelling medieval artisans and journeymen from many different locations: Cologne, Bruges, Burgos.[6] His fanciful speculation unsettles any self-satisfied enjoyment of a narrowly national tradition: 'Perhaps the Muslims played a part in it, . . . with Toledo only a few weeks' horse ride away' ['les musulmans y furent peut-être pour une part . . . Tolède n'étant qu'à quelques semaines de galop'] (*ED*, 191–2). The France of monarchy, he reminds his reader, was created through the sword, public burning at the stake, and the violence of the Crusades, while bourgeois, post-Revolutionary France is similarly grounded in might, although for crusade we now read colonial empire. Any pious recitation of the place-names of old becomes, he insists, a record of barbarism: 'the poets must have a sardonic grin on their faces. This thousand-year-old country smells of the stake: Albi, Montségur, Rouen, Nantes, Paris . . .: those who went to the gallows in Brittany, the drowned of Nantes, not forgetting the besieged of La Rochelle' ['les poètes doivent avoir un rictus sardonique. Ce pays millénaire sent le bûcher: Albi, Montségur, Rouen, Nantes, Paris . . .: les pendus de Bretagne, les noyés de Nantes – encore! – les assiégés de La Rochelle'] (*ED*, 195). While deliberately caricatural, Genet's cavalier history makes the point that edifying national self-images mask a legacy of barbarism.[7] The corollary to this is his proactive defence of the right to difference of Palestinians, Bangladeshis, and Africans.

Genet's appetite for vitriolic denunciation is legendary. Referring to France as a massive colonial power, he writes of being 'crushed by the concept of France' ['écrasé par le concept de France'].[8] Dramatizing his status as a one-time child in care, a product of the *Assistance Publique*, he reflects on the extent of his alienation: 'you would need not just to hate France, not just to vomit it up' ['il faudrait plus que haïr, plus que vomir la France']. He is, he speculates, perhaps 'a Black, with white or pink colouring, but a Black all the same. I do not know my family' ['un Noir qui a les couleurs blanches ou roses, mais un Noir. Je ne connais pas ma famille'].[9] In the tradition of cultural dissidence that we have been exploring, Loti's flirtation with Islam finds a modern-day correlative in the Arabophilia of Genet, whose claimed defection from France outstrips in its venomous intensity anything proposed by his exoticist predecessors.

As early as the *Journal du voleur*, published in 1948, Genet protests his Francophobia and claims a perfected social exclusion:

I could see no diversity in a social order from which I was excluded by virtue of my birth and proclivities. I admired the perfect coherence that rejected me. I was amazed at how the internal structures of a rigorous edifice worked so cohesively against me. . . . That formidable, awesome order . . . had a meaning: my exile.

[Exclu par ma naissance et par mes goûts d'un ordre social je n'en distinguais pas la diversité. J'en admirais la parfaite cohérence qui me refusait. J'étais stupéfait devant un édifice si rigoureux dont les détails se comprenaient contre moi. . . . Cet ordre, redoutable, redouté . . . avait un sens: mon exil.] (*JV*, 192–3)

Social order and the narrator's identity are depicted as polar opposites. The former guarantees and requires a marginalization that is precisely shaped and defined by this essentialized, unshakable coherence. Yet the implication in the self-portrait is that the perception of a social monolith masks the reality of its heterogeneity; and additionally, that constructing the enemy of bourgeois consensus is a *sine qua non* for the theatre of disaffection that Genet promotes. Thus, we have an assiduous cultivation of the rhetoric of exclusion but also the definition of enemies within an antagonistic interdependency.[10]

For Genet, the margins generate their own perverse compensations. Reflecting on the hardships of imprisonment in Mettray, he writes of the furtive pleasure enjoyed at the heart of institutional structures: 'And that life cultivated in the interstices was all the sweeter in that it was stolen from our torturers. By torturers, I mean not just the magistrates but also those responsible for child penal institutions' ['Et cette vie cultivée dans les interstices est d'autant plus chérie qu'elle était dérobée à nos tortionnaires. Je nomme tortionnaires non seulement les magistrats mais les responsables des bagnes d'enfants'][11] The self-dramatizing instinct never abandoned him. In an interview given at a time when he was terminally ill, he addresses his interviewer and the TV crew working there, reinforcing the line of separation in almost self-parodic terms: 'There's a norm . . . where you are located . . . and then there is a margin where I am, marginalized' ['Il y a une norme . . . où vous êtes . . . et puis il y a une marge où je me trouve, où je suis marginalisé'].[12]

Writing in 1971 in support of the Black activist George Jackson, Genet reflects on what he terms the vertiginous space in the Christian West that separates 'Man (who made Humanism possible!) and the Black' ['l'Homme (qui permit l'Humanisme!) et le Noir'].[13] In castigating a white cultural value-system, he addresses the politics inherent in the capitalization of the terms, *Homme* and *Humanisme*, just as Glissant rejects the capitalized History of the dominant.

For Genet, the Palestinians are cast outside the sphere of political respectability. So long as they remain dispossessed, he reflects provocatively, they have his support, to be withdrawn should they obtain political status (*ED*, 282). While the caveat is typically peremptory in its formulation, it again suggests Genet's uncompromising promotion of the margins as a place of inverted privilege and as a pre-condition of his support.[14] But it also signals commitment, for as Colin Davis argues, 'only where responsibility is expected can betrayal be possible'.[15] The margins offer authenticity if we accept Genet's observation that the history propagated by the West induces a form of alienation, the clear inference being that openness to alternative histories is a step beyond falsehood (*ED*, 99). Paradoxically, the urge to expose what is counterfeit preoccupies an author whose work revels in histrionics and explores the intimate connection between political power and theatricality.

ALPHABETS AND THE INSCRIPTION OF POWER

In contrast with the militant sloganizing, moments of penetrating reflection on difference inform *Un captif amoureux*, which comprises elements of travelogue, autobiography, ethnography, and philosophical and political speculation. Genet picks up repeatedly not only on language's inherent ideological contamination but also on the likely limits of his intervention as an outsider in Middle Eastern politics. Intrigued by the threshold between inside and outside, he strives to uncover the interconnectedness of these two styles of living. He questions the separation of Self and Other, inferring the porosity of the categories and seeing in racism the return of the repressed.[16] The margins become, then, the space in which access to what society rejects becomes possible. Genet likens ethnic and national divisions to forms of theatre accommodating privileged inclusions and aggressive exclusions. In particular, he cites the disputed Occupied Territories in Israel and Alsace-Lorraine, identifying these contested interstitial locations as places of possibility, enrichment, and plenitude. The intolerant Jacobin within us who insists on defending borders disappears, he says, as we approach the frontier, along and beyond which totality is possible (*PL*, 146–7; *CA*, 244–5).

Alert to the grammar of centre and periphery, Genet identifies the potential for heterogeneity and sedition within the Self. An alternative, decentred position emerges as the inclusive space capable of retrieving what the centre represses. In *L'Anus solaire*, Bataille reflects on how bourgeois class snobbery is plotted on to the contours of the body. In his uncompromising formulation, 'those in whom the force of eruption is concentrated are necessarily situated below. To the bourgeois, Communist workers are as ugly and dirty as the sexual and lower parts [of the body].'[17] Genet confirms the point anecdotally by pointing to Orientalist leitmotifs in French television advertising of the 1980s. While he finds no overt mocking of Arab culture, he detects a clear subtext concerning the otherness of Arabism. In addition to exotic images of Orientals typically flying on carpets, he cites the example of an advertisement that links camels defecating and the appearance in the desert of a giant packet of Camel cigarettes. For Genet, Western fantasies entail a projection on to the East of the repressed, 'what . . . we can't face up to in ourselves' (*PL*, 257) ['ce que nous n'osons pas voir en nous'] (*CA*, 421).

The Self's need of the Other is graphically illustrated in his reflections on cultural exclusion in the United States:

> In white America the Blacks are the characters in which history is written. They are the ink that gives the white page a meaning. If they ever disappear the United States will be nothing but itself to me, and not a struggle growing more and more dramatic. (*PL*, 213)

> [Les Noirs en Amérique blanche sont les signes qui écrivent l'histoire; sur la page blanche ils sont l'encre qui lui donne un sens. Qu'ils disparaissent, les États-Unis pour moi ne seront plus qu'eux seuls et non le combat dramatique qui devient de plus en plus ardent.] (*CA*, 350)

Sense is thus generated through the imbrication of black and white, the inference being that the white world is incapable of autonomous meaning and existence. In the dialectical processes of history, social advantage necessarily calls up a legacy of suppression, collective amnesia giving way to group memory. Genet's specific insistence on a writerly metaphor recalls the opening line of *Un captif amoureux*, where a Mallarmean 'The page that was blank to begin with . . .' ['La page qui fut d'abord blanche . . .'] becomes rapidly politicized as the author queries the extent to which his work might fail to capture the reality of the Palestinian struggle:

Was the Palestinian revolution really written on the void, an artifice superimposed on nothingness, and is the white page, and every little blank space between the words, more real than the black characters themselves? (*PL*, 3)

[La révolution palestinienne fut-elle écrite sur le néant, un artifice sur du néant, et la page blanche, et chaque minuscule écart de papier blanc apparaissant entre deux mots sont-ils plus réels que les signes noirs?] (*CA*, 11)

The dilemma is not about the limits of mimesis in a dehistoricized setting, *à la* Mallarmé. Rather, the alphabet of black letters on the white page signals explicitly a history of social rejection, the victory of *la page blanche* spelling the triumph of white Occidental hegemony.

Genet proposes variants on the metaphor, speculating that reality lies between the separate letters of the Hebrew alphabet, and retracting the idea that Blacks are the characters on the white page of America. Meaning, he says, falls down the gap between words, and he gives fanciful, arbitrary expression to the idea of in-betweenness when he concedes: 'the truth really lies where I can never quite know it, in a love between two Americans of different colour' (*PL*, 3) ['la réalité étant surtout dans ce que je ne saurais jamais précisément, là où se joue le drame amoureux entre deux Américains de couleur différente'] (*CA*, 12).

The *art poétique* that opens *Un captif amoureux* thus becomes an *art politique*, in which Genet scrupulously points to the limits of his ability to represent the Palestinian revolution. He concedes that its real import may have completely eluded him. Nevertheless, his anxious interrogation of language and representation remains an overtly political statement and becomes potentially a point of departure for sustained, ethical reflection on the West's dismissal of the Other.[18] In the same way, he comments that the black words on the white American page are sometimes erased, but that it is precisely the disappeared, *les disparus*, who form the poem. Ironically, white America, though politically hegemonic, provides the encompassing margin, this time of the page, and the poem 'is written by the absent Blacks – the dead, if you like – the nameless . . . Blacks who wrote the poem, of which the meaning escapes me but not the reality' (*PL*, 218) ['est composé par les noirs absents – vous direz les morts . . . anonymes et dont l'agencement constitue le poème et dont le sens m'échappe mais non sa réalité'] (*CA*, 358). Disappearance, visibility, and meaning born of cultural imbrication are all central, then, to Genet's reflections on power. But in his aggressive politicization of the Mallarmean paradigm, he proposes an inevitable connection between white and black, authority and marginalization. In a picture of continual outmanoeuvring, white power, having been subverted by exclusion, moves in turn to contain that exclusion.

LIBERATION POLITICS, SEXUAL LIBERATION

Being is given to us in an intolerable outflanking of being.

(Bataille)[19]

If the Western bourgeoisie represses what is unpalatable, Genet's evocation of violent Palestinian protest against Israel and its allies is regularly presented as the return of the repressed, in both political and sexual terms. An arresting example of militarism being overlaid with sexual radicalism involves his reflection on the tradition of suicide-bombings. Two Arab women, one an eighty-year-old, the other sixteen, take their own lives in separate attacks on enemy soldiers. The old woman, wearing a corset containing grenades, walks tearfully towards the Amal soldiers who have been firing heavily on the Palestinians and who now move to comfort her; the girl approaches a group of Israeli soldiers. Genet is intrigued by the joyous preparations for the funerals of these female warriors, the militant Islamic suicides prefacing a glorious rebirth. He dramatically conflates his fascination with these reincarnations and Mozart's *Requiem*, which he is listening to on a walkman in his hotel room. In a glorious excision of a Christian setting – there is no church, no cemetery, no priest, no incense, he insists – the Mozart is interwoven with Muslim ceremonial for the dead: 'at the sound of the *Kyrie*, I started to hear a pagan madness' (*PL*, 52) ['dès le *Kyrie* j'entendis une folie païenne'] (*CA*, 89). The troglodytes dance with joy to greet the dead woman. 'Gaiety', 'laughter', 'freedom' (*PL*, 52) ['gaieté', 'hilarité', 'liberté'] (*CA*, 90) are the terms used to capture this extreme moment of release and rebirth.

But the commemoration is doubly provocative, Genet intensifying the momentousness of the occasion through an arresting lateral connection with a young man's sex change, seen as simultaneously monstrous and heroic: 'a joy close to madness when he refers to himself as "she" instead of "he"' (*PL*, 52) ['une joie proche peut-être de la démence quand, parlant de soi il ne dira plus "il" mais "elle"'] (*CA*, 90–1). In this crescendo that is both religious and sexual, collective and intimate, Genet confronts his European addressee with allied forms of miraculous transitionality:

'I am filled with thy joy . . .' 'Farewell to half of me – I die to myself . . .'
    To leave behind the hated but familiar masculine ways is like forsaking the world and going into a monastery or a leper-house. To quit the world of trousers for the world of the brassiere is a kind of death, expected but feared. And isn't it also comparable to suicide, with choirs singing the 'Tuba Mirum'? [. . .] What prevailed was the joy of the transsexual, of the *Requiem*, of the kamikaze. Of the hero. (*PL*, 52–3)

['Ta joie m'inonde . . .' 'Adieu chère moi-même, je meurs à moi-même . . .'
Quitter la démarche virile abhorrée mais connue, c'est laisser le monde pour
le carmel ou la léproserie, quitter l'univers du pantalon pour celui du soutien-
gorge, c'est l'équivalent de la mort attendue mais redoutée et n'est-ce pas
comparable au suicide afin que les chœurs y chantent le *Tuba mirum*?. [. . .]
Joie du transsexuel, joie du *Requiem*, joie du kamikaze . . . joie du héros.] (*CA*,
91)

Private sexual fantasy and public religious ritual are thus overlaid in a
baroque collage of asceticism, destruction, reincarnation, high culture,
and contingent details of Western dress codes. The configuration provides an eloquent example of what Edmund White calls 'the incorrigible
subjective voice that can never be factored into the consensus'.[20] The
cultivation of excess and transgression recalls forcefully Bataille's
preface to *Madame Edwarda*: 'excess is the process whereby being is first
and foremost beyond all limits' (p. 21). The collapsing of borders and categories is thus integral to Genet's dissidence. Similarly, the extremes of
both sexual and religious emotion echo Bataille's observation on the
excesses inherent in pleasure: 'Pleasure would be contemptible if it did
not entail this crushing sense of outflanking [*dépassement*] that is not
exclusive to sexual ecstasy and that the mystics of different religions . . .
have also known' (p. 16).

Genet's reconfigurations provide a radical variant on the quest for
sexual identity in Proust's *Recherche*. For the latter, mapping homosexuality involves a gesturing to the colonial margins. But Proust's hesitant,
oblique subversion becomes the iconoclasm of *Un captif amoureux*. Genet
riskily calls up delirious forms of self-transformation and weaves
together two very different struggles: one involving the politics of gender,
the other, violent Palestinian insurrection. He is at his most mercurial in
these forms of deliberately shocking convergence, where earnest
affiliation to a political cause mutates anarchically into joyous cham-
pioning of the isolated transsexual heroically negotiating new borders of
the body.

The conjoining of social insurrection and sexual transformation
returns in a lengthy description of the workings of Israeli intelligence.
Sexual disguise, Genet notes, is the key weapon in the synchronized killings of three Arab activists, all members of Fatah. In each case, their
assassins are disguised as pairs of transvestite homosexual lovers, who
scandalously embrace outside the homes of the victims before overpow-
ering the guards and carrying out the executions. Genet marvels at the
bravado with which trained soldiers have perfected their lovers' act and

at their meticulous attention to dress, body language, and speech; in short, this is consummate theatre. As he comments wryly, 'And like all works carried out under the aegis of the Beaux-Arts, Murder deserves a medal or two. I imagine six chests were duly decorated' (*PL*, 158–9) ['Comme toute œuvre distinguée par les Beaux-Arts, l'Assassinat exige une décoration, ou plusieurs. Je suppose qu'elles furent accrochées sur six thorax'] (*CA*, 263).

A scandalous form of sexual behaviour provides the cover, then, for counter-insurrection. Notwithstanding Genet's professed Palestinian sympathies, he injects a note of lyrical beauty into these unconventional, ruthless undercover operations. True to his art of 'baroque delirium', he invites his reader to consider the plight of the *authentic* transvestite – the interplay of illusion and reality is acute here – alongside the secret agents who masquerade as such:[21]

The inward laughter of transvestites who never ceased feeling like men may have echoed the terror of real transvestites, afraid of being found out through their voices and gestures. (*PL*, 160)

[Le rire intérieur des travestis qui n'ont cessé de se sentir virils correspondait peut-être à la terreur des vrais travestis qui redoutent d'être découverts à cause de leurs voix . . . comme leurs gestes.] (*CA*, 266)[22]

The layers of disguise and subterfuge in the world of counter-insurrection generate an intense and provocative theatricality. The use of transvestism again demonstrates how imperatives of gender radicalize the representation of militarism and *raison d'état*. Yet by interweaving state terror and sexual pleading, Genet practises a form of exoticism, in which the representation of Middle Eastern *realpolitik* competes with wilful subjectivism. He speculates, arguably parasitically, on the bizarre theatre of the incident: 'The strangeness of their situation lay in the gentle feminine delicacy of their movements, and their transformation from one moment to the next into the precise gestures of murderers – not murderesses' (*PL*, 160) ['Toute l'étrangeté de leur situation venait de la douceur, de la délicatesse féminine de leurs gestes qui, d'un moment à l'autre, avec précision, deviendraient gestes de tueurs, pas de tueuses'] (*CA*, 266–7). The combination of clinical tactical efficiency and sexual taboo, like the invocation of the suicide bombers, underlines how unremittingly personal fantasies are mapped on to the narrative of political and military upheaval. In this powerful interpellation, Genet jolts his reader out of both Eurocentrism and heterosexist complacency.

APPROPRIATION AND EMPATHY

When, with characteristic unpredictability, Genet asserts that he would cease to offer the Palestinians support were they to obtain nationhood, he is flirting with unadulterated exoticist appropriation. This is his provocative way of refusing any form of recuperation, either for himself or the Palestinians, to whom he feels an emotional and sensual attachment. Nevertheless, we need to remember the circumstances in which Genet asked: 'But would I love them were injustice no longer turning them into a vagabond people?' ['Mais les aimerais-je si l'injustice n'en faisait pas un peuple vagabond?'][23] He wrote 'Four hours in Shatila' ['Quatre heures à Chatila'] in September–October 1982, in the weeks following the massacre of Palestinian civilians in Beirut by Lebanese Christian militia, operating under the eyes of the Israeli army of occupation. Genet was in Beirut at the time and was one of the first Western witnesses of the carnage. His powerful testimony is an attempt to exorcize the brutal horror of the event.[24] In the light of this genocidal violence, his insistence on the continuing marginalization of the Palestinians may be read as an expression of love *in extremis* from a writer who himself resisted recuperation back into a domestic cultural context.

Genet underscores the conjunction of love and death in his textual response to the massacres:

Love and death. The two terms immediately go together when one of them is written. I had to go to Shatila to witness the obscenity of love and the obscenity of death. In both cases, the bodies have no longer anything to hide: the postures, the contortions, the gestures, the signs, even the silences are common to both worlds.

[L'amour et la mort. Ces deux termes s'associent très vite quand l'un est écrit. Il m'a fallu aller à Chatila pour percevoir l'obscénité de l'amour et l'obscénité de la mort. Les corps, dans les deux cas, n'ont plus rien à cacher: postures, contorsions, gestes, signes, silences mêmes appartiennent à un monde et à l'autre.] (*ED*, 245)

Thus Genet not only offers a social testimony grounded in the first-hand witnessing of a genocidal act but includes in his account the twin disfigurements of death and love, thus doubly provoking his reader, who is made to confront what the bourgeois traditionally represses.

Critics have defended the author of *Un captif amoureux* against the charge of imaginative parasitism. The Moroccan novelist Tahar Ben Jelloun invokes what he sees as Genet's excluded body: 'Alone in the society that cursed him, Jean Genet has links, but to territories elsewhere'.[25] Similarly, the suggestion that Genet might cynically see in distant *causes célèbres* an opening for insulting a domestic audience is rebutted by Malgorn: 'These texts . . . are not political blank cheques in favour of vaguely exotic causes.'[26] For these commentators, then, Genet's unrelenting campaigning on behalf of the Palestinians escapes the charge of Orientalist self-indulgence. Still, the danger remains that the only forum for the accommodation and representation of the Palestinian struggle is the caricaturally scandalous literary margins occupied by a sexual and moral outlaw. It is as though Genet, scourge of the French establishment, provides a protected space in which to address the explosive Palestinian question. Or, to reformulate the Orientalist paradigm, the only available conduit for causes that threaten Occidental hegemony must double up as a channel for the representation of sexual taboo. Like the contours of Bataille's bourgeois body, the West's distinction between the morally tolerable and intolerable continues to be rigorously defined.

Genet's crusading on behalf of perceived enemies of European values drew the ferocious responses that he no doubt aimed to solicit. In an article of September 1977 entitled 'Violence et brutalité', he scandalized huge sections of the French media by acting as apologist for the militant Red Army Faction in Germany. Jacques Henric slates Genet for his failure to set on record Soviet repression and wonders if, now that sex has become taboo in Genet's writing, political extremism will permit a redirection of sexual energies.[27] Coincidentally, Henric's provocative conflation of libidinal and political imperatives anticipates the subversive combination of sexual and political radicalism that features in *Un captif amoureux*.

GENET THE JANISSARY

When Genet speaks on the plight of immigrants, it is, in the words of Malgorn, not to espouse artificially their cause but to expose the bad conscience of Western history. For Malgorn, the dissident's arguments are affective in that they attack the emotional roots of xenophobia.[28] In *Un captif amoureux*, Genet remains alert to the pitfalls of Orientalism. He confesses to having served, albeit incompetently, as a soldier in Syria in the 1930s, thereby qualifying, he notes humorously, for the role of janissary to the colonizer (*PL*, 333; *CA*, 545). Coming a century after Loti, whose novels were required reading for colonial functionaries and adventurers, Genet mockingly casts himself as guide to Occidental readers of the East. Yet unlike Loti, his role was sanctioned by his Palestinian hosts, who saw him as being well placed to influence opinion in the West.[29]

As an escort-cum-writer, Genet persistently disabuses his public. He criticizes, for example, the manner in which the Palestinian refugee camps with their variegated colours and desert locations have become aestheticized and appropriated by the media:

> We oughtn't to have let their ornamental appearance persuade us the tents were happy places. We shouldn't be taken in by sunny photographs [in glossy magazines]. A gust of wind blew the canvas, the zinc, and the corrugated iron all away, and I saw the misery plain. (*PL*, 12)

> [Nous devions nous défendre contre cette élégance qui eût pu nous faire croire que le bonheur était là, sous tant de fantaisie, tout de même qu'il faut regarder avec défiance les photos des camps au soleil sur le papier glacé des magazines de luxe. Un coup de vent fit tout voler, voiles, toiles, zinc, tôle, et je vis au jour le malheur.] (*CA*, 26)

Genet cautions against a European bourgeois fantasy consuming exploitatively these commodified images of difference. The West's visual sense is indulged and pampered, and a screen thrown over the dereliction of what is persistently viewed as a distant, mythical community.

In Europe's cavalier discarding of nomadic groupings and the unresolved conflicts they symbolize, Genet paints a picture of sedentary indifference. The inhabitants of the camps become

> the discarded refuse of 'settled' nations. These, not knowing how to get rid of their 'liquid waste', discharge it into a valley or on to a hillside, preferably somewhere between the tropics and the equator. . . . the fortified countries and cities, tied to the ground like Gulliver, made use of their nomads – the privateers, the navigators, the Magellans, Vasco da Gamas and Ibn Battutas; the explorers, the centurions, the surveyors – they despised them too. (*PL*, 12)

> [les détritus de nations 'assises'. Ne sachant comment évacuer 'leurs eaux usées', elles les ont abandonnées dans une vallée, sur le flanc d'une colline, et plutôt entre les tropiques et l'équateur . . . les villes et les nations fortifiées, captives au sol de la même façon que Gulliver, si elles utilisèrent leurs nomades: corsaires, navigateurs, magellans, gamas, batoutas, explorateurs, centurions, arpenteurs, les utilisaient en les méprisant.] (*CA*, 25)

Genet offers a scatological restatement of the interconnectedness whereby the Other embodies what the Self represses or discards. He shuttles between opposing positions, decrying European oppression while constructing a celebratory glossary of that tradition's marauding adventurers – who were themselves excluded by their contemporaries.

In his ambiguous linguistic pleasure-taking, he gets promiscuously under the skin of persecutor and persecuted alike.

Genet's pleasure is not restricted, then, to the depiction of dissidents. Television coverage of mass Muslim funerals with coffins being carried aloft becomes a media event rivalling the appeal of huge sporting occasions. He himself confesses that Nasser's funeral in Egypt, with the coffin of the leader borne aloft by the huge crowd, is reminiscent of a rolling maul performed by the New Zealand All Black rugby team: 'I couldn't help thinking of a World Cup in Oriental Funerals' (*PL*, 6) ['Je ne pouvais pas ne pas penser à une Coupe du monde des Enterrements orientaux'] (*CA*, 16). Social and cultural difference is thus converted into visual commodity. The peripheral is divested of political impact and trivialized as bizarre, exotic spectacle. Similarly the Palestinian freedom fighters, the fedayeen, who die for the cause, satisfy the imperious appetite of Western television, which remains indifferent to the significance of the fedaye's self-sacrifice or *don de soi* (*PL*, 124; CA 206). Ensconced in our comfortable domestic interiors, Genet reflects, we turn the page of the newspaper or change frequency on the radio to shut out Asia. The armchair spectator thus performs a banal act of political exclusion.

Sensitive to the ethics of writing about the Other, Genet wonders about the perception that Palestinians might have of him: 'But what did they mean to do with this grey head, with its grey skin, grey hair, grey unshaven beard – this grey, pink, round head forever in their midst?' (*PL*, 83) ['Mais de cette tête blanche, blanche par sa peau, ses cheveux, sa barbe non rasée, blanche, rose et ronde toujours présente au milieu d'eux que voulaient-ils faire?'] (CA 138). Becoming the object of the Palestinian gaze, he inverts the Eurocentric logic that turns the East into spectacle.

Reflecting on the analogous context of his active collaboration with the Black Panther Movement in the late 1960s and early 1970s, Genet writes effusively of his self-realization:

It was like the fulfilment of an old childhood dream, in which strangers, foreigners – but probably more like me than my own compatriots – opened up a new life to me.

This childishness, almost innocence, was forced on me by the Panthers' kindness, which it seemed to me they bestowed on me not as a special favour but because it was natural to them. To be adopted like a child when one was an old man was very pleasant: it brought me both real protection and education in affection. (*PL*, 83)

[Je réalisais là probablement un très vieux rêve enfantin, où des étrangers – mais au fond plus semblables à moi que mes compatriotes – m'ouvriraient à une vie nouvelle. Cet état d'enfance et presque d'innocence m'avait été imposé par la douceur des Panthères, une douceur qui ne m'était pas accordée par privilège, mais de laquelle je bénéficiais puisqu'elle était, me semblait-il, la nature même des Panthères. Or, déjà vieillard, redevenir un enfant adopté, était très agréable puisque c'est grâce à cela que je connaissais une véritable protection et une éducation affectueuse.] (*CA*, 138–9)

While we can object that the antidote to solipsism comes via oneirographic fantasy about the dispossessed, Genet's engagement with cultural difference was sustained. In an inversion of the colonialist topos in which the Other is child-like, he welcomes the undoing of his emotional orphanhood in the West through the affirmation shown him by his Black American hosts. Despite this Romantic affiliation, Genet grasps crucially the limits of his engagement. He rejects exemplary and selfless espousal of a cause, preserving an impregnable zone of separateness in spite of strong feelings of solidarity. The isolation is acutely felt when he is writing in the midst of the fedayeen. It is not his Celtic physiognomy nor some form of insulating goose fat that separates him, he says, but a stronger armour: 'I didn't belong to, never really identified with, their nation or their movement. My heart was in it; my body was in it; my spirit was in it. Everything was in it at one time or another; but *never my total belief; never the whole of myself*' (*PL*, 90) ['ma non-appartenance à une nation, à une action où je ne me confondis jamais. Le cœur y était; le corps y était; l'esprit y était. Tout y fut à tour de rôle: *la foi jamais totale et moi jamais en entier*'] (*CA*, 150; my emphasis).

The scrupulous testing of the discourse of depth and self-giving provides a gauge of Genet's empathy. While in the broad social sense, the West controls the outsider (the Panthers, the Palestinians), Genet espouses the causes of the disenfranchised while remaining in some degree distanced from the faith, the cause, the margin. The detachment is returned to when he asks if his involvement with the struggle for civil rights in the United States – he dropped everything in response to an invitation to get involved there – is not that of the 'natural sham' (*PL*, 149) ['*spontané simulateur*'] (*CA*, 248; Genet's emphasis). Theatricalization is central to self-image here and, by extension, to identification with the Other. Likewise, he sees the invitation to spend time in Palestine as a call to visit the interior of a fiction (*PL*, 149; *CA*, 248). But far from trivializing the Palestinian question, these forthright pronouncements signal Genet's self-critical engagement with the myth-making at work in political and ethnic exclusion.

VOICES AND BODIES: STYLES OF CULTURAL VENTRILOQUISM

Doubts about affiliation to the alluring cause of the marginalized are bound up with broader ontological anxieties. Genet asks if his 'hollow non-life' ['non-vie en creux'] might not further undermine the liberation struggles he is involved with, and wonders if his life might not be like that of the Black Panthers, 'a dream floating on the activity of the Whites' ['un rêve flottant sur l'activité des blancs'] (*CA*, 248).[30] Worse still, he fears being an agent for the dispersal of the cultural claims of the marginal:

a dreamer inside a dream, wasn't I just one more factor of unreality inside both movements? Wasn't I a European saying to a dream, 'You are a dream – don't wake the sleeper!' (*PL*, 149)

[rêveur à l'intérieur du rêve, n'étais-je pas, un de plus, un élément déréalisateur des Mouvements? N'étais-je pas l'Européen qui au rêve vient dire: 'Tu es rêve, surtout ne réveille pas le dormeur'?] (*CA*, 248–9)

Notwithstanding Genet's scrupulous rejection of effortless cultural identification, how appropriate is it to talk of empathy and generosity in this context? Certainly, by refusing the comfortable label of the philanthropic European, Genet problematizes his contact with excluded ethnicities. He claims that Eurocentrism acts like a vice, condemning the dissidents clamped within it to a reenforcement of Western structures. This is Genet at his most scrupulous and most self-undermining. In one sense, he sees himself as finished, destroyed by Europe. He was suffering from serious illness when writing *Un captif amoureux* and the work reflects regularly on mortality. He describes himself as being dead within, while events in the external world advance without him: 'It seemed to me the world changed around me while I stayed inside myself, certain only of having been' (*PL*, 190) ['Autour de moi, me semblait-il, le monde devenait, moi je reposais en moi, certain d'avoir été'] (*CA*, 314). The tone of recrimination is intense as he likens himself to a cadaver killed by the Catholic Church, although in a typically grand flourish, he anticipates the compensation the non-Christian world will bring: 'the cadaver of myself . . . will receive quiet homage from paganism' (*PL*, 190) ['très doucement le paganisme lui [au cadavre] rendra hommage'] (*CA*, 314).

These moments of cultural self-dramatization are offset by expressions of powerful alignment with the Palestinians. Genet associates his newfound commitment with a form of personal resurrection that is both mental and physical. At sixty, he is reinvigorated (there are echoes here of Gauguin's boasts about rejuvenation in Polynesia) and, even allowing for his frequently asserted social isolation, his engagement is energetic. The Palestinian Revolution, he announces, will become his jubilation, while Europe looks on with a mixture of sullenness and condescension:

those who fought in the cause of the Palestinians . . . were regarded in Europe as outcasts without any real identity, without any legitimate link with a recognized country, and above all without a territory belonging to them and to which they belonged, with the usual proofs of existence: cemeteries, war memorials, family trees, legends and, as I was to find out later, strategists and ideologues. (*PL*, 204)

[la cause des Palestiniens . . . était défendue par des hordes qui paraissaient à l'Europe des rassemblements de marginaux, sans véritable identité, sans lien juridique bien établi avec un État reconnu, mais surtout sans territoire bien sûr leur appartenant, mais auquel eux-mêmes appartinssent, territoire où se trouvent habituellement les preuves: cimetières, monuments aux morts, racine des noms de famille, légendes et même, ce que je saurai plus tard: stratèges et idéologues.] (*CA*, 336)

What is disregarded as peripheral, rootless, and ragbag has in fact its own genealogy and traditions, attributes that the nation-states of Europe see as their exclusive birthright. The clear inference is that the West's legality is a licence to subjugate and pillage.

Given Genet's religious and social iconoclasm, his espousal of the Palestinian cause is, on occasions, remarkably solemn and even pious. Claiming a coalescing of the liberation struggle and his own private memory, he observes that, however infantile the statement of affiliation might appear, the struggle is intimately linked to his oldest memories: '"The Koran is eternal, uncreated, consubstantial with God." Setting aside the word "God", their revolt was eternal, uncreated, consubstantial with me. Is that enough to show how important I think memories are?' (*PL*, 211) ['"Le Coran est éternel, incréé, consubstantiel à Dieu." Sauf ce mot, "Dieu", leur révolte était éternelle, incréée, consubstantielle à moi-même. Était-ce assez révéler l'importance que je donne aux souvenirs?'] (*CA*, 348). This may be another self-ironizing gesture of mock conversion. However, the wholesale adoption of a language heavy with religious connotations provides a measure of the author's willingness to embrace alterity. The claimed consubstantiality of personal memory and social identity permits the conjoining of margins and an unequivocal statement of adherence. Remarkably, Genet allows himself to be seduced by religious discourse with its uncompromising appeal to eternal truth. Reduced to a corpse by Christianity, he zealously sees himself restored in the bosom of Islam. And tellingly, the religion of the

Other (no less wedded to absolutes than the Christian mind-set that Genet derides) provides a haven for the cultural discontent. Private mythologies and imperatives thus find an important correlative in the Palestinian struggle for self-determination.

Un captif amoureux may be read as a document of love as its title suggests, with Genet in the lead role of the helpless lover, bound by his admiration for the Palestinian cause and people. Jonathan Dollimore makes the point that, for a writer whose causes have been labelled fascist and racist, 'his *Prisoner of Love* is nothing less than an affirmation of the love that Fanon envisaged and which has sometimes given the dissident their courage'.[31] Genet speculates that the book has assumed a momentum of its own, unblocking fifteen years of self-imposed reticence. Its discontinuities and fragmentation, he explains, are testimony to this effusiveness and unguarded commitment. But in this love affair, he signals a necessary re-evaluation after the intensity of the initial encounter, casting a more sober eye on the Arab world, identifying its divisions and rivalries and thereby debunking some of its cherished myths. Yet while condemned to impermanence, this distinctive alliance involving a disaffected European and an outcast people provides a vibrant example of private and public peripheries overlapping.

The closing of ranks against the West is a persistent gesture in the book. After a night during which the fedayeen successfully defend their camp at Ajloun in Jordan, Genet writes provocatively that, unlike Paris in 1940, Irbid had managed to hold out (*PL*, 170; *CA*, 282).[32] Or again the Palestinians, curious about life in the United States, are entertained by his improbable account of skyscrapers where people defecate at all times of the day and night (*PL*, 223; *CA*, 366). This excremental vision of life in the Western metropolis confirms the place of slapstick in Genet's armoury and recalls his earlier works in which scatology signals a strident refusal of bourgeois respectability.[33] But with typical unpredictability, Genet constructs moments in the text when European high culture and Arab popular ritual coalesce. The rhythmic tapping on the side of the coffins of dead comrades-in-arms, for example, forms a recurring motif in what for Genet is the almost joyful passage in the Kyrie of Mozart's *Requiem* (*PL*, 179; *CA*, 297). The hybridization of aesthetic and political elements marks an oblique engagement with alterity, as Self and Other are drawn into eccentric dialogue.

Genet's self-doubting appears in the description of the bodies of two deceased freedom-fighters for whom he feels a sexual attraction. Dispelling ambiguity, he points out that there was no exploitation during his cohabitation with the guerrillas: 'Prostitution was absent and so was desire' (*PL*, 178) ['la prostitution était absente et tout désir l'était'] (*CA*, 295). By scrupulously addressing the vexed issue of a predatory hedonism, he asserts his sexual responsibility. The imperative is clear: 'to show the kind of self-censorship that hovers over me whenever I write about the Palestinians' (*PL*, 178) ['ne jamais perdre de vue qu'une sorte d'autocensure ne cesse de me surveiller dès que j'écris sur les Palestiniens'] (*CA*, 295).

The emphatic way in which these scruples are voiced marks the contradiction between duty and desire that Genet was singularly aware of. Tangible evidence of this tension lies in the spectacle provided by the bruised body of Hamza, one of the fedayeen tortured by Jordanian troops and for whom Genet develops a special affection:

Hamza's torture-blackened legs, nothing but two huge wounds, were enough for me, though I'd never seen them and knew *they belonged more to the Palestinian people than to me.* (*PL*, 264)

[Les jambes de Hamza noircies par la torture, les plaies qu'étaient ses deux jambes jamais vues, me suffisaient, sachant pourtant que *deux jambes torturées appartenaient plus à la communauté palestinienne qu'à moi.*] (*CA*, 432; my emphasis)

Attracted by Hamza, Genet ambivalently checks his emotion, insisting on the chaste non-spectacle of the Palestinian's body; and in a conscious self-effacement, he acknowledges the greater cause of collective Palestinian grieving.[34] He thus gauges the parameters of European empathy and the concomitant risks of cultural voyeurism. But in wanting to restore the body of Hamza to the dispossessed community, he consciously works to reverse a violent misappropriation. Unlike many of his exoticist predecessors, Genet is highly lucid about these difficulties, commenting deftly on the scope and impact of *Un captif amoureux*: '[may the book] weigh less than the furtive gleam of a fedayee stealing away from Ajloun' (*PL*, 332) ['qu[e le livre] pèse moins que la rougeur furtive du feddai se sauvant d'Ajloun'] (*CA*, 543). The statement marks a nimble attempt to deflect the charge of an expropriative European imaginary.

The same quest for stoicism is reflected in a roll call of honour for those whose acts of defiance against the West, commonly seen as acts of terrorism, are synonymous with sacrificial greatness: Saint-Just, the Black Panthers, the Baader Meinhof, the fedayeen. Genet celebrates the very provisionality of their actions, captured as 'brief flashes against a world wrapped up in its own smartness' (*PL*, 179) ['de brefs éclairs sur un monde aux élégances épaisses'] (*CA*, 297), as well as the exuberance and joy that these ephemeral lives impart. Transparency and elation, lived intensely and fleetingly, thus stand in confrontation with the opaque, sedentary refinements of the dominant.

In the same vein, the Palestinian revolution is conceived of as an isolated body with diminished internal circulation, living a painful diaspora and contending with attacks from all sides (*PL*, 200; *CA*, 329–30). Dispossession engenders depression, the corollary being that the search for autonomy mirrors the quest for mental and physical health: 'Homeland and health were lacking' (*PL*, 265) ['La nation et la santé étaient à retrouver'] (*CA*, 433). A pathology would thus be remedied with the securing of nationhood.

Refusing to see the Palestinian question as a form of spectator sport, Genet protests that the revolution reverberates within him (*PL*, 264; *CA*, 432). Deeply ingrained cultural differences nevertheless persist, Eastern and European attitudes to death, for example, accentuating the cultural divide. Thus his commemoration of an individual soldier runs counter to the collectivization of loss that marks the Palestinian struggle. Hence one combatant's reproach: 'You can't mourn just one fedayee' (*PL*, 265) ['Tu ne peux pas porter le deuil d'un seul feddai'] (*CA*, 434).

Culturally sanctioned forms of group identity help underline Genet's marginal position. In his commemoration of Hamza and his mother, the couple who come to dominate *Un captif amoureux*, he opts for Western-style individualization. Nevertheless, betrayal, which elsewhere Genet brazenly proposes, now assumes awesome proportions for a writer keen to promote the Palestinian cause.[35] Struggling to honour adequately the memory of Abou Omar, one of the strategists in the struggle, he is seized with grave misgivings:

Is it a ghost speaking? I'm not sure I haven't made him into a marionette, the sort of doll whose slack lips showmen, and liars too, manipulate. It's difficult not to play the ventriloquist when you're making a drowned man, or a man who was shot, talk. (*PL*, 306)

[Est-ce une ombre qui parle? Je ne suis pas sûr de n'avoir pas fait de lui une marionnette dont par les moyens des montreurs, des menteurs aussi, j'en fais bouger les lèvres molles. Il est difficile de n'être pas ventriloque quand on fait parler un noyé ou un fusillé.] (*CA*, 500)

Political and affective sympathy for the marginalized ensures Genet's scrupulous exploration of the culture confronting him in *Un captif amoureux*. In that sense, the ventriloquism that he fears encompasses not just the living speaking about the dead but also the West's impersonation of the East.

LANGUAGE AND AUTHORITY

The stealing or masking of voices can be tied to other manipulations of language that Genet identifies. As the West appropriates the discourse of moral authority, Israel wins the war of words against those labelled terrorists. The point is confirmed in Genet's ironic bow to what he labels that country's linguistic acuity:

Very smart of Israel to carry the war right into the heart of vocabulary, and annex the words holocaust and genocide. The invasion of Lebanon didn't make Israel an intruder or predator. The destruction and massacres in Beirut weren't the work of terrorists armed by America. . . . Words are terrible, and Israel is a terrifying manipulator of signs. (*PL*, 325–6)

[Admirable Israël portant la guerre au cœur même du vocabulaire afin d'annexer . . . le mot holocauste et le mot génocide. . . . L'invasion du Liban ne fit d'Israël l'intrus ni le prédateur; la destruction ni les massacres de Beyrouth ne furent les actes de terroristes armés par l'Amérique. . . . Les mots sont terribles en ce sens qu'Israël est un terrifiant manipulateur de signes.] (*CA*, 532–3)

Discursive power enables the oppressor to monopolize moral value and authority. Continuing his metalinguistic speculation, Genet proposes an indictment of the social exclusion and racism institutionalized in the French language. In a settling of old scores, he evokes the spectacle of French refugees fleeing from the Nazis. Whereas he is scrupulous and empathic in his evocation of Palestinian suffering, the plight of France in 1940 awakens no such generosity of feeling. The sight of a French refugee carefully untying a cardboard case of clothes prompts Genet to reflect that something of the same care has gone into the compilation of the nation's language:

how careful this sensitive nation is of its language, in which Berber means barbarian, hashischin an assassin, Andalou a vandal, Apache an apache. . . . (*PL*, 337)

[comme ce peuple délicat prend soin de sa langue où: Berbère égale barbare, hachischin, assassin, Andalou, vandale, Apache, apache. . . .] (*CA*, 552)

In Genet's primarily linguistic contestation, the debacle of 1940 becomes retribution for the tyranny laid bare by etymology. The panoply of state power includes, then, the linguistic infrastructure that delivers denigration and marginalization.

Writing *Un captif amoureux*, Genet confesses to seeing France as increasingly remote. Unlike the East, it becomes shrouded in mist as he asserts: 'And I became a stranger, a foreigner, to France' (*PL*, 338) ['Et je devins étranger à la France'] (*CA*, 553). Genet does not idealize his role. In protesting that his intention is not to betray the facts (*PL*, 308; *CA*, 504), he disregards mimetic fidelity, conceding that he brings to his narrative on Palestine his own emotional baggage, a conjunction that is presented in almost oneiric terms. The disparate nature of his fractured existence fuses with what he terms the continuity of Palestinian life, and he concludes frankly: 'This is *my* Palestinian revolution, told in my own chosen order. As well as mine there is the other, probably many others' (*PL*, 309) ['*ceci est ma révolution palestinienne* récitée dans l'ordre que j'ai choisi. À côté de la mienne il y a l'autre, probablement les autres'] (*CA*, 504; Genet's italics).

In his review of *Un captif amoureux*, Bertrand Poirot-Delpech justifiably sets Genet's promotion of Palestine squarely within the French exotic tradition of Loti, Gide, Montherlant, Céline, and Malraux.[36] Yet it would be oversimplifying to see him merely replicating the excesses of his predecessors. Loti offers an aggressively superficial account of non-European lifestyles, while exoticists such as Montherlant struggle to develop an inchoate ethics of difference. Genet is both more versatile and self-aware, pluralizing perspectives and developing what in another context Clifford calls 'an "ethnography" of conjunctures'.[37] He expresses a political engagement that encompasses both engaged reportage on the Palestinians and a far-reaching interrogation of French domestic culture.[38] And much more actively than his predecessors, he spells out, sporadically and yet incisively, the ethical dilemmas raised by exoticist identification.

STAGES OF IDENTITY

The mythologies that sustain the West ideologically are repeatedly targeted in *Un captif amoureux*. In conversation with the Sudanese soldier Moubarak, who fights on the side of the Palestinians, Genet discovers the conceptual gap separating European and African. For Moubarak, the revolution must remain all trance and dance, with rationalizing seen as a bizarre, foreign instinct (*PL*, 296–7; *CA*, 484). While the risk of an exoticist caricature of African attitudes is clear, the exchange enables Genet to establish critical detachment from the rationalist teleology of European narrative. He dismantles many of his ingrained attitudes and links himself to Moubarak, as the latter reconstructs his abandoned childhood in a way that mirrors Genet's own. And when we remember Genet's quip that he himself is a black with pink skin, we can appreciate the transracial bonding:

I'd been thinking only of my own solitude, but now Moubarak's suddenly struck me. If he wore his colour and his ritual scars arrogantly, it was because they were the symbol of his uniqueness here, and of a loneliness that abated a little only when he was with me. (*PL*, 195)

[Alors que je ne songeais qu'à la mienne, la solitude de Moubarak . . . me sautait à la gorge. S'il portait avec arrogance sa couleur et ses cicatrices rituelles, c'est qu'elles étaient la marque, ici, d'une singularité, donc sa solitude, qui ne cessait un peu qu'auprès de moi.] (*CA*, 322)

In a similar scene announcing Genet's reaffiliation, he recalls the visit of a group of Black Panthers to address a 3,000-strong student gathering at Yale and the ideological impasse this produces. As students betray their tribal markings in the form of a barrage of questions fine-tuned in a millennial Christian mindset (*PL*, 219; *CA*, 359), the Panthers reject the rules of European disputation that have legitimized enslavement and tyranny. Only when the edifice of rationalism crumbles, they insist, will they engage in dialogue:

'When everything's tottering, even verified verities, it makes you laugh. So we're going to laugh! Revolution is the happiest time of our lives.' (*PL*, 219)

['Quand tout chancelle, quand les vérités qui furent vérités vérifiées chancellent, cela fait rire: donc on va rire! La révolution est la période la plus joyeuse de la vie.'] (*CA*, 360)

A solemn, moribund world order ends and the moment of liberation becomes carnivalesque. Like the dancing of the blacks referred to by Moubarak, laughing becomes a weapon of contestation in the hands of the marginalized.[39]

But as Genet astutely observes, carnival is also associated with awesome state power. Television coverage of the funeral of the assassinated Egyptian President Sadat prompts Genet to reflect on the puppet-like performance of the French President. Surrounded by police bodyguards, Mitterrand moves slowly forward, so slowly that we have the impression he is gliding along on roller skates:

that carnival image. . . . The President was like a marionette . . . and it was from the police that he derived his strength. . . . But better than any theory this image showed that might came before right . . ., the second proceeding from the first via sateen sleeves. (*PL*, 254) [cette image de carnaval. . . . [L]e président, marionnetté par la police, tirait d'elle son pouvoir . . . je savais que cette image même, mieux qu'une théorie l'eût fait, était la démonstration que la force prime le droit. . . . La force précédait le droit qui, grâce à des manchons de lustrine, découlait d'elle.] (*CA*, 416–17)

Genet not only alerts the reader to the intense theatricality of the moment (the sateen sleeves are those of the puppet Mitterrand) but also sees, in the authoritarianism marking the scene, that international politics is a form of *grand guignol* with deeply serious consequences.

Beyond the staged, constructed phenomenon that is national authority, Genet is frank about his own role, conceding that, in his writing, he too is a puppet-master, resurrecting the figure of the dead Palestinian activist Abou Omar and ventriloquizing his speech. He confesses to practising this impersonation without misgivings, his reader's hypocrisy matching his own. Still, in spite of his apparent self-deprecation, he sees merit in his string-pulling: 'Through what I make him say, Abou Omar comes back to life' (*PL*, 255) ['Par ce que je lui fais dire Abou Omar *revit*'] (*CA*, 417; Genet's emphasis). Scruples about authorship, then, do not invalidate the transmission of the broader political message. But in this knowing expropriation, an ethical sensitivity to alterity is at work.

Carnival, dance, and puppeteering are all part of Genet's arsenal in the onslaught against a tradition that he is committed to excoriating. In the laughter of revolution, the mythologies underpinning nation and Europe are deconstructed. The irreverence is taken further when Genet recalls a visit to Japan in 1967 that triggers deliverance from a restrictive European coil. A solitary word of farewell pronounced by the air hostess – *sayonara* – acts as an effective antidote to layers of European culture:

The word made me feel my body being stripped bit by bit of a thick black layer of Judæo-Christian morality, until it was left naked and white. I was amazed at my own passiveness. (*PL*, 44)

[À partir de ce mot, je fus attentif à la manière dont s'enlevait par lambeaux de mon corps au risque de me laisser nu et blanc la noire et certainement épaisse morale judéo-chrétienne. Ma passivité m'étonnait.] (*CA*, 77)

The author, describing his body as having been subjected to a long and degrading siege, has anticipated that removing these cultural accretions will be traumatic, and yet the process begins with a gentle linguistic stimulus, the single word of Japanese purifying the surface of his being and releasing him from a moral system that remains, he boasts, only skin-deep.[40] While declaring his immunization, Genet still re-enacts his indoctrination and the drama of Eurocentrism.

Contesting cultural assumptions, he speaks of thumbing his nose at polite society and adopts the language of defecation to shatter the decorum masking cultural triumphalism. The writer expels from his body the 3,000-year-old worm of European civilization, and with it a burdensome morality. A hierarchy of taste is thus discarded, the scatological metaphor underscoring a cultural evacuation that is intensely liberating. As Genet says less provocatively elsewhere, the drawing of France and Europe will be erased and, in the blank space of liberty, his experience of Palestine will be inscribed (*PL*, 373; *CA*, 609).

Calculated exaggeration is part of a conscious strategy for the staging of the margins. Scanning the potentially explosive interface between cultural centre and periphery, *Un captif amoureux* regularly uncovers the theatre that underpins ideology. The connection with Genet's plays is also clear, for here too, social authority is shown to be inextricably bound up with the studied construction of appearances.[41]

RELOCATING THE CIVILIZED

If Genet criticizes the Western indifference that consigns the Palestinians to being 'a race of shadows' (*PL*, 280) ['un peuple d'ombres'] (*CA*, 458), he also looks critically at the internal politics of the Middle East. Referring to Jordanian society, in which the Palestinian refugees are despised and marginalized, he constructs a fantasticated cityscape in which the splendour of life at the royal Palace is juxtaposed with living conditions in the Palestinian shanty town and the adjoining redlight district. Insisting on the chaotic interconnectedness of palace, *bidonville*, and brothel, he provides a provocative account of this scene of radical cultural difference. In a baroque configuration, sexual desire, whether pursued in the palace or the brothel, draws together these ostensibly divorced spaces. Of the brothel, he writes:

Everyone felt relieved at his own rottenness, soothed at escaping from moral and aesthetic effort. What crawled towards the brothels was a mass of desires craving quick fulfilment. . . . If a stranger, Arab or otherwise, came here, he'd see the survival of *a closely guarded civilization*, one with a familiar, almost pious contact with rejection, with what Europe calls dirt. . . . The absence of morality scares everyone but it doesn't put them off. . . . What's needed for that: to do away with the pride of self, of having a surname, a first name, a family tree, a country, an ideology, a party, a grave, a coffin with two dates. (*PL*, 60–1)

[En pourrissant, chacun se sentait soulagé, donc apaisé, d'échapper à l'effort moral et esthétique, les bordels ne voyaient avancer vers eux qu'une reptation de désirs à

calmer vite. . . . Si l'étranger – arabe ou non – pouvait venir jusqu'ici il verrait la
survivance au bordel d'*une civilisation bien gardée*, celle du contact familier, presque
pieux avec le rejet, ce que l'Europe nomme le sale. . . . L'absence de morale effraie
mais ne dégoûte personne . . . Ce qu'il fallut pour arriver à ça, abolir la fierté d'être
soi, d'avoir un nom, un prénom, une lignée, une patrie, une idéologie, un parti, une
tombe, profiter d'un cercueil avec deux dates.'] (*CA*, 103–04; my emphasis)

Unlike the equally chaotic space of Jupien's male brothel in *Le Temps
retrouvé*, the brothels of Amman provide, in Genet's teasing formulation,
'only married, patriotic, Swiss mountain love' (*PL*, 60) ['l'amour matri-
monial, national, montagnard suisse'] (*CA*, 103)! Genet's signature is
plainly visible in this extended evocation: the sideswipe at European
good taste and heterosexuality; the denial of social role and of nationhood to the marginal; and the provocative use of oxymoron, both in the
elevation of Europe's detritus to a form of piety and in the brothel, seen
as the locus of civilized values.

While the risk is that the fantasia becomes another Orientalist cameo
à la Loti, Genet gets beyond exoticist flirtation in the scathing critique of
social division that he proposes. The baroque magnificence of the palace
forms a stage that the professional dramatist cannot resist dissecting:

Erotic fantasies were more intricate and more sought after in the bedrooms and
corridors of the Royal Palace, with its mirrors, whole walls of mirrors, in which
the smallest caress was repeated to infinity – that infinity where you can make
out every detail of a tiny ultimate image. The mirrors were set at strange angles
designed to include a view of the shanty town. Need it be said that the residents
of the Palace were more sophisticated than those of the shanty town? And did
the people of the shanty town know they were in the mind of the Palace, min-
istering to its pleasure? (*PL*, 60)

[Les fantaisies érotiques étaient plus travaillées – et recherchées – dans les chambres et les couloirs du Palais royal, où les miroirs, des murs entiers de miroirs où
la moindre caresse se reproduisait à l'infini, jusqu'à cet infini où l'oeil distingue
le détail d'une presque ultime image devenue minuscule, sous des angles inat-
tendus mais espérés pour finalement cadrer la vue qu'on désire: le bidonville.
Ou ailleurs. Faut-il dire que les gens du Palais étaient plus raffinés que ceux du
bidonville? Et ceux du bidonville savaient-ils qu'ils existaient dans la cervelle du
Palais, entretenant son plaisir?] (*CA*,103)

In this highly polemical picture of sexual decadence, Genet crafts simultaneously a piece of engaged literature and an intricate game of mirrors.
If sex as enjoyed by the stateless in the brothel is condoned as a release
from someone else's morality, scandalous indulgence in the palace is presented as confronting and requiring, at its point of climax, the concentrated, intensely visualized reality of material poverty that is the shanty

town. In engineering this elaborate play of mirrors, Genet constructs a theatre of narcissism for the palace-dwellers and identifies, though never piously, with the dispossessed of the shanty town. In his contentious, risky conflation, the uprooting of the stateless finds a perverse echo in the decentring of palace residents through erotic desire. *Un captif amoureux* thus displays a deeply radical political purpose in highlighting the twin provocations of political violence and sexual expression. At the same time, Genet obliges his Western reader to confront the world of Arab politics in terms of its internal heterogeneity and social injustice, and not as a cultural monolith lending itself to mythopoeic generalization.

PIETY AND PROVOCATION

While voicing disaffection with the West, he also problematizes any easy cultural migration. Notwithstanding his campaigning on behalf of groupings such as the Panthers and the Palestinians, he observes in an interview that, while he contests white interests, he still enjoys the protection that comes with being born white and belonging to the dominant: 'I am on both sides' ['Je suis des deux côtés'].[42] Genet revels in fanciful speculation. In a manner reminiscent of Gauguin's desire for insertion in Polynesian culture or Loti's dream of subsumption into the Ottoman Empire, he fantasizes about his adoption by the Black Panthers. 'I had a black father' (*PL*, 261) ['Mon père était noir'] (*CA*, 427), he suggests flirtatiously, referring to the young activist David Hilliard, who takes the much older Genet under his wing. But while prey to exotic fantasy, he reflects fastidiously on the limits of European engagement with a culture that has historically been denigrated. Even the best European, he says in relation to the Palestinian and other revolutions, remains a spectator looking on from a plush stage box in the theatre (*PL*, 264; *CA*, 432). In this self-castigating logic, the European is sidelined but significantly the liberation movement pursues power in a potently theatrical manner.[43]

An uneasiness regularly accompanies Genet's quest for allegiance. Following a period of absence from the Middle East, he finds himself back among the Palestinians and confesses: 'I've never thought of myself as a Palestinian. But there I was at home' (*PL*, 344) ['je ne me suis jamais cru palestinien, cependant: j'étais chez moi'] (*CA*, 562). A lucid acknowledgement of cultural difference does not exclude what, for the self-professed vagabond, is a sense of belonging.

The desire for adoption acquires mythopoeic status in *Un captif amou-reux* in the obsession with the young fedayee, Hamza, and his mother. Genet remarks on the brevity of his encounter with them (a single over-night stay, when Hamza goes off on military patrol while he, now visibly ageing, is offered hospitality by Hamza's mother). With hindsight, the episode acquires a symbolic potency for the European outsider, who can only do justice to Hamza and his mother by invoking the figures of Christ and Mary in the *Pietà*.[44] For fourteen years, he explains, he returned periodically in search of the couple, this being the central quest for the *prisoner of love* that he has become: 'That head [of Hamza's mother] was inside me' (*PL*, 353) ['Cette tête était en moi'] (*CA*, 578). The addictive search brings closure to the text.

While the encounter is reconfigured within a pointedly Judæo-Christian cultural matrix, Genet remains characteristically uneasy about the risk of a clichéd European narcissism. His instinct is deliber-ately to unsettle the cultural icon, appealing to archetypes and desanc-tifying the image by seeing it as potentially Oedipal:

Which came first, the group often known as a *Pietà*, depicting the Virgin Mary and her divine Son, or some other image farther back in time and in some place other than Europe, Judæa or Palestine? In India, perhaps. Or perhaps rather in every man.

And should so many precautions be taken against incest, if it was commit-ted, unknown to the Father, in the intermingled dreams of mother and son?

. . . it is very strange, that for me the seal, the emblem of the Palestinian Revolution was never a Palestinian hero or a victory like Karameh, but that almost incongruous apparition: Hamza and his mother. *That was the couple I needed, for in a way I'd cut it out to suit myself.* (*PL*, 176–7)

[Mais qui fut premier: le groupe souvent nommé *Pietà*, de la Vierge et de son divin Fils, ou plus haut dans le temps et ailleurs qu'en Europe, Judée et Palestine? Aux Indes, par exemple mais alors peut-être en tout homme, et faut-il tant se préserver de l'inceste s'il eut lieu, à l'insu du Père, dans la confusion des rêveries de la mère et du fils. . . . le mystère est grand ici: le sceau de la Révolution palestinienne ne me fut jamais un héros palestinien, une victoire (celle de Karameh par exemple) mais l'apparition presque incongrue de ce couple: Hamza et sa mère, et *c'est ce couple que je voulus car, en quelque sorte, je l'aurai découpé à ma mesure.*] (*CA*, 292; my italics)

Genet's ploy is deeply subversive. By allowing incest to defile the holy image of broken son and inconsolable mother, he transgressively eroti-cizes the icon. As a dissident, he remains deeply self-aware, admitting frankly that choosing the couple is an act of arbitrary excision from a broad historical continuum. Such free association does not impinge on the Palestinian Revolution, which will, he insists, pursue its independent course (*PL*, 374; *CA*, 611).

In this scrupulous self-examination, Genet confesses to the preying role of his desires. The figure of Hamza exerts an undeniable attraction on him, yet he suppresses his sexual feelings. The Palestinian experience has changed him, he asserts, in that the lexicon of social cohesion previously discarded in a spirit of revolt acquires new meaning in the Palestinian context: 'heroes, martyrs, struggle, revolution, liberation, resistance, courage . . . homeland and fraternity' (*PL*, 272) ['héros, martyrs, lutte, révolution, libération, résistance, courage . . . patrie et fraternité'] (*CA*, 445). By now entertaining the mystique surrounding such ideologically resonant terms, Genet flirts with the idea of his social incorporation. In this memorable curb on his disaffection, it is as though the Palestinians succeed in extricating him from a peripheral isolationism. Yet in concluding with stubborn elusiveness that the linguistic sign conceals vacuity ('I know there's nothing behind such words' (*PL*, 272) ['je sais que derrière de tels mots il n'y a rien'] (*CA*, 445)), Genet confirms that his affiliation is always provisional.

While doubting his ability to write the Palestinian struggle, he freely pursues forms of personal reverie that trigger suggestive cultural connections. Exploring the rhapsodic memory of being with the fedayeen in the forests near Ajloun, he proposes two working definitions of the term *fête*:

the fire that warmed our cheeks at being together despite the laws that hoped we'd have deserted one another. Or as the escape from society into a place where people were ready to fight with us against that society. (*PL*, 367)

[le feu qui nous chauffe les joues d'être ensemble malgré les lois qui nous espèrent dans la déréliction; ou encore une autre [définition]: s'échapper de la communauté afin de rejoindre un lieu où, contre elle nous retrouverons des complices.] (*CA*, 599)

Common to both definitions is the idea of the group, marginalized from without or self-marginalizing and free from the weight of law and community. Genet's privileged forest-dwellers comprise a deliberately heterogeneous band: the fedayeen gathering on the banks of the Jordan; the clandestine night-time burial of a Jew in Occupation France, with a small congregation of seven musicians, each of whom arrives silently from a different direction, before they play a piece of Offenbach and disperse without exchanging words; and the inspirational sight of the ageing mother of Hamza. They all participate in a fête that is simultaneously a form of vigil for the dead: 'In fact, every fête is at once jubilation and despair' (*PL*, 367) ['en effet, toute fête est simultanément jubilation et désespérance'] (*CA*, 599). But, in a mercurial style that recalls the brothel-keeper Jupien's talk of vice and virtue in Proust's *Recherche*, Genet, sensing too much piety, appends to his string of nighttime encounters a perverse counterpart, the night-life of the Bois de Boulogne:

Of course it's understood that the words nights, forests, septet, jubilation, desertion, and despair are the same words that I have to use to describe the goings-on at dawn in the Bois de Boulogne in Paris when the drag-queens depart after celebrating their mystery, doing their accounts and smoothing banknotes out in the dew. . . . Any celebration of a mystery is dangerous, forbidden. But when it takes place it's a fête. (*PL*, 367–8)

[Étant bien entendu que les mots nuits, forêts, septuor, jubilation, déréliction, désespérance sont les mots mêmes dont je dois me servir afin de dire les désordres au petit matin du bois de Boulogne à Paris où et quand les travelos en repartent après avoir célébré leur mystère, et qu'ils font leurs comptes, défroissant dans la rosée, les billets de banque. . . . Toute célébration d'un mystère est dangereuse; interdite mais qu'elle ait lieu c'est la fête.] (*CA*, 600)

This provocative rhapsody is a celebration of marginal figures, excluded on account of their religion and ethnicity (the Jew), their armed resistance (the Palestinians), their exemplary dedication (the Mother straight out of a *Pietà*), their dubious occupation (the drag-queens of the Bois de Boulogne). In this poignant and baroque analogizing, Genet revels in the dangers of perverse collocation. By drawing together exemplary mother and transvestite, Jewish burial ritual and prostitution, he plays with transgressive dislocation and outlawed pleasure. What society dismisses as moral dereliction, Genet reconstructs as mystical celebration.

*

The extended reflection on the marginalization of the Palestinians and the Black Panthers in *Un captif amoureux* is simultaneously an analysis of Western culture and of the myths, icons, and language that sustain it. In the text's regular metalinguistic interludes, Genet reviews glossaries of exclusion; he contests the hegemony of heterosexism; he invokes European cultural icons and norms (the tradition of the *Pietà*, the Mozart, the reflections on baroque art); he performs a visual analysis of Western leaders on the so-called world stage (a metaphor that Genet reinvigorates by exploring incisively the theatre inherent in political power). As a trenchant cultural analyst, he underlines the necessary interrelatedness of Middle East and West, of Black and White, of

would-be centre and margins, health and detritus. The point is illustrated in a December 1983 interview for Austrian radio, in which Genet
concurs with Layla Shahid that the Palestinian question has its roots in
the Jewish question, that Europe's shameful legacy of anti-semitism has
been transported to Palestine, now a dumping ground for the by-products of European political calamity.[45] It is the return of the political
repressed at a geographical remove.

Critics have often delighted in denying Genet his right to difference
by asserting his inalienable Frenchness.[46] Yet he energetically counters
Western complacency and conveys metaphorically the appeal of the
Other. Acting as antidote to the heaviness of the Occident is his idea of
a playful lightness. Crucially, he does not equate such play with an
absence of impact nor are its adherents condemned to oblivion. The
lightness of the fedayeen is for Genet a mark of their strength: 'The fact
that they were like ghosts, appearing and disappearing, lent them a life
more powerful than that of things . . . whose image is there all the time'
(*PL*, 302) ['D'être ainsi, spectres apparaissant, disparaissant, leur donnait
cette force convaincante d'une existence plus forte que les objets dont
l'image demeure'] (*CA*, 493). Similarly, his minute description of the
elaborate gestures of Palestinian card-players and dice-throwers is not
intended to trivialize difference but rather to convey liberation from
restrictive utilitarianism. Seeing the Other as a dream floating on the
surface of Western reality, appealing to the flagrant emptiness of gesture
and the ephemerality of appearance, to the revolution as a 'poetical
revolt, an "act"' (*PL*, 149) ['révolte poétique et jouée'] (*CA*, 248) or as
theatre predicated on an absence of being (*PL*, 263; *CA*, 430) – these are
Genet's highly imaginative and often ludic ways of celebrating cultural
difference.

The same off-centredness is invoked in more private contexts.
Beyond forms of political exclusion working at a global level, he especially surveys hierarchies in Western sexual morality. Manoeuvres such
as his conflation of suicide bomber and transsexual have prompted the
criticism that his engagement is capricious and subjectivist. Layla
Shahid, however, rejects the idea that Genet's campaigning on behalf
of the Palestinians gave oblique expression to his homosexuality,
arguing that *Un captif amoureux* demonstrates deep responsibility and
seriousness.[47]

While Shahid's glowing endorsement is to be expected (she cam-
paigned actively with him and they witnessed together the aftermath of
the Shatila massacres in Beirut in 1982), Genet's self-assessment is intri-

guing. Writing with disarming modesty about his ephemeral involvement, he contrasts his flurry of activity in the Middle East with the sense of impending death:

inside me lay the corpse I'd been for a long while. . . . Everything jolted along, and me with it, a parcel and at the same time a human being, a name and a tomb, a parcel and a corpse, eating, looking, laughing, whistling and loving left, right, and centre. It seemed to me the world changed around me while I stayed inside myself, certain only of having been. (*PL*, 190)

[à l'intérieur de moi reposait le mort que j'étais depuis longtemps . . . tout se déplaçait avec des heurts en me déplaçant quand je n'étais qu'un colis et pourtant un être humain portant mon nom et ma tombe, un colis et un mort qui mangeaient, regardaient, riaient, sifflaient, aimaient à tort et à travers. Autour de moi, me semblait-il, le monde devenait, moi je reposais en moi, certain d'avoir été.] (*CA*, 313–14)

Genet's perspective, signalling both his own demise and new political beginnings, combines grandeur and modesty. Aware that there is no easy cultural migration (no Loti-style new dress, new identity), he nevertheless displays an isolation in the face of death and a self-fascination that would not be out of place in Loti. The subjectivist elements in *Un captif amoureux* ensure that the engagement with forms of political marginality remains necessarily provisional: 'never my total belief; never the whole of myself' (*PL*, 90) ['la foi jamais totale et moi jamais en entier'] (*CA*, 150). The Palestinian periphery, then, is where France's dissident, however committed, asserts the limits of his empathy.

Conclusion

O, yonder, yonder! to scalp myself and tear away this European mind!

[Oh! là-bas, là-bas! m'y scalper de mon cerveau d'Europe!]

(Laforgue)[1]

'In their revolt, the Palestinians have assumed this weight – oh! I worry about being too literary – but they have assumed the weight of Cézanne's canvasses' ['les Palestiniens, dans leur révolte, ont pris ce poids – oh! j'ai peur d'être très littéraire – mais ils ont pris le poids des toiles de Cézanne'].[2] Genet's scruples about blunting the immediacy and impact of contemporary history suggest an awareness of the pitfalls facing the European who attempts to write cultural otherness. By retaining the Cézanne analogy, he nevertheless indulges the temptation to aestheticize. But his hesitation hints at an ethical concern not shared by his exoticist predecessors. Not that he refrains from aggressively free association in *Un captif amoureux*, yet the association is often directed against European self-congratulation. Thus when he splices private sexual fantasies and moments of violent Palestinian insurrection, he is clearly targeting both bourgeois heterosexist orthodoxy and *raison d'État*.

Alongside such provocation, which risks appropriating the Other to unsettle narcissistically one's own culture, the itinerant dissident in Genet strains to bring about a form of cultural self-emptying. Implicitly, he proposes a retroactive education of exoticists such as Loti, Gauguin, and Montherlant when he insists on the limits of empathy and problematizes the notion of unfettered access to a commodified alterity. His scrupulous insistence on the autonomy of the Other is signalled in his depiction of the tortured fedayee, Hamza. The bruised body, he notes, is not available to the Western onlooker but rather belongs to the Palestinian people. The body thus becomes emblematic of attitudes towards the Other. The urge to appropriate it is a reflex response of

166

Eurocentrism. Whether it be the sculptural body of the Polynesian in Gauguin or the fantasmatic bodies of Aziyadé and Rarahu in Loti or Rahma in *La Rose de sable*, the will to manipulate and control in these transracial liaisons delivers a reified alterity. By casting Hamza and his mother as a replica of the *Pietà*, Genet himself lapses, knowingly and often apologetically, into such manipulation. But the self-awareness of his gesture reflects a postcolonial revaluation. As Seán Hand observes in his discussion of Leiris's *L'Afrique fantôme*, the reconfiguration of political power in the wake of decolonization entails 'an anguished intellectual process of dispossession'.[3] Genet's Palestinian narrative spells a double dispossession: the marginalization of the camp-dwellers and the hesitation of the European Arabophile inhibited by memory of the West's punitive legacy.

A feared loss of possession is also central to the symptomatology of Camus's *Le Renégat*, which enacts a struggle for supremacy between two competing cultural legitimacies. Here, European colonial fantasy unfolds around the vulnerable body of the disfigured missionary. Likewise, anxiety about colonial self-definition is concretized in the search for missing or elusive bodies in *Le Premier Homme*: the hitherto-neglected remains of Cormery *père* in the Saint-Brieuc cemetery, the unidentified graves of colonial ancestors in Algeria, and the phantom-like Muslims who disappear into their barricaded homes at night, having fascinated Cormery by day. With the body becoming a repository of cultural insecurity, the retrieval of Self and an inchoate ethnic curiosity are central to Camus's quest narrative.

Late nineteenth-century ethnography was similarly fixated with a corporeal possession of the Other. The *Exposition Universelle* of 1889 involved the public display of African and Asian tribespeople on the Esplanade des Invalides. Commenting on the ethnic exhibition, Auguste Vitu wrote: 'It seems that savagery possesses an irresistible attraction for people weary of an extreme and advanced civilization.'[4] Vitu's typecasting echoes the assertive binarism of his contemporary, Gauguin, whose commodification of difference becomes a parody of cultural enquiry. A few years earlier, in 1883, a group of Singhalese and Araucanians were on view in the Jardin d'Acclimatation, an event recorded in Proust's novel where the crude Mme Blatin indulges her racist voyeurism with the greeting to one of the human exhibits: '"Good morning, nigger!"' (*RMP*, 1, 577) ['"Bonjour, négro!"'] (*RTP*, 1, 526). But as the Narrator delights in recounting, the reply comes back: '"Me nigger; you old cow!"' ['"Moi négro . . . mais toi chameau!"'].

Proust's ability to ridicule the culturally dominant by recording their crude responses to difference goes well beyond anecdote. His Narrator exposes what is arbitrary, obsessive, and congealed in anti-semitism and xenophobic nationalism, while demonstrating, in an unsettling Protean way, insider knowledge of the energies at work in these perversions. As with Gide, Montherlant, and Genet, the depiction of homosexuality in the *Recherche* releases an anxious exoticism. Proust's homosexuals form a procession of spectral presences, barely visible in a French domestic context and coming out in Orientalist or remote colonial landscapes. As a cartographer of desire, he assigns a heroic homosexuality and a heterosexist xenophobia to distinct terrains while subversively tunnelling between them.

Laforgue's desire for violent cultural mutilation and his wholesale adoption of masks provides a frenetic variant on the claimed appetite for radical difference that runs from Loti to Genet. Other works not considered here explore the same much-vaunted encounter with difference in a French context: the Surrealists' promotion of the primitive, Leiris's *L'Afrique fantôme*, Bardamu's African adventures in Céline's *Voyage au bout de la nuit* (including the perverse cultural reversal whereby he, the white European, is sold into slavery), and Michaux's *Un barbare en Asie*. Variations on Laforgue's inhibiting *cerveau d'Europe* are to be found in Loti's nostalgia and Gauguin's petulance, and in the restlessness and ambivalence with which Proust, Montherlant, Camus, and Genet all review metropolitan culture. Yet the crucial question is the extent to which their iconoclasm and gesturing towards otherness ever become relationality. As would-be cultural dissidents, they may puzzle over difference and its translatability. More regularly, they appropriate it unproblematically, so that whether they see it as compensatory, salvational or degraded, the hyperbole in their negativity and positivity marks an absence of encounter. However much they voice dissatisfaction with their own cultural legacy, the Europhobes' often crude response to otherness confirms their entanglement in a Francocentric legacy. As with Laforgue's dreamer in the 'Rêve de Far West' – 'there I shall be king! . . .' ['là-bas je serai roi! . . .'] – the lure of the exotic regularly translates into a narcissistic arrogance in respect of the availability of the Other. We have seen myriad examples of this: Loti's call to the Other to fill the void of his being, the magisterial tone of Gauguin's exile as captured by Segalen in *Le Maître du Jouir*, the leitmotif of the kingdom in Camus's defence of the French Algerians in *L'Exil et le Royaume*, the spectacle of Montherlant's protagonist buoyed up by the discourse of the *mission ci-*

vilisatrice. And yet Montherlant's declared aim was to write an anticolonialist account of the French protectorate in Morocco centred on the newly enlightened figure of Auligny, Camus imagines a fraternity involving Muslims and French Algerians, Gauguin insists on a cultural relativization in which the European becomes a savage, and the hero of *Aziyadé* is a Turcophile who dies in the uniform of the Sultan's army. Both in their adulation and denigration of the Other, they struggle to engage dialectically with difference.

While Genet is a maverick figure, his achievement is to reflect on otherness in an often highly lucid and sensitive manner. Writing in a post-colonial world, he champions the Palestinians, while describing his ambivalent relationship with them. Admittedly, the image of the seduced European conveyed by the title, *Un captif amoureux*, suggests that Genet may be a latter-day Loti. With both authors, we have the cultivation of the fantastic in the respective figures of the cultural transvestite and the transsexual; the intense theatricality and self-consciousness of the poses struck; and the celebration of whimsicality and surface. On the stage of the exoticist's self-fascination, then, the Other is consigned to the wings. But crucially, it is in the declared provisionality of Genet's identification with the dispossessed ('never the whole of myself' (*PL*, 90) ['et moi jamais en entier'] (*CA*, 150) that we see acknowledged not only the impossibility of cultural migration and indeed the refusal to forfeit his eccentric identity but also the will to see the Other as being similarly elusive. With Genet, then, we have the apparent paradox whereby the West's moral outlaw provides an ethical lead in the reflection on difference.

The workings of cultural prejudice are also laid bare in *A la recherche du temps perdu*. When Proust sets out to counter the prevailing doxa by seeking legitimacy for homosexuality, he strains to imagine where his reflection will take him: 'Perhaps, to form a picture of [the homosexual], we ought to think, if not of the wild animals . . . then at least of the negroes whom the comfortable existence of the white man renders desperately unhappy' (*RMP*, II, 647) ['Peut-être, pour les peindre, faut-il penser sinon aux animaux . . . du moins aux noirs, que l'existence confortable des blancs désespère'] (*RTP*, III, 26). Initiating this reckless writerly trajectory, Proust's 'Peut-être' sets in train a homoerotics that becomes transracial. Yet projecting on to the black African the otherness of homosexual desire is wholly arbitrary. The link is meaningful but only syllogistically in that, within the European mindset of Proust's day, black Africa and would-be aberrant sexuality are both consigned to the order of taboo. Moreover, the connection signals only a feigned reciprocity. For unbeknown to himself, the quasi-animalized African is the mute third party in a triangle designed to deliver collusion between Proust's Narrator and his bourgeois reader.

The image of Proust the writer bearing the dubious gift of homosexuality-by-association to a nameless, unsuspecting African recalls a detail in his biography. Part of the Grand Hotel in wartime Cabourg (which will become Balbec in the *Recherche*) was converted into a military hospital and Proust writes of his regular visits to see the hundreds of wounded soldiers, among them Senegalese and Moroccan troops, and of bringing them gifts (numerous games of draughts and about sixty packs of cards, he estimates in a letter to Madame de Madrazo).[5] How we read the cameo provides a marker for our reading of cultural marginality more generally. Seen from the angle of cultural predation, Proust's act signals the exoticist indulging in paternalistic charity and enjoying the crude visual spectacle of ethnic difference. More naively (or is it more ethnocentrically?), his gesture may be read as Samaritan giving. But our critical scepticism as we reflect on the meaning of Proust's gesture is conditioned by the broader tensions identified in the literary responses to difference that we have explored. In a postcolonial age of suspicion coming in the wake of colonial exclusion, we look back to see, along with the incontestable vocabularies of denigration and incomprehension, the inchoate awareness of the Other and the workings of an anxious exoticism. Nostalgia, uneasiness, curiosity, and transracial fantasy are no substitutes for relationality, nor are they preludes to it. Yet the authors considered here articulate important ambiguities that both define colonialism's culture and hold the capacity to dismantle it.

Notes

INTRODUCTION

1 Genet's hitherto unpublished text of August 1971, 'Après l'assassinat', is reproduced in *ED*, 105–108, here 108.

2 *Les Damnés de la Terre*, p. 57.

3 Sartre, *Saint-Genet: comédien et martyr*. As Colin Davis reminds us, Sartre, accepting the inevitability of betraying Genet, insists that he will at least be faithful to himself (Sartre, *Saint-Genet*, p. 646). See Davis, 'Genet's *Journal du voleur* and the Ethics of Reading', p. 54.

4 Sartre, *Orphée Noir, Situations III*, p. 232.

5 *Situations III*, pp. 232, 265.

6 Arnaud Malgorn, *Jean Genet: qui êtes-vous?* p. 16. Sabra and Shatila were the sites of the massacres of Palestinians in Lebanon in 1982. Genet was a key witness, visiting the Shatila camp in the immediate aftermath of the killings. See his 'Quatre heures à Chatila', *ED*, 243–64.

7 For the English translation of Proust's novel, I use the three-volume *Remembrance of Things Past* (Harmondsworth: Penguin, 1989), which is based on the translation of C. K. Scott Moncrieff and Terence Kilmartin, revised by D. J. Enright.

8 Camus, *Actuelles III: Chroniques Algériennes (1939–1958)* in *Ess.*, 887–1018.

9 Geoffrey Bennington, 'Postal Politics and the Institution of the Nation', in *Nation and Narration*, ed. Homi K. Bhabha, pp. 121–37, here p. 121.

10 Edgar Morin, *La Méthode*, vol. 1, *La Nature de la nature* (Paris: Seuil, 1981; first published 1977), pp. 203–4 (my emphasis), quoted in Bennington, 'Postal Politics and the Institution of the Nation', pp. 121, 133. Bennington also refers to Derrida and the idea of the hinge (*la brisure*) as developed in *De la grammatologie* (Paris: Minuit, 1967), pp. 96–108.

I WITHOUT OBLIGATION: EXOTIC APPROPRIATION IN LOTI AND GAUGUIN

1 The original French reads: 'Chacun appelle barbarie ce qui n'est pas de son usage', 'Des cannibales', p. 254. Translation taken from Montaigne, *Essays*, trans. J. M. Cohen (London: Penguin, 1958), p. 108.

2 Victor Segalen provides a bibliography of French and English travel writing on Polynesia, including that of Cook and Ellis, in his *Les Immémoriaux, OC*, 1, 247–8.

3 Diderot, *Supplément au Voyage de Bougainville*, pp. 968–9.

4 Glossing Freud's notion of *unheimlich* (the uncanny, the weird), Kristeva writes: '*death* and [the] *feminine*, . . . the final and . . . the original absorb and constitute us, and trouble when they disappear', *Étrangers à nous-mêmes*, p. 274 (Kristeva's italics).

5 Diderot, *Supplément*, pp. 987–92.

6 See Peter Brooks, *Body Work: Objects of Desire in Modern Narrative*, p. 197.

7 Kirk Varnedoe, 'Gauguin', in *'Primitivism' in Twentieth-Century Art*, ed. William Rubin, p. 181.

8 For a trenchant discussion of Freud's hypotheses both in *Totem and Taboo* and *Civilization and its Discontents*, see Marianna Torgovnick, *Gone Primitive: Savage Intellects, Modern Lives*. Torgovnick notes the conflation of the primitive and the neurotic in *Totem and Taboo* and contests Freud's attribution to the Other of the infantile, the repressed, and the feminine, *Gone Primitive*, pp. 204–8.

9 In 'Pensers Païens', a form of philosophical dialogue in the style of Diderot's *Supplément*, Segalen quotes an imaginary Polynesian who laments the dissolution of local culture caused by Western colonization.

10 See Bruno Vercier's highly informative introduction in his edition of *Le Mariage de Loti*, p. 15.

11 Quoted in Alain Quella-Villéger, *Pierre Loti: le pèlerin de la planète*, p. 83. Quella-Villéger concedes that Lyautey's boast to Claude Farrère may be no more than a half-truth.

12 The expression is Segalen's. See Victor Segalen, 'Gauguin dans son dernier décor', *OC*, 1, 290. In *Le Mariage de Loti* we read: 'Tahitians have a character not unlike that of small children' ['Le caractère des Tahitiens est un peu celui des petits enfants'] (*ML*, 74).

13 Letter of 18 October 1907, quoted in Segalen, *OC*, 1, 105.

14 Page references are to the 1901 La Plume edition of *Noa Noa*, which contains the chapters of both Gauguin and Morice. For a detailed account of the three sharply diverging editions of the work, see Nicholas Wadley's indispensable *Noa Noa: Gauguin's Tahiti*, pp. 7–9.

15 Quoted in Alison Fairlie, *Leconte de Lisle's Poems on the Barbarian Races*, p. 394.

16 Lesley Blanch, *Pierre Loti: Portrait of an Escapist*, p. 75.

17 Quoted in Alain Quella-Villéger, *Pierre Loti: le pèlerin de la planète*, p. 92. For the material that follows on Loti's role in the Annam crisis of 1883, I have borrowed heavily from Quella-Villéger's account of the episode.

18 Quella-Villéger quotes from letters of 3 January and 7 November 1912, *Pierre Loti: le pèlerin de la planète*, p. 94.

19 *Le Discours sur le colonialisme* (1955), quoted in Quella-Villéger, *Pierre Loti: le pèlerin de la planète*, p. 105. Quella-Villéger does not set out to canonize Loti and indeed condemns the author's pillaging in the ruins of pagodas in the wrecked town of Ma-Kung in the Pescadores Islands in 1885. Yet he is keen to demonstrate Loti's ethical misgivings about the impact of colonization.

20 Todorov, *Nous et les autres: La Réflexion française sur la diversité humaine*, p. 346.

21 'The only urgent thing is decor'; cited on the jacket cover of Quella-Villéger's *Pierre Loti: le pèlerin de la planète*.

22 Viaud disguises his identity in several ways. The novel was never ascribed to him. Initially, it was attributed simply to 'l'auteur d'*Aziyadé*', the latter novel having been published a year earlier. In later editions of *Le Mariage de Loti*, the name Pierre Loti appears on the title page. Vercier makes the point that, as a naval officer, Viaud was not free to claim authorship of these fictions of adventure and desire (*ML*, 29).

23 The detail is taken from Blanch's engaging account of Loti's background, *Pierre Loti: Portrait of an Escapist*, p. 9.

24 Barthes, *New Critical Essays*. Subsequently cited in the text as *NCE*.

25 See the discussion of Genet in the Introduction, p. 1.

26 The relationship with Hatidjè is documented in chapter 3 of Quella-Villéger ('Amours sur le Bosphore'), *Pierre Loti: le pèlerin de la planète*, pp. 75–90.

27 Quoted in Quella-Villéger, *Pierre Loti: le pèlerin de la planète*, p. 84.

28 Todorov contrasts the xenophilia of much of Loti's exotic fiction with the xenophobia to be found in the colonial novel, *Le Roman d'un spahi*. See *Nous et les autres*, p. 351.

29 Bongie sees Peyral as epitomizing a colonialism that has come to stay, 'the first in a new breed of colonial heroes [yet] also the last avatar of the exotic subject', *Exotic Memories*, p. 103.

30 Glissant, *L'Intention poétique*, p. 219.

31 Torgovnick, *Gone Primitive*, p. 247.

32 Todorov, *Nous et les autres*, p. 354.

33 J.-A. Moerenhout, *Voyages aux Îles du Grand Océan*, 1, 498.

34 Gauguin was reading Moerenhout in 1891 and early in 1892 (see Alan Wilkinson, *Gauguin to Moore: Primitivism in Modern Sculpture*, p. 39). The title page of Moerenhout's work captures the ambitious scope of his investigations: *Voyages to the Islands of the Great Ocean, containing new documents on their physical and political geography, the language, literature, religion, customs, and traditions of their inhabitants; with general consideration given to their trade, history, and government, from the earliest times to the present day.*

35 Beyond Gauguin, André Breton, for example, insists on the inseparability of Oceanic art and the development of Surrealism. See Wilkinson, *Gauguin to Moore*, p. 16.

36 In chapter 1 of *Noa Noa* authored by Charles Morice, there is an echo of Moerenhout in the reference to Polynesian culture and 'the glorious frisson of its ancient greatness, . . . the fatal marks of its present agony' ['le frisson glorieux de ses grandeurs anciennes, . . . les marques fatales de sa présente agonie'] (*NN*, 6).

37 This theory of geophysical apocalypse enjoyed credence among nineteenth-century commentators on Polynesia. See Fairlie, *Leconte de Lisle's Poems on the Barbarian Races*, pp. 191–2.

38 Gauguin makes the point in *Avant et Après* that, for the European, cannibalism is taboo until he finds himself abandoned on a raft! (*AA*, 238).

39 Projecting Moerenhout's anxieties forward, we see *fin-de-siècle* primitivism and subsequent developments such as Surrealism provoking paranoid expressions of Western cultural insecurity. For consideration of theories of cultural calamity circulating in the inter-war years, including Oswald Spengler's *The Decline of the West* and Henri Massis's *The Defence of the West*, see Barrie Cadwallader's very lucid *Crisis of the European Mind*.

40 Segalen's unfinished *Le Maître du jouir*, written in 1907–08, was edited by Henri Bouillier and published for the first time in Segalen, *OC*, I, 302. Bouillier notes the promotion of Gauguin to the rank of a superhuman sitting in judgement on a culture of disabling morality.

41 Segalen, *OC*, I, 302.

42 Moerenhout quotes extensively from Cowper's *The Task* and from chapter 2 of Delille's *Jardins* of 1782 in *Voyages*, II, 174–5.

43 ['Terrible itching for things unknown']. Gauguin's expression features in a letter to Emile Bernard in the summer of 1889, quoted in Cachin, *Gauguin: 'Ce malgré moi de sauvage'*, p. 63.

44 Cachin, *Gauguin*, p. 60.

45 Pascal Ory makes this point in his *L'Exposition Universelle*, pp. 94–5, adding ironically that showing exotic human specimens was the 'pursuit to its extreme limits of the logic of illusionism', pp. 100–01.

46 Varnedoe, 'Gauguin', p. 179.

47 Letter of 23 November 1893, *Camille Pissarro: lettres à son fils Lucien*, ed. John Rewald (Paris: Albin Michel, 1950), p. 217, quoted in Varnedoe, 'Gauguin', p. 187. Varnedoe comments that Gauguin's primitivism was a mere façade and based on half-truths (p. 179).

48 Wayne Andersen refers to Gauguin's syphilitic condition on arrival in Polynesia and sees his behaviour as rivalling those Europeans he most despised, the missionary-conquerors who brought disease and social disintegration. Andersen writes: 'Unconsciously he continued to revert to the romantic concept of savagery, which glorified as "natural" what modern society perceived as sin', *Gauguin's Paradise Lost*, p. 10.

49 Gauguin in an interview with Jules Huret, *L'Echo de Paris*, 1891; quoted in Cachin, *Gauguin*, p. 67.

50 Charles Harrison, Francis Frascina, and Gill Perry, *Primitivism, Cubism, Abstraction*, p. 8. Cachin's chapter heading 'Premiers Bretons, Premiers Tropiques' captures the sense of exotic continuity between the Breton and the Tahitian periods. See also Gauguin's letter of March 1888 from Pont-Aven to Schuffenecker, quoted in Cachin, *Gauguin*, p. 37.

51 See Robert Young's discussion of the centrality of Darwinism to nineteenth-century notions of race in *Colonial Desire: Hybridity in Theory, Culture and Race*, pp. 11–15.

52 Gauguin, *Lettres de Paul Gauguin à Émile Bernard 1888–1891*, p. 128.

53 Letter of Gauguin to Strindberg (5 February 1895); quoted in Cachin, *Gauguin*, pp. 168–9.

54 *Lettres de Paul Gauguin à Émile Bernard*, p. 99.

55 Robert Young cites Condorcet's 'Outline of the Intellectual Progress of Mankind' of 1795 as an example of progressivist history in his *Colonial Desire*, pp. 32–3.

56 Letter of 14 November 1902, *Lettres de Gauguin à Daniel de Monfreid*, p. 232.

57 *Lettres de Gauguin à Daniel de Monfreid*, p. 190.

58 Well aware of the opprobrium that he incurred on abandoning his Danish wife Mette Gad and their five children as well as a career in finance, Gauguin raged in a letter to Monfreid in the year before his death: 'What does it matter! Let us leave these filthy bourgeois where they belong – even if they are our children – and carry on with the work we have begun' ['Qu'importe! et laissons ces sales bourgeois – même s'ils sont nos enfants – à leur sale place et continuons l'œuvre commencée'], *Lettres de Gauguin à Daniel de Monfreid*, p. 192.

59 See especially chapter 6 of Brooks, *Body Work*.

60 Reflecting on sexual norms as a mode of social control, Sander Gilman considers the place of the asexual and the androgynous in *Difference and Pathology: Stereotypes of Sexuality, Race, and Madness*, p. 25. See also Wadley's exploration of androgyny, *Noa Noa: Gauguin's Tahiti*, p. 74.

61 In later chapters, we shall be considering the depiction of sexually ambiguous bodies in Proust, Montherlant, and Genet.

62 In a letter to Madeleine Bernard, the younger sister of Émile Bernard, Gauguin enjoins her to consider herself an androgyne: 'the soul, the heart, in short all that is divine must not be *enslaved* to matter, that is to say the body. A woman's virtues are entirely similar to those of man and are Christian virtues' ['l'âme, le coeur, tout ce qui est divin enfin, ne doit pas être *esclave* de la matière, c'est à dire du corps. Les vertus d'une femme sont semblables entièrement à celles de l'homme et sont les vertus chrétiennes'], *Lettres de Paul Gauguin à Émile Bernard 1888–1891*, p. 59; Gauguin's italics. Sweetman refers to the 'discomforting homoeroticism of the Jotefa experience', *Paul Gauguin: a Complete Life*, p. 367.

63 Freud, *Civilization and its Discontents*, p. 316.

64 *Ibid.*, p. 306.

65 *Ibid.*, pp. 251–9.

66 We find the same brusque self-deprecation in *Avant et Après* with its regular refrain: 'This is not a book' ['Ceci n'est pas un livre']. Gauguin also stresses his mother Aline's upbringing in Lima and how he spent his early childhood there (between 1849 and 1855), undergoing the influence of the Inca civilization. In a letter of February 1888 to his wife, he writes of the two natures within him, the sensitive being and the Indian; and writing to Émile Bernard from Arles, where he was staying with Van Gogh in late 1888, he contrasts Van Gogh's Romanticism with his own primitive state (Cachin, *Gauguin*, pp. 50, 53).

67 Wadley, *Noa Noa: Gauguin's Tahiti*, p. 125.

68 In Wadley's terms, the work highlights 'both the confusion and the artifice surrounding his quest for a new identity', *Noa Noa*, p. 144.

69 Wadley, *Noa Noa*, p. 145.
70 Gauguin's explanation to Morice is quoted in Wadley, *Noa Noa*, p. 124.
71 Malingue observes: 'In this admirable composition, the presence of Meyer de Haan, which is shockingly ugly, is technically justified as it gives balance to the overall layout', *La Vie prodigieuse de Gauguin*, p. 277.
72 Segalen, *Le Maître-du-Jouir*, *OC*, I, 309.
73 *Lettres de Gauguin à Daniel de Monfreid*, p. 233.
74 *Ibid.* In his letters to Monfreid, Gauguin repeatedly enquires about the pricing and slow sales of his work. The sale of *Nevermore* prompts him to remind Monfreid that the latter had doubted the wisdom of inscribing this literal title on the canvas itself. Gauguin congratulates himself, speculating that the title, which carries its own linguistic exoticism, was a decisive factor in the sale of the painting (*Lettres de Gauguin à Daniel de Monfreid*, p. 135). For the painter, *Nevermore* captures 'a certain barbarian luxury of past years' (quoted in Lawrence and Elizabeth Hanson, *The Noble Savage: a Life of Paul Gauguin*, p. 258). Cachin sees in the title 'Nevermore' an echo of the poem by Poe translated by Mallarmé, *Gauguin*, p. 114.
75 Charles Morice, *Le Soir*, 28 June 1895. Quoted in Malingue, *La Vie prodigieuse de Gauguin*, p. 224. Less reverentially, Jules Renard notes in his *Journal* that Daudet derided Gauguin for endlessly talking of abandoning Europe without ever getting round to it (Malingue, *La Vie*, p. 224).
76 The text, originally intended as a preface to a re-edition of *Noa Noa*, was written during the First World War and used as a preface to the correspondence between Gauguin and Monfreid.
77 Quoted by Bouillier in Segalen, *OC*, I, 103.
78 James Clifford, *The Predicament of Culture*, p. 161.

2 EXEMPLARY INCLUSIONS, INDECENT EXCLUSIONS IN PROUST'S *RECHERCHE*

1 The quotation is taken from a manuscript draft in *Cahier 25*, reproduced in *RTP*, II, 942.
2 Sweetman, *Paul Gauguin*, p. 152.
3 See *CSB*, 337.
4 See Proust's letter to his mother of 5 September 1888 in which he enthusiastically likens reading *Le Mariage de Loti* to the pleasurable drinking of tea, *Corr.*, I, 108–10. Mme Proust's letter of 23 April 1890 contains a substantial quotation from Loti's *Le Roman d'un enfant*, which her son had encouraged her to read, *Corr.*, I, 136–8.
5 See George D. Painter, *Marcel Proust: a Biography* (London: Chatto & Windus, 1989), II, 115.
6 *Corr.*, XIX, 243–4. Vandérem's piece appeared in the *Revue de Paris*, 15 April 1920. Alec Hargreaves is nevertheless right to stress the limitations of Loti's fiction when compared with Proust's, *The Colonial Experience in French Fiction*, p. 84.

7 See Antoine Compagnon's indispensable introduction to *Sodome et Gomorrhe* in *RTP*, III, especially III, 5, n. 2, and III, 10, n. 1.

8 See the chapter 'Freud and Proust' in Bowie, *Freud, Proust and Lacan: Theory as Fiction*. Bowie's epigraph taken from Adorno has a clear bearing on the present discussion: 'In psychoanalysis nothing is true except the exaggerations', p. 67.

9 *Freud, Proust and Lacan*, p. 77.

10 Proust's landscape recalls that encountered by Marlow leading the expedition upriver in equatorial Africa: 'we glided past like phantoms, wondering and secretly appalled' provides a typical instance of exoticist *Schadenfreude*. See Conrad, *Heart of Darkness*, p. 186.

11 The words 'Mané, Thécel, Pharès' [Counted, Weighed, Divided] form literally the 'writing on the wall' that announces to Belshazzar his impending punishment, namely the dividing up of his kingdom.

12 Fredric Jameson, *Modernism and Imperialism*, p. 7.

13 *Ibid.*, pp. 11–12.

14 See, for example, Bowie, *Freud, Proust and Lacan*, pp. 76–82.

15 As Genet reminds us, while the term 'apache' means a Parisian hooligan, etymologically it denotes the Native American tribe of the same name (*PL*, 337; *CA*, 552). Genet sees the slide from ethnic label to term of abuse as signalling a more general tradition of Western intolerance.

16 *NCE*, 116. As Barthes insists, desire requires, and finds its pure form in, unreality.

17 *Civilization and its Discontents*, pp. 293–4; quoted in Torgovnick, *Gone Primitive*, p. 194.

18 Edward Said makes the point in *Orientalism*, pp. 176–7.

19 See the extract from *Carnet* 3 reproduced in *RTP*, IV, 786–7 under the title 'M. de Charlus et Paris en guerre'.

20 See the Pléiade editor's note referring to the plight of 'la belle Zobéide' (*Les Mille et Une Nuits*, 33e et 34e nuit, 66e nuit), *RTP*, IV, 1244.

21 A special number of the Belgian review *Variétés* of June 1929 features an imaginary planisphere ('The World at the time of the Surrealists') in which France is reduced to Paris, Greece and Italy disappear, the Soviet Union encroaches on Europe, and locations associated with a primitive exotic such as Melanesia, Peru, and Mexico are enormous. See the *Dictionnaire Général du Surréalisme et de ses environs*, ed. Adam Biro and René Passeron (Paris: PUF, 1982), p. 80.

22 Chapter 4 considers French colonial culture in Algeria with reference to Camus.

23 Albert Memmi, *Le Racisme*, p. 66.

24 Fraser, *Proust and the Victorians*, p. 220.

25 Jonathan Dollimore, *Sexual Dissidence: Augustine to Wilde, Freud to Foucault*, p. 313.

26 To borrow Paul Julian Smith's valuable gloss on Lacan: 'Meaning can only point towards the goal it always fails to reach. Thus for Lacan, language is

a letter of love. . . . This (untranslatable) letter of love is a love without essence, a love within language: the passion of the signifier as it works (on) the body', *The Body Hispanic*, p. 104.

27 Writing about the pain and disappointment of life, Freud evokes Fontane's 'auxiliary constructions'. Charlus's abuse provides a provocative example of one such palliative or 'substitutive satisfaction', *Civilization and its Discontents*, p. 262.

28 The Pléiade edition cites the early twentieth-century historian F. de Rochegude's account of the fate of the Jew Jonathas, who was executed in 1290 (*RTP*, III, 1619, n. 2 to III, 492). Desecration of the eucharistic host was a familiar charge in the history of European anti-semitism.

29 Dollimore identifies the religious heretic and the wayward woman, Satan and Eve, as two outstanding types of pre-modern perversion, Dollimore, *Sexual Dissidence*, p. 27.

30 M. Foucault, *The History of Sexuality* (New York: Vintage Books, 1980), p. 101; quoted in Dollimore, *Sexual Dissidence*, p. 225.

31 Leiris, *Langage Tangage ou Ce que les mots me disent*, p. 40. We can contrast this allergy with Levinas's view of peace entailing 'the prior and non-allergic presence of the Other', *Littérature et infini: Essai sur l'extériorité* (The Hague: Martinus Nijhoff, 1971), p. 174; quoted in Colin Davis, 'Genet's *Journal du voleur* and the Ethics of Reading', p. 60.

32 Leiris writes of the revelatory power of word association: 'Then language is transformed into an oracle and we find a thread, however tenuous, to guide us through the Babel of our minds.' 'Propos recueillis par Madeleine Chapsal', *Quinzaine Littéraire*, 14 (15–31 October 1966).

33 *Langage Tangage*, p. 47. It is difficult to convey in translation the dense word-play of the original.

34 The authoritative reference point here is Said, who defines Orientalism as 'shaped to a degree by the exchange with power political . . ., power intellectual . . ., power cultural (as with orthodoxies and canons of taste, texts, values), power moral', *Orientalism*, p. 12. See also Compagnon, *Proust entre deux siècles*, especially his chapter on Proust and Racine in which the role of Nissim Bernard is discussed, pp. 65–107.

35 See Hayden White, 'The Forms of Wildness', p. 25.

36 While the colony is a far cry from Proust's Balbec hotel, Fanon highlights the foreigner-as-vermin motif in the colonizer's refutation of contact with the colonized: 'Values . . . are irremediably poisoned and infected as soon as they come into contact with the colonized people', *Les Damnés de la Terre*, p. 72.

37 Writing about the value systems inherent in the work of F. R. Leavis, Mulhern identifies its restrictive cultural parameters: 'The governing values . . . are class-restrictive, (hetero)sexist and ethnocentric. The "human" image is caught in a sepia print of family life in lower-middle-class England.' See 'English Reading' in *Nation and Narration*, ed. Bhabha, pp. 250–64, here p. 259.

38 The intolerance of the *courrières*, while represented anecdotally, reinforces the theoretical notion of an imperialism of the same. Robert Young explores the theory in his discussion of Levinas's critique of the primacy of History in his *White Mythologies*, p. 15. That the maids' references to the Other are fraught with verbal violence registers symptomatically the impossibility of a total occlusion of alterity.

39 *Civilization and its Discontents*, p. 305.

40 The term is used by Bhabha in 'DissemiNation: Time, Narrative, and the Margins of the Modern Nation', p. 299. Drawing on Poulantzas, Bhabha writes of 'an eternity produced by [the nation's] self-generation'.

41 Foucault, 'Space, Knowledge, and Power', interview with Paul Rabinow, *The Foucault Reader*, p. 246.

42 Foucault, 'Of Other Spaces', p. 23. The original French text formed the basis of a 1967 lecture.

43 I have in mind especially Eve Kosofsky Sedgwick's 'Epistemology of the Closet'.

44 Julia Kristeva, *Le Temps sensible: Proust et l'expérience littéraire*, p. 62.

45 'Of Other Spaces', p. 26.

46 Kristeva, *Le Temps sensible*, p. 67.

47 Leiris, *Glossaire j'y serre mes gloses*, p. 116.

48 Kristeva, *Le Temps sensible*, p. 128; my italics.

3 CLAIMING CULTURAL DISSIDENCE: THE CASE OF MONTHERLANT'S
LA ROSE DE SABLE

1 Montherlant, *Le Maître de Santiago*. Quoted by the author in his 'Avant-propos' of 1967 to *La Rose de sable* (*RS*, 14).

2 Montherlant, 'Avant-propos', *RS*, 10.

3 Montherlant writing in *Comœdia*, 1 March 1932; quoted by Michel Raimond in his 'Notice' to *La Rose de sable*, in Montherlant, *Romans II*, 1257.

4 Fearing that his manuscript might be destroyed, Montherlant made available to friends in 1938 a limited edition of sixty-five copies of the second half of the novel, *Mission providentielle*. In 1954, Plon published Part One under the title *L'Histoire d'amour de La Rose de sable*.

5 Reading *La Rose de sable* biographically, Larguié sees the young girl Rahma as the transposition of an adolescent male; quoted in Raimond, *Les Romans de Montherlant*, pp. 121–2.

6 Quoted in Catherine Hodeir and Michel Pierre, *L'Exposition coloniale*, p. 122. Gide asks how many more lives need to be lost to ensure the future prosperity of French Equatorial Africa and speaks of 'morally unacceptable' practices, *Voyage au Congo* suivi de *Le Retour du Tchad*, pp. 223–6, here p. 225.

7 See James Clifford, *The Predicament of Culture*.

8 Kyria writes that the novel might have galvanized those who doubted the morality of colonization, *Combat*, 21 March 1968. See also Raimond's editorial note in *Romans II*, 1271. Raimond cites similar misgivings voiced by

Pierre-Henri Simon (*Le Monde*, 16 March 1968) and Jean de Beer (*Les Nouvelle Littéraires*, 14 March 1968). The latter suggests the potentially momentous impact of Montherlant's colonial fiction, saying that publication in the 1930s might have changed the course of events. Raimond contrasts Montherlant's silence with Gide's contemporaneous critique of colonialism in his *Voyage au Congo*.

9 Lyautey, quoted in *RS*, 323. The original source is L.-H.-G. Lyautey, *Lettres du Tonkin et de Madagascar (1894–1899)*, II, 285. The work contains twenty-eight black-and-white sketches of colonial locations drawn by Lyautey himself and fourteen colour maps of Indo-China and Madagascar.

10 Claude Farrère writes obsequiously of the general: 'at the present time, our Africa cannot do without Lyautey the African. . . . In truth, one cannot avoid the comparison between Scipio, conqueror of Carthage, and Lyautey, conqueror of Fez and Marrakesh', *Lyautey l'Africain*, p. 29.

11 Rom Landau, *Moroccan Drama, 1900–1955* (London: Robert Hale, 1956), p. 93; quoted in Scham, *Lyautey in Morocco*, p. 29.

12 Barthes, 'Grammaire africaine', in *Mythologies*, pp. 137–44, here p. 137.

13 *Le Chaos de la Nuit, Romans II*, 912. Reflecting on Lyautey's growing disaffection from metropolitan life in the inter-war years, Celestino observes that he conquered Morocco only to be defeated by France. Celestino cites the words attributed to Lyautey on his death bed, 'I am dying of France' ['Je meurs de la France'], highlighting another dimension of the deep-seated alienation generated by the colonial mindset.

14 Lyautey, *Paroles d'action*, pp. 342, 346.

15 Lyautey's later fame no doubt explains the republication of the text in the year after his death (Paris: Plon, 1935). Page references given in the text are to this edition. As Alan Scham notes, while the original article was published anonymously, Lyautey's promotion was rapid thereafter, *Lyautey in Morocco*, p. 6.

16 Quoted in Hodeir and Pierre, *L'Exposition coloniale*, p. 26.

17 Liauzau's assessment that the period shows the first, abortive glimpses of anticolonialism is corroborated by *La Rose de sable*. See *Aux origines des tiers-mondismes: colonisés et anticolonialistes en France (1919–1939)*, p. 9.

18 Henri Cartier, *Comment la France 'civilise' ses colonies*, p. 78. I am grateful to Abigail Descombes for bringing this invaluable source to my attention. See also Barthes's 'Grammaire africaine', p. 138.

19 Quoted in Hodeir and Pierre, *L'Exposition coloniale*, p. 103.

20 The text is reproduced in Maurice Nadeau, *Histoire du Surréalisme* suivie de *Documents surréalistes* (Paris: Seuil, 1964), pp. 325–7. See also a second tract, 'Premier Bilan de l'Exposition coloniale', pp. 330–2.

21 The Surrealists labelled the exhibition 'the Luna-Park of Vincennes', Nadeau, *Histoire du Surréalisme*, p. 327.

22 Barthes, 'Grammaire africaine', p. 139.

23 Gallieni's instructions are dated 22 March 1898 in Lyautey, *Lettres du Tonkin*, II, 282.

24 *Ibid.*, 285.

25 Letter from Lyautey to Albert de Mun, 10 October 1912; cited in Pierre Lyautey (Lyautey's nephew), *Les Plus Belles Lettres de Lyautey*, p. 117.

26 Quoted in Scham, *Lyautey in Morocco*, p. 11. Scham notes how the Sultan of Morocco complained to the Quai d'Orsay about the unofficial incursion of 1903 that was aimed, or so Lyautey claimed, at countering Moroccan dissidence (pp. 10–11). We have already seen Montherlant's Celestino take a jaundiced view of Lyautey's claims in *Le Chaos de la nuit* (see above, note 13).

27 The prominence given to Lyautey sets militarism at the heart of *La Rose de sable*. In a related context, Seán Hand explores the intertextual links between Leiris and the writings of Gallieni, arguing that the military mentality is 'the real, repressed phantom of *L'Afrique fantôme*'. See Hand, 'Phantom of the Opus', p. 178.

28 *Ibid.*, p. 186.

29 I am indebted to Patricia O' Flaherty for this information and for her many detailed suggestions on this chapter.

30 *Culture and Imperialism*, p. 69.

31 Nicholas Thomas refers to Stephen Greenblatt's work on the conquest of the New World, and in particular to his identification of the ambiguities of possessiveness and wonder in respect of the Other, *Colonialism's Culture*, p. 69.

32 Foucault, *Discipline and Punish*, p. 136.

33 Montherlant, *Service Inutile* in *Essais*, p. 585; quoted by Raimond in *Romans II*, 1252.

34 True to his Communist convictions, Cartier claimed that the Soviet Union had succeeded in breaking this cycle of repression, *Comment la France 'civilise' ses colonies*, p. 82.

35 Fanon adds that the colonized 'object' will become human in the course of liberating itself, *Les Damnés de la Terre*, p. 67.

36 Glissant, *L'Intention poétique*, p. 28.

37 Pierre Sipriot refers to Montherlant's promiscuous lifestyle in North Africa under the assumed name M. Millon (*Montherlant sans masque*, II, p. 33).

38 In characterizing perversion in Shakespearian England, Dollimore refers to the paradigm of 'paranoia, displacements, and disavowals around images of the perverse', *Sexual Dissidence*, p. 28.

39 In Dollimore's words, 'the proximate is often constructed as the other, and in a process which facilitates displacement. But the proximate is also what enables a tracking-back of the "other" into the "same"', *Sexual Dissidence*, p. 33.

40 James Clifford uses the term 'oneirography' with reference to Leiris's *L'Afrique fantôme*, *The Predicament of Culture*, p. 169.

41 The expression is Said's, *Culture and Imperialism*, p. 89.

42 Fabian, *Time and the Other: How Anthropology makes its Object*, p. 143.

43 *Ibid.*, p. 164.

44 In the colonialist lexicon, Barthes highlights *honneur*, *destin*, and *mission* as magical, mystificatory terms ('des mots *mana*') requiring no definition, 'Grammaire africaine', pp. 138–40.

45 Letter of 10 October 1912, quoted in Scham, *Lyautey in Morocco*, pp. 25–6; my italics.

46 Todorov explores the recurring opposition between native matter and European form as used in Sepúlveda'a sixteenth-century account of the Spanish colonization of the Americas, *The Conquest of America*, p. 153.

47 Clifford, *Predicament of Culture*, p. 11.

48 At Montherlant's request, Odinot read the manuscript of *La Rose de sable* shortly after it was completed. In his travelogue of a rudimentary sociological kind, *Le Monde marocain*, Odinot appeals to philanthropic idealism in defining the concept of the protectorate: 'The difference between a colony and a protectorate is as great as that between a slave bought at the market and a legitimate wife, married in accordance with the rites', p. 54. In common with *La Rose de sable*, Odinot's writings, which explore cultural conflict between French and Muslim value systems, confirm a Eurocentric narrowness. His novel *Géranium, ou La Vie d'une femme marocaine* sees the difficulties involved in a Franco-Muslim marriage as mirroring the broader challenges posed by the French protectorate. For a detailed discussion of Odinot's friendship with Montherlant, see Raimond's editorial notes, *Romans II*, 1260–5.

49 Camus's *L'Étranger* provides an analogous case where the denouement heralds the death of the European. Common to both texts is the fantasy of a sacrificial, would-be innocent colonial presence. The same delusional scenario features in *Aziyadé*, where the death of Loti provides a variant on the topos of the European's generous gift of Self.

50 Kristeva, *Le Temps sensible*, p. 67.

51 Quoted from *Lettres de guerre du Capitaine Robert Dubarle* (Paris: Perrin, 1918). Montherlant sees Dubarle's text, composed at the front in World War I, as an invocation to the fatherland.

52 Freud observes that the child's super ego is formed not on the image of the parents but on the image of their super ego, and thus becomes the channel of tradition and of value judgements surviving across the generations. See J. Laplanche and J.-B. Pontalis, *Vocabulaire de la psychanalyse* (Paris: PUF, 1967), p. 473.

53 Fabian, *Time and the Other*, p. 165.

54 Todorov refers to the 'extreme, and exemplary, encounter' between European and Native American at the time of the Spanish colonization (*The Conquest of America*, p. 5), cited in Thomas, *Colonialism's Culture*, p. 69.

4 CAMUS AND THE RESISTANCE TO HISTORY

1 Camus, *Le Minotaure*, *Ess.*, 813; Derrida, *Le Monolinguisme de l'autre*, p. 73; Derrida's emphasis.

2 Camus's *Misères de la Kabylie* was originally published in serial form in the newspaper *Alger Républicain* in June 1939. The articles are included in *Actuelles III: Chroniques Algériennes 1939–1958*, *Ess.*, 887–1018.

3 Barthes, *Mythologies*, trans. Annette Lavers, p. 151.

4 See Glissant, *L'Intention poétique*, p. 28.

5 The text is contained in *L'Été, Ess.*, 846–50.

6 *Mythologies*, p. 151.

7 One of the most forthright critics of Camus's legacy, Edward Said, writes: 'from [Camus's] work, the facts of imperial actuality, so clearly there to be noted, have dropped away', *Culture and Imperialism*, p. 208.

8 I return to the figure of the Tower of Babel in my discussion of *La Chute*.

9 R. D. Laing, *The Divided Self*, p. 44.

10 Sartre, 'Préface' to Memmi, *Portrait du colonisé précédé de Portrait du colonisateur*, p. 28.

11 The 'solitude of the column' anticipates suggestively the solitude of the *colon* as explored in *Le Premier Homme*.

12 *Mythologies*, p. 155. The search for a fixity of identity in Camus's geological imaginary provides an instance of what Barthes, glossing Freud's pleasure-principle, calls 'the clarity-principle of mythological humanity', p. 143, n.

13 See the closing section of *Le Mythe de Sisyphe, Ess.*, 196.

14 *Mythologies*, pp. 152–3; the italics are Barthes's.

15 Barthes asks the question: 'What [is] more "political" than the sea celebrated by the makers of the film *The Lost Continent*?' in his discussion of exotic myth, *Mythologies*, p. 144.

16 See Said, 'The Politics of Knowledge', p. 21.

17 The term 'constellation of delirium' is Fanon's and is quoted by Bhabha in his Foreword to *Black Skin, White Masks*, p. xiv.

18 Glissant, *L'Intention poétique*, p. 13.

19 O'Brien refers to the combination of nightmare and idyll in Camus's feelings about Algeria, *Camus*, p. 69.

20 The imaginary world of *Le Renégat* provides a variant on what Bhabha sees Fanon achieving in his *Black Skin, White Masks*: 'It is through image and fantasy – those orders that figure transgressively on the borders of history and the unconscious – that Fanon most profoundly evokes the colonial condition', 'Foreword', p. xiii.

21 Clifford uses the term with reference to the fiction of Conrad and Malinowski in *The Predicament of Culture*, p. 105.

22 Said, *Culture and Imperialism*, p. 215.

23 Gilman, *Difference and Pathology*, p. 24.

24 We find a suggestive variant on the theme of European alienation in North Africa in Derrida's reflection on his status as Franco-Maghrebin: 'I have only one language, and it is not my own' (*Le Monolinguisme de l'autre*, pp. 15, 42). Given the ambiguity in the term *langue* (denoting both language and tongue), the mutilation of the renegade's tongue captures metaphorically an identitarian conflict analogous to the one addressed by Derrida.

25 In his conclusion to *Civilization and its Discontents*, Freud sees the workings of that collective pathology in twentieth-century conflicts between nations, p. 339.

26 Imperialism, Said argues, has thrived on such invented essences as Oriental, Frenchness and Africanness, 'The Politics of Knowledge', p. 21.

27 'The Politics of Knowledge', p. 26.

28 See the extracts from Camus's *Nouvelles de l'exil*, dated February 1952 and quoted by Roger Quilliot in Camus, *TRN*, 2044.

29 *Black Skin, White Masks*, p. 23.

30 See Freud's 'Thoughts for the Times on War and Death', written in 1915, p. 76.

31 A similar use of heliocentrism as a vehicle for cultural narrowness marks the opening pages of *La Rose de sable* (see above, chapter 3).

32 The words attributed to Christ on the Cross are recorded in Matthew 27:46: 'And about the ninth hour, Jesus cried with a loud voice, saying . . . "My God, my god, why hast thou forsaken me?"'

33 Brooks uses this formulation in his review of modern critical responses to Richardson's *Clarissa*. See *Body Work*, p. 33.

34 O'Brien, *Camus*, p. 84.

35 The deep-seated territorial anxiety in the colonial psyche is symbolized by the precarious shoreline, lying between the desert and the sea. It gives resonance to the insurrectionist slogan of the Algerian War, 'Les Français à la mer!' ['Into the sea with the French!'].

36 Defending his counter-reading of Camus, Said argues: 'a correlative way of interpreting Camus's novels . . . would be as interventions in the history of French efforts in Algeria', *Culture and Imperialism*, p. 212. Jeanyves Guérin points out that France was hostile to decolonization in the post-War period, citing approval in the Communist press for the brutal repression of the uprising in Sétif in 1945 as a marker of the political consensus of the time. While the Communists were later to break ranks, metropolitan France was not interested in Algeria until late 1955, when the impact of the war began to influence public opinion. See the chapter 'L'Algérie au cœur' in Guérin, *Camus: Portrait de l'artiste en citoyen*, pp. 238–60.

37 Typical of the criticisms levelled against Camus was Simone de Beauvoir's scathing dismissal of him as 'that just man without justice' ['ce juste sans justice'], quoted in O'Brien, *Camus*, p. 84. See also Todd, *Albert Camus: une vie*, especially chapters 42 ('1er Novembre 1954) and 43 ('L'Algérie n'est pas la France').

38 *Camus*, p. 85.

39 It is worth remembering that Camus had originally intended to include *La Chute* in the *L'Exil et le Royaume* collection, where Algeria is pre-eminent.

40 Foucault, *Discipline and Punish*, p. 304.

41 Meursault refers to the guillotine as a 'work of precision, finite and gleaming' ['ouvrage de précision, fini et étincelant'] (*TRN*, 1204).

42 *Discipline and Punish*, p. 305.

43 O'Brien, *Camus*, p. 82. The contradictory imperatives of justice and family fuelled Camus's dilemma.

44 For the story of the Tower of Babel, see Genesis 11: 1–9.

45 *L'Intention poétique*, p. 20. Glissant adds that in the absence of relation to the Other, our world becomes totalitarian. There is a potentially very suggestive connection here with Clamence's mock omnipotence and his manipulative use of monologue. See also Blanchot's 'La Confession dédaigneuse'.

46 In notes for this unfinished novel, Camus writes of extending the engagement with Africa beyond furtive day-trips to the unpopulated interior. In the planned closing section, Jacques would explain to his illiterate mother (in stereotypical terms, we may infer) the Arab question, the nature of Creole civilization, and the destiny of the West (*PH*, 307). This exposure to otherness is proposed by the mature narrator, who envisages breaking out of populist Arabophobic narrowness.

47 Barthes, *Mythologies*, p. 96.

48 Abdul JanMohammed, *Manichean Aesthetics: the Politics of Literature in Colonial Africa* (Amherst: University of Massachusetts Press, 1983), p. 280; quoted in Bill Ashcroft, Gareth Griffiths, and Helen Tiffin, *The Empire Writes Back*, pp. 81–2.

49 Gilman, *Difference and Pathology*, p. 213.

50 See Genesis 3: 16–19.

51 Camus's often-cited reference to Meursault as 'the only Christ we deserve' ['le seul christ que nous méritions'] (*TRN*, 1929) confirms the author's desire to adapt Christian cultural markers. The recycling of religious discourse to advance secular positions continues when he argues in *L'Exil et le Royaume* that his kingdom is of this world and in the choice of biblical titles and names such as *Jonas*, *Le Premier Homme*, and Jean-Baptiste Clamence.

52 Fabian stresses the ideological importance of these different times in his *Time and the Other*, p. 27.

53 Camus uses the term to denote the inhabitants of the working-class district of Belcourt in Algiers in *Noces* (*Ess.*, 72).

54 Interview of 20 December 1959, published in *Venture*, Spring–Summer 1960 and reproduced in *Ess.*, 1925–8 (1925). Guérin reminds us of Camus's comparison between Algeria as a land of immigration and the United States and draws a parallel between the outlook of *pieds noirs* such as Veillard who work the land and the pioneering mentality of Steinbeck's and Cauldwell's protagonists, 'Des *Chroniques Algériennes* au *Premier Homme*. Pour une lecture politique du dernier roman de Camus', pp. 5–16, here p. 8.

55 O'Brien refers to Camus's 'terrible, hollow, public rhetoric of these last years', *Camus*, pp. 85–6.

56 Matthew 5: 5.

57 Camus delivered his 'Appel pour une trêve civile en Algérie' in Algiers on 22 January 1956, against a background of hostility and mounting violence (*Ess.*, 991–9). For a detailed account of this episode, see Todd, *Albert Camus: une vie*, pp. 623–30.

58 Stora, 'La Guerre d'Algérie quarante ans après: connaissances et reconnaissance', p. 138.

59 Bhabha's subtle formulation, 'How can a human being live Other-wise?', is applicable to the challenge facing Camus's *petit colon*, 'Foreword', p. xxv.

5 PERIPHERIES, PUBLIC AND PRIVATE: GENET AND DISPOSSESSION

1 Both epigraphs are taken from *Un captif amoureux* (*CA*, 424, 458; *PL*, 259, 280).
2 Barthes, *NCE*, 116.
3 Information taken from Albert Dichy's 'Chronology', in Edmund White, *Genet*, p. xxx.
4 Quoted in Arnaud Malgorn, *Jean Genet: qui êtes-vous?* p. 164.
5 Derrida, *Glas* (Paris: Denoël, 1981), p. 50, quoted in Hadrien Laroche, *Le Dernier Genet*, p. 7. In the original formulation ('il saute partout où ça saute dans le monde'), Derrida plays on the double meaning of the verb *sauter*, to jump up, to explode.
6 The article was published in *L'Humanité*, 30 June 1977; reproduced in *ED*, 191–7.
7 Dichy reminds us of Genet's comment to Bertrand Poirot-Delpech that the 'Cathédrale de Chartres' piece was written tongue-in-cheek. See Dichy's editorial note, *ED*, 382.
8 See Genet's interview of December 1983 with Rüdiger Wischenbart and Layla Shahid Barrada for Austrian radio and the German daily *Die Zeit*, *ED*, 269–96, here p. 273.
9 Genet's interview with Hubert Fichte in December 1975 was published in *Die Zeit* and is reproduced in *ED*, 141–76, here p. 149.
10 See Patrice Bougon's discussion of the idea of 'close enemies' in 'The Politics of Enmity', p. 154.
11 Taken from Genet's working notes for the 'Entretien avec Antoine Bourseiller' (Summer 1981), reproduced in *ED*, 400, n. 18.
12 'Entretien avec Nigel Williams' filmed in the summer of 1985 for BBC 2, *ED*, 297–306, here p. 305.
13 Genet, 'Pour George Jackson', *ED*, 83–7, here p. 83.
14 Edmund White finds in this statement an indication of Genet's anarchic impulse. See his 'Introduction' to Barbara Bray's translation of *Un captif amoureux*, *PL*, xi.
15 See Davis, 'Genet's *Journal du voleur* and the Ethics of Reading', p. 60.
16 'La Ténacité des Noirs Américains', published in *L'Humanité*, 16 April 1977; reproduced in *ED*, 185–9, here p. 188.
17 Quoted in Laroche, *Le Dernier Genet*, p. 23.
18 Colin Davis reflects on Genet's investigation of the link between literature and ethics, 'Genet's *Journal du voleur* and the Ethics of Reading', p. 61.
19 See Bataille's preface to *Madame Edwarda*, p. 16. In its original formulation, the oxymoron reads: 'L'être nous est donné dans un dépassement intolérable de l'être.'
20 White, 'Introduction', *PL*, xiii.
21 Poirot-Delpech applies the term *délire baroque* to Genet in his obituary article in *Le Monde*, 16 April 1986, pp. 1, 19.
22 The English translation and the original diverge somewhat at this point in the text.

23 'Quatre heures à Chatila', *ED*, 243–64, here p. 254.
24 In his editorial notes, Dichy explains how the rawness of the experience drives Genet's text beyond traditional generic boundaries, *ED*, 404–5.
25 Tahar Ben Jelloun, 'Pour Jean Genet', reproduced in *ED*, 392.
26 *Jean Genet: qui êtes-vous?* p. 145.
27 An abbreviated version of Henric's article, 'Monsieur Jean Genet, nouveau patriote', is reproduced in *ED*, 391–2.
28 *Jean Genet: qui êtes-vous?* p. 145.
29 When Genet died, Arafat observed that his help to Palestinians in their hour of need would not be forgotten, *Humanité-Dimanche*, 20 April 1986.
30 I offer my own translation of what is a crucial statement for my overall argument.
31 Dollimore, *Sexual Dissidence*, pp. 355–6. In a similar vein, Genet's friend Layla Shahid, writing just after the appearance of *Un captif amoureux*, refers to its author's real engagement: 'To come as he did in 1970 was a political act. But staying on was something other than that. It amounted to an act of love', quoted in Mathieu Lindon, 'Un livre qu'Arafat lui a demandé d'écrire', *Libération*, 26 May 1986, p. 35.
32 Genet confessed to experiencing delight at the humiliation of his long-standing enemy, France, in 1940: 'I could only worship [the Austrian corporal] who had brought about the humiliation of France' ['je ne pouvais qu'adorer [le caporal autrichien] qui avait mis en oeuvre l'humiliation de la France'], 'Entretien avec Hubert Fichte', December 1975, *ED*, 149. While statements such as this exposed him to the charge of harbouring Nazi sympathies, the context for the remark is crucial, Genet referring to his orphanhood and to his deep-seated hatred of French institutions as a child.
33 We find a celebrated example of this in Tableau 14 of *Les Paravents*, where Nestor and his fellow-soldiers pass wind in what is mockingly touted as a generous, patriotic salute to the deceased Lieutenant.
34 White sees the tension, while stressing that 'Genet seeks . . . to honour the collective emergency, but in the end he remains true to his equally radical (and politically rooted) need for independence. Fidelity to oneself is treachery to the group', 'Introduction', *PL*, xiii.
35 Genet regularly refers to the pleasures of betrayal. In his *Journal du voleur*, for example, he writes of wanting to emulate the admirable moral solitude of those who desert from the army (*JV*, 48).
36 '*Un captif amoureux* de Jean Genet: le théâtre des opérations', *Le Monde*, 6 June 1986, pp. 1, 19.
37 Stressing the place of translation and transplanting, Clifford insists that modern ethnography must work constantly between cultures, *The Predicament of Culture*, p. 9.
38 For consideration of the interface between writing and political commitment, see Bougon, 'The Politics of Enmity'.
39 Genet also focuses on the joy of the student protests of May 1968 in Paris. In his first political article, 'Les Maîtresses de Lénine', published in *Le Nouvel*

Observateur, 30 May 1968 (*ED*, 29–31), he pays tribute to the student leader, Daniel Cohn-Bendit, and writes of the elegance of Paris in revolt and of the elation he experiences on returning there (*ED*, 31).

40 For a highly developed celebration of the cultural otherness of Japan and release from the tyranny of the same, see Barthes's *L'Empire des signes* (Paris: Skira, 1970). Abdelkebir Khatibi discusses this aspect of Barthes's work in *Figures de l'étranger dans la littérature française*, pp. 65–70.

41 See, for example, the overdetermination of ethnic difference in *Les Nègres*, the theatricalization of decolonization in *Les Paravents*, and the incisive reflections on role-play in *Le Balcon*.

42 'Entretien avec Bertrand Poirot-Delpech', *ED*, 227–41, here p. 238.

43 As Genet suggests to Hubert Fichte, 'power cannot do without theatricality. . . . Power shelters behind some kind of theatricality'; quoted in David Walker's introduction to *Jean Genet: 'Le Balcon'*, p. 12.

44 The capitalization of 'Sa Mère' (*CA*, 432) already suggests the elevated, near sacred status of the mother/son couple. The English translation omits the capitalization (*PL*, 264).

45 'Entretien avec Rüdiger Wischenbart et Layla Shahid Barrada', *ED*, 295–6.

46 See, for example, Alain Bosquet, who argues in his review of *Un captif amoureux* in *Le Figaro Littéraire* (9 June 1986) that, however much Genet may protest, he remains wedded to a French tradition that is rationalist, didactic, and humanist.

47 Shahid is quoted in Lindon, 'Un livre qu'Arafat lui a demandé d'écrire', 35.

CONCLUSION

1 Jules Laforgue, 'Rêve de Far West', quoted in Roger Mathé, *L'Exotisme d'Homère à Le Clézio*, pp. 152–3.

2 Interview with Rüdiger Wischenbart and Layla Shahid (*ED*, 279), quoted in Félix Guattari, 'Genet retrouvé', p. 33.

3 Hand, 'Phantom of the Opus', p. 190.

4 See editor's note, *RTP*, I, 1380, n. 3 to I, 526.

5 See *Corr.*, XIV, 45–6. It was during one such visit that Proust heard the 'Bonjour, négro!' story, which he transposes to the 1883 Jardin d'Acclimatation exhibition (see note 4).

Bibliography

PRIMARY TEXTS

Camus, Albert. *Essais*. Paris: Bibliothèque de la Pléiade, 1965.
    Le Premier Homme. Paris: Gallimard (Cahiers Albert Camus VII), 1994.
    Théâtre, Récits, Nouvelles. Paris: Bibliothèque de la Pléiade, 1962.
Gauguin, Paul. *Avant et Après* [1910]. Paris: La Table Ronde, 1994.
    Lettres de Gauguin à Daniel de Monfreid, précédées d'un *Hommage à Gauguin* par
    Victor Segalen, ed. Mme A. Joly-Segalen. Paris: Falaize, 1950.
    Lettres de Paul Gauguin à Émile Bernard 1888–1891. Geneva: Cailler, 1954.
Gauguin, Paul and Charles Morice. *Noa Noa*. Paris: La Plume, 1901.
Genet, Jean. *Un captif amoureux*. Paris: Gallimard (Folio), 1986.
    L'Ennemi déclaré, ed. Albert Dichy. Paris: Gallimard, 1991.
    Journal du voleur. Paris: Gallimard, 1949.
    Les Paravents [1961]. Paris: Gallimard (Folio), 1981.
Loti, Pierre. *Aziyadé* [1879]. Paris: Flammarion, 1989.
    Madame Chrysanthème [1887]. Paris: Flammarion, 1990.
    Le Mariage de Loti [1880]. Paris: Flammarion, 1991.
    Le Roman d'un spahi [1881], in *Romans*. Paris: Omnibus, 1989.
Montherlant, Henry de. *Romans II*. Paris: Bibliothèque de la Pléiade, 1982.
    La Rose de sable. Paris: Gallimard (Folio), 1968.
    Service inutile in *Essais*. Paris: Bibliothèque de la Pléiade, 1963.
Proust, Marcel. *Correspondance*, ed. Philip Kolb, 21 vols. Paris: Plon, 1970–93.
    Contre Sainte-Beuve. Paris: Bibliothèque de la Pléiade, 1971.
    À la recherche du temps perdu, 4 vols. Paris: Bibliothèque de la Pléiade, 1987–9.

SECONDARY MATERIAL: BOOKS AND ARTICLES

Andersen, Wayne. *Gauguin's Paradise Lost*. London: Secker & Warburg, 1972.
André, Serge. *L'Imposture perverse*. Paris: Seuil, 1993.
Ashcroft, Bill, Gareth Griffiths, and Helen Tiffin. *The Empire Writes Back: Theory
    and Practice in Post-colonial Literatures*. London and New York: Routledge,
    1989.
Barthes, Roland. *Fragments d'un discours amoureux*. Paris: Seuil, 1977.

Nouveaux Essais Critiques, published with *Le Degré zéro de l'écriture*. Paris: Seuil, 1972; *New Critical Essays*, trans. Richard Howard. New York: Hill and Wang, 1980.

Mythologies [1957]. Paris: Seuil, 1970. Partial translation *Mythologies*, Annette Lavers. London: Granada, 1973.

Bataille, Georges. *Madame Edwarda, Le Mort, L'Histoire de l'œil*. Paris: Pauvert (Editions 10/18), 1979.

Ben Jelloun, Tahar. 'Pour Jean Genet'. *Le Monde*, 24 September 1977, p. 2.

Bhabha, Homi K. 'Foreword: Remembering Fanon', in Frantz Fanon, *Black Skin, White Masks*, trans. Charles Lam Markmann, pp. vii–xxvi.

'DissemiNation: Time, Narrative, and the Margins of the Modern Nation', in *Nation and Narration*, ed. Bhabha, pp. 291–322.

Bhabha, Homi K., ed. *Nation and Narration*. London: Routledge, 1990.

Blanch, Lesley. *Pierre Loti: Portrait of an Escapist*. London: Collins, 1983.

Blanchot, Maurice. 'La Confession dédaigneuse', in *Les Critiques de notre temps et Camus*, ed. Jacqueline Lévi-Valensi, pp. 91–7. Paris: Garnier Frères, 1970.

Bongie, Chris. *Exotic Memories: Literature, Colonialism, and the Fin de Siècle*. Stanford: Stanford University Press, 1991.

Bougon, Patrice. 'The Politics of Enmity', in *Genet: In the Language of the Enemy*. *Yale French Studies*, 91 (1997), pp. 141–58.

'Translation, Tradition and Betrayal: From Political Commitment to Literary Freedom in Genet's *Les Paravents*'. *Parallax*, 4, 2 (1998), pp. 129–44.

Bowie, Malcolm. *Freud, Proust and Lacan: Theory as Fiction*. Cambridge: Cambridge University Press, 1987.

Proust among the Stars. London: HarperCollins, 1998.

Brooks, Peter. *Body Work: Objects of Desire in Modern Narrative*. Cambridge, Mass.: Harvard University Press, 1993.

Cachin, Françoise. *Gauguin: 'Ce malgré moi de sauvage'*. Paris: Gallimard (Découvertes), 1989.

Cadwallader, Barrie. *Crisis of the European Mind: a Study of André Malraux and Drieu La Rochelle*. Cardiff: University of Wales Press, 1981.

Cartier, Henri. *Comment la France 'civilise' ses colonies*. Paris: Bureau d'Editions, Saint-Denis, 1932.

Clifford, James. *The Predicament of Culture: Twentieth-Century Ethnography, Literature, and Art*. Cambridge, Mass.: Harvard University Press, 1988.

Coe, Richard N. *The Vision of Jean Genet*. London: Peter Owen, 1968.

Cohen-Solal, Annie. 'Jean sans Terre', review of *Un captif amoureux*. *Le Nouvel Observateur*, 23 May 1986, pp. 100–02.

Compagnon, Antoine. *Proust entre deux siècles*. Paris: Seuil, 1989.

Conrad, Joseph. *Heart of Darkness and Other Tales*. Oxford: Oxford University Press, 1990.

Cruickshank, John. *Montherlant*. Edinburgh: Oliver and Boyd, 1964.

Davis, Colin. '*Un captif amoureux* and the Commitment of Jean Genet'. *French Studies Bulletin*, 23 (1987), pp. 16–18.

Davis, Colin. 'Genet's *Journal du voleur* and the Ethics of Reading'. *French Studies*, 48, 1 (January 1994), pp. 50–62.

Deguy, Michel. 'La "pietà" de Jean Genet'. *La Quinzaine Littéraire*, October 1986, pp. 14–15.

Derrida, Jacques. *Le Monolinguisme de l'autre*. Paris: Galilée, 1996.

Dichy, Albert. 'Chronology', in Edmund White, *Genet*, pp. xiii–xxxv.
'Genet, Ecrivain?' *Europe*, 808–09 (August–September 1996), pp. 3–7.

Diderot, Denis. *Supplément au Voyage de Bougainville* [1798] in *Oeuvres*. Paris: Bibliothèque de la Pléiade, 1951.

Dine, Philip. *Images of the Algerian War: French Fiction and Film, 1954–1992*. Oxford: Clarendon Press, 1994.

Dollimore, Jonathan. *Sexual Dissidence: Augustine to Wilde, Freud to Foucault*. Oxford: Oxford University Press, 1991.

Fabian, Johannes. *Time and the Other: How Anthropology makes its Object*. New York: Columbia University Press, 1983.

Fairlie, Alison. *Leconte de Lisle's Poems on the Barbarian Races*. Cambridge: Cambridge University Press, 1947.

Fanon, Frantz. *Les Damnés de la Terre*, with a preface by J.-P. Sartre. Paris: Gallimard (Folio), 1961.
Peau Noire, Masques Blancs. Paris: Seuil, 1952; *Black Skin, White Masks*, trans. Charles Lam Markmann. London: Pluto Press, 1986.

Farrère, Claude. *Lyautey l'Africain*. Abbeville, F. Paillart, 1922.

Foucault, Michel. *Surveiller et Punir*. Paris: Gallimard, 1975; *Discipline and Punish: the Birth of the Prison*, trans. Alan Sheridan. Harmondsworth: Penguin, 1991.

Foucault, Michel. 'Des Espaces Autres' [1967], *Architecture-Mouvement-Continuité* (October 1984), pp. 46–9; 'Of Other Spaces', *Diacritics: a Review of Contemporary Criticism*, 16, 1 (Spring 1986), pp. 22–7.

Fraser, Robert. *Proust and the Victorians: the Lamp of Memory*. London: Macmillan, 1994.

Freud, Sigmund. *Civilization and its Discontents* [1930]. London: Penguin Freud Library, 1991, vol. 12, pp. 243–340.
Group Psychology and the Analysis of the Ego [1921]. London: Penguin Freud Library, 1991, vol. 12, pp. 91–178.
'Thoughts for the Times on War and Death' [1915]. London: Penguin Freud Library, 1991, vol. 12, pp. 57–89.

Gates, Jr., Henry Louis, ed. *'Race', Writing, and Difference*. Chicago: University of Chicago Press, 1986.

Gide, André. *Voyage au Congo* [1927] suivi de *Le Retour du Tchad* [1928]. Paris: Gallimard, 1995.

Gilman, Sander L. *Difference and Pathology: Stereotypes of Sexuality, Race, and Madness*. Ithaca: Cornell University Press, 1985.

Glissant, Édouard. *L'Intention poétique*. Paris: Seuil, 1969.
Poétique de la relation. Paris: Gallimard, 1990; *Poetics of Relation*, trans. Betsy Wing. Ann Arbor: University of Michigan Press, 1997.

Gontard, Marc. *Victor Segalen: Une esthétique de la différence*. Paris: L'Harmattan, 1990.

Guattari, Félix. 'Genet retrouvé'. *Revue d'études palestiniennes*, 21 (Autumn 1986), pp. 27–42.

Guérin, Jeanyves. 'Des *Chroniques Algériennes* au *Premier Homme*. Pour une lecture politique du dernier roman de Camus', *Esprit*, 211 (May 1995), pp. 5–16.
  Camus: Portrait de l'artiste en citoyen. Paris: Bourin, 1993.

Hand, Seán. 'Phantom of the Opus: Colonialist Traces in Michel Leiris's *L'Afrique fantôme*'. *Paragraph: a Journal of Modern Critical Theory*, 18, 2 (July 1995), 174–93.

Hand, Seán, ed. *Mapping the Other: Anthropology and Literature's Limits. Paragraph: a Journal of Modern Critical Theory*, 18, 2 (July 1995).

Hanson, Lawrence and Elizabeth. *The Noble Savage: a Life of Paul Gauguin.* London, Chatto & Windus, 1954.

Hargreaves, Alec G. *The Colonial Experience in French Fiction: a Study of Pierre Loti, Ernest Psichari and Pierre Mille.* London: Macmillan, 1981.

Harrison, Charles, Francis Frascina, and Gill Perry. *Primitivism, Cubism, Abstraction: the Early Twentieth Century.* New Haven: Yale University Press, in association with the Open University, 1993.

Henric, Jacques. 'Monsieur Jean Genet, nouveau patriote', *Libération*, 21 September 1977, p. 14.

Hentsch, Thierry. *L'Orient imaginaire: La Vision politique occidentale de l'Est méditer-ranéen.* Paris: Minuit, 1987.

Hodeir, Catherine and Michel Pierre. *L'Exposition coloniale.* Brussels: Editions Complexe, 1991.

Horne, Alistair. *A Savage War of Peace: Algeria 1954–1962.* London: Macmillan, 1977.

Jameson, Fredric. *Modernism and Imperialism.* Derry: Field Day, 1988.

Khatibi, Abdelkebir. *Figures de l'étranger dans la littérature française.* Paris: Denoël, 1987.

Knight, Diana. *Barthes and Utopia: Space, Travel, Writing.* Oxford: Clarendon Press, 1997.

Kosofsky Sedgwick, Eve. 'Epistemology of the Closet'. *Raritan* (Spring 1988), pp. 39–69.
  Between Men: English Literature and Male Homosocial Desire. New York: Columbia University Press, 1985.

Kristeva, Julia. *Étrangers à nous-mêmes.* Paris: Gallimard (Folio), 1988.
  Le Temps sensible: Proust et l'expérience littéraire. Paris: Gallimard, 1994.

Laing, R. D. *The Divided Self: a Study of Sanity and Madness* [1960]. Harmondsworth: Penguin, 1965.

Laroche, Hadrien. *Le Dernier Genet: Histoire des hommes infâmes.* Paris: Seuil, 1997.

Le Bot, Marc. *Paul Gauguin: Noa Noa, Voyage de Tahiti.* Paris: Editions Assouline, 1995.

Leiris, Michel. *Glossaire j'y serre mes gloses* [1939] in *Mots sans mémoire.* Paris: Gallimard, 1969.
  Langage Tangage ou Ce que les mots me disent. Paris: Gallimard, 1985.
  Cinq études d'ethnologie [1951, 1966]. Paris: Denoël, 1969.

Liauzau, Claude. *Aux origines des tiers-mondismes: colonisés et anticolonialistes en France (1919–1939)*. Paris: L'Harmattan, 1982.

Lindon, Mathieu. 'Un livre qu'Arafat lui a demandé d'écrire'. *Libération*, 26 May 1986, p. 35.

Lyautey, L.-H.-G. *Lettres du Tonkin et de Madagascar (1894–1899)*. 2 vols. Paris: Armand Colin, 1920.

    Paroles d'action: Madagascar-Sud-Oranais-Oran-Maroc. 1900–1926. Paris: Armand Colin, 1927.

    Le Rôle social de l'officier. Paris: Plon, 1935 (first published in the *Revue des Deux Mondes*, 15 March 1891).

Lyautey, Pierre. *Les Plus Belles Lettres de Lyautey*. Paris: Calmann-Lévy, 1962.

Malgorn, Arnaud. *Jean Genet: qui êtes-vous?* Lyon: La Manufacture, 1988.

Malingue, Maurice. *La Vie prodigieuse de Gauguin*. Paris: Buchet/Chastel, 1987.

Martin, Andrew. *The Knowledge of Ignorance: from Genesis to Jules Verne*. Cambridge: Cambridge University Press, 1985.

Mathé, Roger. *L'Exotisme d'Homère à Le Clézio*. Paris: Bordas, 1972.

Memmi, Albert. *Portrait du colonisé* précédé de *Portrait du colonisateur*, with a preface by J.-P. Sartre [1957]. Paris: Gallimard, 1985.

    Le Racisme. Paris: Gallimard, 1982.

Michel, Jacqueline. 'Sur les traces d'un paysage français dans l'œuvre de Montherlant', *Travaux de linguistique et de littérature*, 16, 2 (1978), pp. 155–78.

Milianti, Alain. 'Le Fils de la honte: notes sur l'engagement politique de Jean Genet'. *Revue d'études palestiniennes*, 4 (Winter 1992), pp. 205–12.

Moerenhout, Jacques-Antoine. *Voyages aux Îles du Grand Océan*. 2 vols. Paris: Arthus Bertrand, 1837.

Montaigne, Michel de. 'Des Cannibales' in *Essais*, Livre I, pp. 251–63. Paris: Garnier-Flammarion, 1979.

O'Brien, Conor Cruise. *Camus*. Glasgow: Fontana, 1972.

Odinot, Paul. *Le Monde marocain*. Paris: Marcel Rivière (Librairie des Sciences Politiques et Sociales), 1926.

    Géranium, ou La Vie d'une femme marocaine. Rabat: F. Moncho, 1932.

Ory, Pascal. *L'Exposition Universelle*. Brussels: Editions Complexe, 1989.

Poirot-Delpech, Bertrand. Obituary article on Jean Genet. *Le Monde*, 16 April 1986, pp. 1, 19.

    '*Un captif amoureux* de Jean Genet: le théâtre des opérations'. *Le Monde*, 6 June 1986, pp. 21, 28.

Prochaska, David. *Making Algeria French: Colonialism in Bône, 1870–1920*. Cambridge: Cambridge University Press, 1990.

Quella-Villéger, Alain. *Pierre Loti l'incompris*. Paris: Presses de la Renaissance, 1986.

    Pierre Loti: le pèlerin de la planète. Bordeaux: Aubéron, 1998.

Rabinow, Paul, ed. *The Foucault Reader*. London: Penguin, 1984.

Raimond, Michel. 'Notice' for *La Rose de sable*, in Montherlant, *Romans II*, 1251–93.

    Les Romans de Montherlant. Paris: SEDES, 1982.

Read, Barbara, ed., with Ian Birchall. *Flowers and Revolution: a Collection of Writings on Jean Genet*. London: Middlesex University Press, 1997.

Said, Edward. *Culture and Imperialism* [1993]. London: Vintage, 1994.

Orientalism [1978]. London: Penguin, 1985.

'The Politics of Knowledge'. *Raritan: a Quarterly Review*, 11, 1 (Summer 1991), pp. 17–31.

Sartre, J.-P. *Orphée Noir* in *Situations III*. Paris: Gallimard, 1949.

Saint Genet: comédien et martyr. Paris: Gallimard, 1952.

Scham, Alan. *Lyautey in Morocco: Protectorate Administration 1912–1925*. Berkeley and Los Angeles: University of California Press, 1970.

Schmid, Marion. 'The Jewish Question in *A la Recherche du temps perdu* in the light of Nineteenth-Century Discourses on Race'. *Neophilologus*, 83 (1999), pp. 33–49.

'Ideology and Discourse in Proust: the Making of "Monsieur de Charlus pendant la guerre"'. *Modern Lanuage Review*, 94, 4 (1999), pp. 961–77.

Segalen, Victor. *Essai sur l'exotisme* [1955], in *Œuvres Complètes* (Paris: Laffont, 1995), I, 745–81.

'Gauguin dans son dernier décor' [1904], in *Œuvres Complètes*, I, 287–91.

'Hommage à Gauguin' [1918], in *Œuvres Complètes*, I, 349–73.

Les Immémoriaux [1907], in *Œuvres Complètes*, I, 107–286.

Le Maître-du-Jouir, in *Œuvres Complètes*, I, 293–348.

'Pensers Païens' [1975], in *Œuvres Complètes*, I, 383–93.

Sharabi, Hisham. Review of Jean Genet, *Un captif amoureux*. *Journal of Palestinian Studies*, 16, 4 (Summer 1987), pp. 129–32.

Sipriot, Pierre. *Montherlant sans masque*. 2 vols. Paris: Laffont, 1982, 1990.

Szyliowicz, Irene L. *Pierre Loti and the Oriental Woman*. London: Macmillan, 1988.

Smith, Paul Julian. *The Body Hispanic: Gender and Sexuality in Spanish and Spanish American Literature*. Oxford: Clarendon Press, 1989.

Sprinker, Michael. *History and Ideology in Proust: 'A la recherche du temps perdu' and the Third French Republic*. Cambridge: Cambridge University Press, 1994.

Stora, Benjamin. 'La Guerre d'Algérie quarante ans après: connaissances et reconnaissance'. *Modern and Contemporary France*, NS2, 2 (1994), pp. 131–9.

Sweetman, David. *Paul Gauguin: a Complete Life*. London: Hodder & Stoughton, 1995.

Thomas, Nicholas. *Colonialism's Culture*. Cambridge: Polity Press, 1994.

Todd, Olivier. *Albert Camus: une vie*. Paris: Gallimard (Biographies), 1996.

Todorov, Tzvetan. *La Conquête de l'Amérique: La Question de l'autre*. Paris: Seuil, 1982; *The Conquest of America: the Question of the Other*, trans. Richard Howard. New York: HarperPerennial, 1992.

Nous et les autres: La Réflexion française sur la diversité humaine. Paris: Seuil, 1989; *On Human Diversity: Nationalism, Racism, and Exoticism in French Thought*, trans. Catherine Porter. Cambridge, Mass.: Harvard University Press, 1993.

Torgovnick, Marianna. *Gone Primitive: Savage Intellects, Modern Lives*. Chicago: University of Chicago Press, 1990.

Varnedoe, Kirk. 'Gauguin', in *'Primitivism' in Twentieth-Century Art: Affinity of the*

Tribal and the Modern, ed. William Rubin, pp. 179–210. New York: Museum of Modern Art, 1984.

Vaughan, Megan. *Curing their Ills: Colonial Power and African Illness*. Cambridge: Polity Press, 1991.

Wadley, Nicholas, ed. *Noa Noa: Gauguin's Tahiti*. Oxford: Phaidon, 1985.

Wake, Clive. *The Novels of Pierre Loti*. The Hague/Paris: Mouton, 1974.

Walker, David H. 'Introduction', *Jean Genet: 'Le Balcon'*, pp. 1–39. London: Methuen, 1982.

White, Edmund. *Genet* [1993]. London: Picador, 1994.

White, Hayden. 'The Forms of Wildness', in *The Wild Man Within: an Image of Western Thought from the Renaissance to Romanticism*, ed. Edward Dudley and Maximilian E. Novak. Pittsburg: University of Pittsburg Press, 1972.

Wilkinson, Alan G. *Gauguin to Moore: Primitivism in Modern Sculpture*. Toronto: Art Gallery of Ontario, 1981.

Young, Robert J. C. *Colonial Desire: Hybridity in Theory, Culture and Race*. London: Routledge, 1995.

White Mythologies: Writing History and the West. London: Routledge, 1990.

Index

196